SWITCHES

--------------------☼--------------------

FROM THE BLOCK
TO THE
WHITE HOUSE

Switches
From the Block to the White House

Published by
Anthony Johnson

ISBN: 978-0-6151-5242-4

Graphic Design: Marion Designs, Atlanta, GA
Photography: Anthony Johnson/Marion Designs

Printed in the United States

Distributed by: www.lulu.com

Acknowledgment:

-------------------☼-----------------

I sincerely thank everyone who played a part in my upbringing and growth. With your guidance, I'll continue to strive to do my best and to avoid the many pitfalls that plague a number of my childhood friends. A special thanks to my family, friends, mentors, disciplinarians, and personal lifelines.

Disclaimer:

Table of Contents

--------------------☼--------------------

Preface

-------------------☼-------------------

Yᵒᵘ are about to embark on a journey that will bring back fond memories of the past while taking you to places that you never thought existed. My journey is typical of many who dared to venture out from urban environments. The difference was in the choices I made and the vehicle I chose, allowing me the opportunity to shake it up a bit, try new things, and see exotic places.

I ventured out to find a life for myself after high school, somewhere away from the urban version of the wild, Wild West. I realized after my departure how much I hated drama – not the usual "He Said/She Said" type, but real, life-or-death drama. It was my eternal enemy. I couldn't stand to see another friend or acquaintance die at the hands of someone with a short temper or a foolish jealousy streak. I grew tired of the grotesque assaults and murders that had made Detroit notorious. We had everything from the Cinder Block Murderer, who dropped cinder blocks on his victims' heads, to the rampage of Alton Coleman. He committed hideous crimes of convenience based on what he needed at that moment. If he needed gas, he'd kill someone at a gas station to get it. If he wanted sex, he'd rape and kill the next woman he saw.

The media, and society to a certain degree, seemed to glorify these lunatics as heroes. At least it seemed that way. They earned street credibility that they didn't necessarily seek. Ironically, Mr. Coleman received little media coverage when he was executed a few years ago.

Homophobia ran rampant in my neighborhood. We had to be *real* men. Never mind the sky-blue, crushed-velvet maxi-coats we wore. I was an adult before I realized that nearly every gay man who didn't have the skill to hide it perfectly would be found murdered. We never talked about it, but we knew why.

It didn't take much to provoke a life-altering event in my neighborhood. One false move and it was over. One wisecrack to the wrong person on the wrong day and it was over. One stepped-on shoe and it was over. One sly look at someone else's woman and someone was dead.

I perceived the common denominator in these events to be *switches*. Life's all about the choices we make or the switches we flip. We have access to a series of switches that can be turned on or off by natural instinct. These switches are mental, and in most cases used immediately. We can flip switches and instantly change our lives for good or bad. I flipped switches whenever I chose not to ride in certain cars. I could sense when the people in them were going to do something treacherous. Switches were flipped on my behalf when others chose to put me out of a car. Switches allowed me the strength to cut friendships when I realized these so-called friends could cause me to lose my life or freedom. It's all about what we want out of life and what we're willing to part with. If keeping it real is more important than freedom or success, that's a choice we must make. Personally, I'll deal with a momentary loss of respect or street credibility instead.

If you are on a job interview, remember to turn off the slang and street attitude switch; it's critical to your employment. If you find yourself in an unsavory environment or situation, it may behoove you to turn on your *street* switch; it may keep you alive by putting a momentary pause in your adversary. If you are kicking it with the boys from the block, it's fine to relax and be yourself. They knew your gangster potential, or lack thereof, before you knew it. Contrary to popular opinion, everyone doesn't want you to fail. Many will live their lives vicariously through your excursions. We can feel a sense of accomplishment when someone we know makes it in sports, music, business, or just out of the neighborhood.

We have to learn how to step up to the plate when it's time. We have to remember that a choice may dictate the next 30 years of our lives, or the lives of our loved ones. The Supreme Being provides the tools and the opportunity, but we choose the switches and deal with the consequences.

If my writings paint clear portraits that place you on a tropical island or in the hull of a ship, I've done what I set out to do. If you can relate to the way things used to be, or laugh at a situation that was similar to your previous experiences, I've succeeded. So sit back, enjoy, and sail away.

Chapter 1
Where are These People?

-------------------☼-------------------

How do I explain memories that must have occurred before the age of 18 months? I feel extremely weird when I recall visual bits and pieces – snapshots of life without many people. I was born in 1962, but I can recall things that must have happened in 1963. I recall holding myself up in my wooden crib with the prison bars and crying, but I don't recall anyone coming to get me. Although I remember that dark-green room vividly, I don't recall any food or humans. Since I couldn't have paid the rent, I suppose it wasn't *my* house. Did I live there alone? Where was everyone? Maybe it was child abuse? No way. That didn't exist before the 80s. I suspect it was called, "I ain't spoiling that boy."

I have a total of four memories before the age of three, and prior to moving to my childhood home. I recall playing on a dirt hill with my sister Vera – at least that's what I learned her name to be. She's the second-oldest of my four siblings and six years older than me. I think she played with me the most in those early years. I can recall another home with a screened-in front porch. I know the entire family had to sleep on that porch one night due to the lack of central air-conditioning. It was more likely a broken fan. That's the only time I can recall the family all together in one place.

Last, but not least, I remember drinking hot cocoa. My parents didn't buy the pre-sweetened kind in the yellow can with the rabbit on it. They bought Hershey's Cocoa in the dark-brown can. This kind had film floating on top. This cocoa issue stuck with me because my nose bled into it. The one thing I can

1

remember enjoying had to be taken away from me. I didn't know much, but I knew that this blood thing wasn't supposed to happen. To this day, I look down into every hot beverage I drink.

I suppose if there had been people around, I could have navigated that cocoa pitfall. It's highly likely that they were standing right there all along. I don't recall having diaper rash. That must have been a wonderful thing. I wonder what experiences the kids today may have. We probably look like cartoon characters to them, with our purple hair, nose rings, and tattoos. Since I made it through my crib incarceration and the chocolate ordeal, whoever lived with me did a wonderful job. I survived to move to the next location.

Chapter 2
Diversity – The Beginning of the End

-------------------☼-------------------

It was 1966 and it was the home that would take me into adulthood. Our neighborhood was an orchard. There were large fruit trees in every backyard. I could smell the invigorating scents from the Wonder Bread bakery around the corner. Maybe it wasn't the bakery around the corner after all. It could have been the continuous stream of pies and cakes that our next-door neighbors passed to my mom over the fence every couple of days.

I looked forward to playing in the backyard because the McAfee's would say, "Go get your momma." They were an older white couple who were probably in their 60s. Today's lack of trust would persuade people to take the cake and throw it in the trash as soon as they returned to their home.

If I had known the word *diversity* in 1966, I wouldn't have used it. It was easier to say *mixed*. Mixed was the best way to portray Detroit's Lemay Street. Blacks and whites were not the only neighbors present. There was also the Yee family. They lived in a big, red-brick warehouse with industrial-strength window screens. There had to be 20 of them. They were Chinese.

I can recall the whole family walking or riding old bikes down our street to play tennis at Joy Junior High School's tennis court. This was before the days of Kato, *Kung Fu*, and *Enter the Dragon*. We weren't rocket scientists, but no one in the neighborhood messed with this crew. Since I never saw a Yee on the tennis circuit, I guess that they were less than terrific at it. To be honest,

3

they didn't need tennis at all. A Yee served as valedictorian at nearly every graduation ceremony. I can recall every one of them receiving four-year scholarships to the schools of their choice.

As a youth, I never knew or understood why every non-African American family moved one by one. I can't recall the day the McAfee's moved. I think they did so in the middle of the night. Diversity, my ass – no more pies! I wonder how they felt before they left. Was it something we did as a family? I doubt it. The pies never stopped coming until the day they left. I suppose it had something to do with all of the fires from the riots that I observed from my window around 1967-68.

I recall my father listening to his police scanner. I remember watching the Army tanks that resembled my toys driving down the streets. I think there is a super-8 movie of me sitting on one of the tanks with a soldier somewhere in my family movie vault, or, should I say, junk drawer.

As a kid, I would browse through the scrapbooks that my parents put together to document the murders of JFK, Dr. Martin Luther King, Jr., and Robert F. Kennedy. I never recall seeing my parents and siblings cry about these assassinations. I learned early on that Martin Luther King was someone quite different and important. I also learned that the same individuals, who I looked up to, the Detroit Police, played a part in the riots' development.

The riots resulted from a raid on an after-hours drinking joint. The police expected to arrest a few individuals and discovered nearly 90 people inside. Their tactics and demeaning language towards the arrestees incited groups of individuals who had quickly gathered around the scene. After the police had left, a group of former patrons broke into an adjacent clothing store, and the rest is history – the military presence, 43 people dead, 1189 hurt, more than 7000 arrested, and multitudes of small businesses destroyed, businesses that would never return.

This group of arrests served as the straw that broke the camel's back for years of shootings, beatings, and generally demeaning behavior by police towards the citizens of Detroit. As a youth, we were taught to be afraid of *The Big Four* and *S.T.R.E.S.S.* Why should a kid less than six years old be afraid of individuals that he saw on TV protecting and serving? I couldn't understand it. They could kill you and not serve a day in jail for it.

4

The Big Four were tough Detroit Police officers who drove around four-deep in huge, dark, unmarked cars. They would jump out on individuals or groups of African Americans to ask for IDs or to beat their heads in – with little in between. They routinely called these citizens "boy" or "nigger."

STRESS took these tactics to another level. They were the precursor to today's SWAT Teams. I had never heard of the word "stress" in my life before these guys arrived. I do recall going to a rally at the University of Detroit as a child to stop STRESS. They have Stop Stress rallies today, but these are geared towards hypertension and anxiety. If I told a six-year-old today to be afraid off stress, the kid would ask for some quiet time.

I always believed that the police were right and the bad guys must have done something wrong. The bad guys in most cases were black. At least that's who I saw being arrested. Seeing these images constantly had me afraid of the police and people outside of Lemay Street in general. It also forced me to think that maybe I was bad as well.

The scrapbooks displayed images that would stay inside my head forever. I can never forget the little girl laying her head on the lap of her black-veiled mother. The picture became a Pulitzer Prize-winning image of Coretta Scott King consoling five-year old Bernice King. I never understood why my parents would save this negative stuff in those large, green books with black construction-paper pages held together by string. I soon understood that my parents were newshounds. We were the only family in the neighborhood who would mouth the words, "It's educational" to our friends. We didn't know what the hell that meant, but my parents preached it in our house often. Our family was the black CNN of the 60s. We had news 24 hours a day, with newspapers in the day and police scanners at night. I'm a news junkie now. Not only do I need to know what's going on in the world, I've told my daughter, "It's educational" so much that she probably hates news. I do seek out humorous stories in the midst of all the negativity to balance out my mind. No one can read straight negativity all the time and continue to be sane.

The downsizing of the non-black population in my neighborhood would affect me for years to come. It probably played a part in my desire to get out of there myself. When it was all said and done, the only diversity that remained after 1968 was the Worde family and, you guessed it, the Yees.

If you think the rapper Eminem has street cred, you haven't seen Mark Worde. Mark was basically raised black. Mark was too cool. Back in the day, we'd say, "He had a pimp." That's a slick walk in street lingo. I don't think Mark was ever considered white by anyone in the neighborhood, or the entire city for that matter. It was even funnier when Mark visited other neighborhoods with us. There were more double-looks than you can shake a stick at. He was one of us, and to this day he still is. Mark still lives on Lemay. While most of us have grown up and out, Mark is holding down the fort and building computers for folks in the hood. God bless him.

When I recently knocked on Mrs. Worde's door to advise her of my endeavor and to seek Mark's permission to use his name in my book, his mother said, "Oh hell, Eminem," and let me in. Go figure. You think she's heard this before? Considering Mark's in his 40s and the rapper is barely 30, maybe he should pay Mark royalties.

Chapter 3
Fifty Homes, Fifty Stories
-------------------☼-------------------

Lemay is an amazing street. Located on Detroit's lower East Side, it sits between a major highway, a bus terminal, and railroad tracks. The street was so long that there were two blocks in one. There were separate worlds and separate mentalities. The kids at opposite ends of the block never got along. Individually, we could hang with someone from the other end, but if we were with a group there would be problems. We challenged each other in everything. We could field two separate football or baseball teams. We could field a whole basketball elimination tournament from one street. It was weird. We didn't hate each other, but it was extremely competitive.

With the exception of pineapples and oranges, every type of fruit tree you can imagine existed in a 10-house radius. One of our neighbors had a concord grape vine. Concords are the bitter, purple grapes that pop directly out of their skin. They were small because we raided the vine each year before they matured.

There was one home directly behind ours that had an extremely huge cherry tree. We raided that one at our own risk because the owner had dogs and threatened to shoot us if we came into his yard, but we did it anyway. Apple and plum trees were commonplace, but they had more worms in them than seeds. We had to take little bites, as a big bite would guarantee eating at least half a worm, so it was one tiny bite and toss it. After six apples or so, we could say we had an apple.

The King family (Hot Dog's house), had a luscious plum tree. They lived three houses to the left and on the same side. They were cool; we didn't have to break into their yard to eat fruit, and we were allowed to climb to the top of the tree if we wanted to. No problem. Hot Dog's real name is Michael King, but he was the fattest kid on our part of the block. When speaking of Lemay, we must distinguish between what part of the block a person lived on.

Besides Hot Dog, there were such other nicknames as Pee Wee, A/Ron, Frog, Mister, and Mane. It took years to learn someone's real name – especially if they were not in school regularly. There were no Laquitas, Sheniquas, or Uniquas. There were Rosas, Lindas, Lillys, and Suzies. Kids were named after baby dolls or action figures, not kings or queens.

The Stotts' family lived in the first house. I think it was at least nine of them. They were well-known for eating grease sandwiches. Just in case you don't think you read this correctly, I said *grease sandwiches*. Chicken or pork chops leave crumbs floating around in about two inches of cooking oil, lard in most cases. The Stotts' lined up with a loaf of bread and commenced sopping bread into this grease and then ate it. It seemed to be a family treat, because they were extremely happy to do it. After watching this, we would leave the house to avoid losing our lunch, so to speak. To this day, no one I talk to believes this story unless they lived on Lemay.

Two houses down from them were one of the later additions to Lemay, the Gardener's. It was about 10 of them. They had so much traffic that they had to replant the grass each year. They tried hard, but never really got the yard to match their name. They would rope their yard off with clothes lines to keep people off of their weeds – I mean grass. Most of the rooms in their house were crammed with clothes. I stood up most of the time when I visited them because they didn't have many places to sit. I didn't want to sit on someone's bed – well, I did, but I was too young – and Ms. Gardener rarely left the chair on her porch or the sofa in her living room.

Next door to them was Thunder. Even though I was a kid, I do remember that she was pretty. She lived with her two sons, and was the youngest of the adult women in the neighborhood. I do not know how she got her name. Since no one ever asked, I didn't either. It couldn't have been too bad of a reason.

Next door to Thunder was Mr. Bear. His real name was Mr. Grissom and he was the big teddy bear of the block. He was a tremendous family man with a sweet wife and great kids. We played together daily. Ms. Vera lived next to them. She was an older lady who lived alone and was a friend of my mom's. The Thomas family lived in the next home. I spent my childhood there, practically living there. My sister Vera married into this family and they remain close in-laws.

Most of my immediate friends were less than great students, making it to high school but not graduating for various reasons. Therefore, anatomy was not an everyday subject around my neighborhood unless it dealt with women. I recall Sammy (Pee Wee) Thomas, who was around 18 at the time, coming up to us, rubbing his throat, and asking with great seriousness, "Hey, are this my lungs?" We looked at each other with amazement as he finished his statement by saying, "Because if they are, they hurt like a motherfucker."

The Lewis' lived next to the Thomas'. It was 14 kids in this family. I was just as close to them as to the Thomas' My niece Tisha, who is a schoolteacher in Detroit, was born out of a relationship between my brother Mark and Regina Lewis, who graduated high school with me. The Lewis' were the comedians of the block. I hung out with Johnny, Bobby, Derrick (Monster), and Vincent (Hook). His head was shaped like a question mark. We used to say, "If you cut the back off his head off, you'd miss his neck."

Marlon (RIP) was the funniest of all. Marlon would put Martin Lawrence or Chris Rock out of business. On one occasion, a group of us were standing on the corner near a Yield sign. Marlon looked at the sign, looked at us, and yelled to the top of his lungs.

We asked, "What in the hell is wrong with you?"

He said, "It said Yell!" He was totally serious.

For comic relief, the Lewis' would give the Wayans' Family from *In Living Color* a run for their money. They were the kings of slang. Ironically, some of their ramblings have found their way into the mouths of Snoop and Ice Cube. Culture travels west.

There was always something to drink or smoke nearby. They were the only people on the block who didn't need a reason to have a party. Having teenage sisters didn't hurt the atmosphere either.

The Oliver's lived in the next house. Michael Oliver was one of the boys. He was the first one of our group to drive and have his own car. I was grown and in the service before I had my first car. Michael was the only boy and he had at least five sisters who all looked like supermodels, being extremely tall and lovely. I don't think they dated the guys on our street. At least, none of us dated them, as far as I can recall. Well, maybe one. I do recall Mr. Bear's son Michael possibly dating Mertice, but it was a no-go for the rest of us. Like it or not, they were above our level.

Corky and Jackie Washington lived in the next house. Jackie had a light complexion, wore glasses, and had class. Her parents kept her in the house most of the time, but I think Marlon had special access to the back door. I'm still trying to figure out how the classiest lady on the block could hook up with the wildest guy in the neighborhood. I suppose it's true that opposites attract. Jackie's brother Corky could have his own chapter in this book. He was hilarious, but not on purpose. He wasn't the most coordinated guy on the block. While running one time, he tripped on a curb at full blast and went airborne, flying headfirst into the pole of a stop sign. How ironic is it to get stopped by a stop sign. He didn't get hurt, or, if he did, he didn't show it. There isn't a person on my block who doesn't recall this story. We don't think it has ever happened anywhere else at any time in the world.

Corky was a flamboyant dresser. On one occasion he spotted a group of us sitting on a porch in suits after burying one of our friends. He exited his car and greeted us, immediately reaching inside the car to show us a sample of his fine haberdashery. He pulled out this sky-blue suit and a pair of dark-purple suede shoes. As we looked at each other in disbelief, we noticed that his pants were slowly slipping off of the hanger and were nearly in the street, but no one said a word.

Corky said, "Hey Ya'll, do these shoes match this suit?"

We said, in amazing unison, "No, they match the purple house behind you!"

They actually matched that house perfectly. It was uncanny. We suspected he thought his light-blue suit was light-purple, or vice versa. He looked a bit disappointed at our response. Then he also noticed that his pants were in the street. I suppose all of the laughter didn't make matters better. He got back in the car and drove off.

Ironically, a few years ago I discovered that Corky was working as an exotic dancer. This would be akin to seeing the comedian Sinbad in a leopard thong – a true Kodak moment.

With all of Corky's coordination shortcomings, he was one of the kindest and most intelligent guys on our block. That's why he is one of the survivors that I truly respect and love dearly. We're all old now and none of us are coordinated, so Corky gets the last laugh.

It's important to note that I only mentioned less than 10 of the 40 houses on one side of the street. The laughs that came out of these homes haven't been matched in my entire adulthood. This proves that our world was both small and large at the same time.

My side of the street was no slouch, either. The Spike's family rented the corner house. They were a comical family of eight who lived in a tiny house that seemed too small to accommodate visitors. I can't recall going inside more than twice.

By this time, the McAfee's had moved and I missed their cakes and pies. Lilly and Robert Buthia bought the next house. Lilly was the first fly mom I ever saw. She was prettier than Thunder, but she had major attitude. I was scared of her. She was the type of neighbor who would tell your parents on you and cause a beat down. The Buthia's had two little girls, Roberta and Randa. Roberta was a year younger than me and feisty like her mom. Randa was a typical five-year-old who mainly played in the house.

The worst spanking I ever received came from an incident at the Buthia's. My Sister Brenda babysat Roberta and Randa. My brother Mark and I had been busy playing in the nicely renovated attic. The next thing I knew, one of the girls had closed the door and turned the lock. It was one of those old skeleton locks.

My brother and I looked at each other and yelled to the top of our lungs, "Brendaaaa!"

Our sister ran upstairs and said from the other side, "What's wrong?"

We told her that one of the girls had closed the door and that the lock was broken and we couldn't get out. All I could think about was our parents blaming us boys and suggesting that we'd had other intentions with these girls. That wasn't the case,

11

because we were at that hate-girls age and we were trying to make them leave us alone.

Thinking quickly, I yelled out the window for Pee Wee to go next door and get my father's big ladder from the side of the garage. Pee Wee got the ladder and placed it against the house. I was out of there in two seconds flat. My wimpy brother was scared of heights and refused to go down the ladder. During this whole time, Brenda was trying to work the lock from the other side. She eventually got it to work, but it was too late. Lilly was home and so was my father, and the beat-down commenced. Later that day, I was on the porch and I saw Lilly.

She asked, "Did your daddy beat you?"

I said, "Yes ma'am."

She said, "Good."

I think that was the last time I saw Lilly, mainly on purpose.

The Magee's lived next door to the Buthia's. One warning here: do not park in front of Ms. McGee's house. Period. Case closed. Well, not exactly closed. Especially, don't park there after she has shoveled the snow from in front of her *two* spaces (we were one-car families at this time) and installed her lawn chair barricade. You may get shot. Now the case is closed.

Ed Davis lived next door to Ms. McGee. Ed was a nice family man and autoworker. He had a lovely wife and a young son and daughter. Ed Davis, Jr. was the backup running back to Tyrone Wheatley for the University of Michigan. He made it to the Detroit Lions, but things didn't pan out in the pros. I heard he received his Masters Degree and is doing well. God bless them as well for living that close to Ms. McGee and not developing any issues.

She could be extremely funny and quite nice, but it wasn't smart to cross her. If someone crossed her, it was on. She always liked me because I hung with her son Otis. The last time I saw Otis, he had an ax wound in the middle of his forehead; I have no clue why.

Hot Dog lived next to him. Hot Dog wasn't exactly fat. We have to place this in the right perspective. We were active, sports-playing kids. He was a bit chubby, but to the rest of us he was Fat Hot Dog.

The next house belonged to the Humphrey's. It was 10 of them. They were good friends to everyone, but anyone who picked them up on the way to school would be late. The only household I've seen that mirrors theirs was the family in *Home Alone* before the flight. The kids in that family were late every day of the school year. I suggested that they wake up at three in the morning to ensure that everyone would get out on time. I hung with Terrance and Junior mostly. Their sister Valerie looked like Diana Ross, but better.

Valerie was the mother of Marlon's child. She was feisty as well. If you can imagine Diana Ross beating people asses, that's Valerie. She could fight almost as well as the guys. Regina and Rosa Lewis could scrap as well. Edie and Cathy Gardener were lovely girls as well, but would knock a person through a brick wall. Wanda and Phyllis Stott could pin Hulk Hogan's shoulders to a mat.

Pricilla Spikes, who was about 5 feet 10 inches and 180 pounds – in sixth grade, I must add – actually swung me around by my hair like a helicopter during a fight in a classroom. I don't think she liked me very much. I didn't want to fight her because she was a girl – well, actually, because she was twice my size, but I had no choice after she swung on me. She tried to jump on my girlfriend Christine, who lived a few blocks away. Christine had long black hair and looked like a full-blooded Indian. I got beat up trying to help Christine, but she eventually beat Pricilla on her own. Hell, I should have stayed out of it. I suppose if I was a human helicopter, I may have lost that one.

There were 40 additional homes and 40 separate stories to accompany them. These non-paid comedians, and the firm parents who molded them, established a level of laughter and camaraderie that was not present on the surrounding blocks. At least camaraderie from each end of the block. Keep in mind, we didn't get along with the other end of the street. We didn't hang together until we were older and gang life forced us into one group.

Chapter 4
Before the Street Lights Come On
---------------------☼---------------------

H aving a large street with many kids is a wonderful way to grow up. There was nothing that we didn't do and no game that we didn't play. If we didn't have a field or were too lazy to walk to one, we played where we lived and with what we had. One good thing about playing outside was that we didn't have to return until the streetlights came on. Every one of our parents told us not to let the street lights catch us. That's probably why we enjoyed blackouts so much.

It took years into adulthood to figure out their rationale behind this. I guess they took that time to get some. Since none of us could imagine our parents "doing it," it never dawned on us as children. I did have one clue. I recall the night when my mom yelled out of the window for us to come in the house. Two seconds later, my father yelled out, "Ya'll can stay outside." We were so happy to stay out past the streetlights coming on that I was grown when I sorted it all out. I suppose as many children as lived on our block, they must have been created by some means.

It was nothing wimpy about guys playing hopscotch, jacks, or jumping rope on this block. The same was true for the girls, who played basketball with us. Ironically, they were not the last people picked to join the teams. We created games. Two-square was king. Two-square is a game played with any bouncing ball, preferably a basketball. It was similar to table tennis, using the crack in the sidewalk as the net between two courts. Somehow, we turned this game into 40 Squares. We could either challenge the person in the square in front of us to take their position or we could keep the person behind us from advancing. The person in the first square was called the King. If they lost that position, they had to go to the back of the line, which got longer and longer as new players joined in.

If we were really bored, we played *that's my car*. This game was easy. Each person had the opportunity to say that the next car to drive down the street was his or hers. The fun began when someone discovered the next car was a *hooptie*, aka a 1919-get-out-and-push. We played a game called *rock teacher*. In this game, the students would sit on the first step on a porch and the kid being the teacher would hide a rock behind his or her back in a hand. If we picked the hand with the rock, we graduated to the next grade, or the next highest stair.

Now that I think of it, we must have been bored to death and our creativity took over. Remember, there were no Game Boys, Nintendos, or X-Boxes. No Maddens or interactive fighting games. Whatever we did came completely out of our imaginations. I wonder why our generation seems to be the most creative in the workforce. We can sit in front of a computer terminal and produce things from scratch.

We also played *strike-em-out* by painting a strike zone on the side wall of the paint shop on the corner. The wall served as the hind-catcher. Unfortunately, there were many windows nearby and this game only lasted a couple of summers. In addition, we didn't want to break the kitchen window in the Stott's household, which was next door to the paint shop. Who knows, maybe the ball would've fallen into that skillet of pork chop grease and someone would've received third degree burns. We had to think of something else.

We were a baseball neighborhood, so we thought of another game. If someone had concrete stairs in front of their home, we played *Home Run Derby*. We pitched the ball off of the stairs, and if it bounced over our head it was a home run. If it hit the ground it was a base hit. We had to use tennis balls or other small rubber balls to get the perfect bounce. The right bounce could cause the fielder to get run over by a car as he chased the ball into the street. No one under the age of 35 drove down Lemay at less than 30 mph.

The game of all games on Lemay was *Finders*. I have no clue how this was created, and it is best described as team hide-and-seek. We would pick teams and flip a coin to see which group would hide first. The boundary would be a 20-house radius, and backyards were in play. This was an amazing game. I think we put kick-the-can out of business. It would go on for hours and would not end until darkness, or when every member was located, or at least when most of them were located. There was always someone on the team that no one liked, and we'd forget about them on purpose and leave them in their hiding place until they decided to come out on their own. At that point, the game would be over and they'd be arrogant enough to believe that they'd had the best hiding place. Of course, we'd say, "You sure did." Others would end the game after their partner was pregnant. I think more than a few babies were made during Finders. Some couples are still missing to this day.

Basketball was an integral part of growing up. Unfortunately, we had no basketball rims. The first rim was a blue plastic milk crate. We nailed it to a pole in the alley and played on it for two years. At some point one of our resident geniuses located an old bicycle rim and we at least had something round to shoot at. A year or so later someone found a real rim with nets that we thought was the recipient of a monster dunk in another life. We used this for years until a half-court was built at St. Margaret Mary's Catholic School at the other end of the street.

Some of my best times were spent in search for the perfect candy bargain. It is amazing what we could buy for a penny. We were rich if we had more than a nickel to spend on candy. One of our biggest scams to get candy was to attend church. It was a sure way to get at least 50¢ from our parents. Since my parents attended church outside of the neighborhood, the kids attended church alone, which was perfect. We would put 25¢ in the pot and keep the other 25¢. If I didn't have cousins attending the same church, I might not have shown up at all. We could buy a bag full of candy for a quarter. We could also buy a Hostess cake and a pop. My favorite after-church treat was a Suzie Q and a Pepsi. The Pepsi came in a long-neck glass bottle. The Suzie Q cost 10¢ and the soda pop was 15¢. What a scam!

Today, penny candy costs at least a quarter each. I saw someone recently purchase one Now-or-Later for a dime. In the 60s and 70s, the entire pack cost a nickel. We would literally buy the store out and trade another kid for a particular kind of candy or candy bar. Unfortunately, they usually only wanted to part with the sticky candy necklace with the sweat and lint on it. You know the kind – the colorful button-looking candy on the elastic string. I think we ate more dirt, wax, and paper than we ate candy. I mention wax because of the Kool-Aid inside the wax container. We would drink the juice and chew the wax until the taste of the Kool-Aid was gone. We would, in turn, melt the wax with a lighter and pour it in our hands. A kid can peel it completely off and give it to the next one. A single Kool-Aid container could last on the block for three days.

Karate became a passion for the entire block during the surge of Bruce Lee movies. We had karate camps similar to the ones we saw in *Enter the Dragon*. We broke boards, bricks, hands, and heads. We kicked, flipped, and slipped. No one got badly hurt, but we realized that it was dangerous to make nun chucks out of sawed shovel handles, chains, and nails. A few people got popped in the head, but nothing major, thank heavens.

The one thing we did regularly was race. I'm not talking about 10-year-olds. Every age group raced. I think we had a few world-class runners, but no one owned a stopwatch to prove it. It's hard to time someone on broken Timex wristwatches or those newfangled LED watches that were as big as a bar of soap. We raced barefooted or with Mr. Basketballs. No one could afford Kinney Shoes NBAs or the top-of-the-line Converse All-Stars. Mr. Basketballs were green and made of canvas; they were the shoes that caused a kid to hit the wall under the basket when going for a lay-up. We literally couldn't stop. They had no traction whatsoever. The ankle patch would fall off and everyone would draw a black star on them to make them look like All-Stars, but we could always tell they were Mr. Basketballs. I wonder if the youth of today would just plain jump off a bridge if their parents made them wear Mr. Basketballs. We didn't have Air Jordans. We had Air Basketballs. They said, "basketball," and the holes in the bottom let air in. That was as close as we could get.

If the streetlights were not our signal to go in the house, Corky's aunt was the other. That lady was different. She was like one of the old folks on TV. She reminded us of the Jeffersons' grandmother. At 7:00 p.m. she would open the door, look out, and yell to the top of her lungs, "Corky Baby, Jackie Baby, come and get your din-din."

Are you serious? Two doors down, the entire neighborhood was perched on the Lewis' porch and she was yelling this stupid saying. Corky and Jackie were at least 13 and 14 when this happened, and it went on for years. We didn't dog them much on this because we continued to wait for their cousin, Berry Gordy, to send us some free tickets to a Motown concert. He never did. I seriously doubted that Corky and Jackie attended any concerts for free, either. At least, that's what most of us thought.

Lemay was a broke-down Atlantic City, home to the neighborhood gamblers. The guys on my street bet on everything. They would bet on the color of the next car to drive down the street. My brother was a notorious dice-shooter, and so was my brother-in-law Bill. They would start gambling Friday evening and go the weekend without stopping or eating. I hope you noticed that I didn't list drinking. After they'd won everyone's money, Bill and Mark would battle between themselves. On Saturday afternoon, Bo would arrive. Bo was an older, working-class brother who doubled as a professional gambler. Each week, Bo would allow the minions on my block to win each other's money, then arrive before sundown Saturday to win their money by pitching pennies (while they bet 20-dollar-bills), or later that evening by shooting dice. I would watch this hard-earned money change hands all weekend and then see Bo arrive to clean up. They never caught on, and Bo raked in the catch by noon each Sunday. I don't know how Bo ended up financially, but I suspect he stressed out a few loved-ones along the way.

Riding bikes had a special place in our hearts. We rode for miles. Today, bikes are top sellers, but you can't get a parent to let their kid ride past their cul-de-sac. We rode to Belle Isle Park, located near the river, or to Metropolitan Beach, which was 30 miles away. The only thing we didn't do was to let someone else ride our bikes. Chances were great that either they would steal them or they'd be taken away from them.

On one occasion, a member of the notorious Tyer Family asked to ride my brother's bike that he'd let me borrow. It was a brand-new white 10-speed. I had two options: say no and get the beat-down, or let him ride it. I decided to let Rodney Tyer ride it. Let me put this in perspective. The Tyer Family had at least 12 to 14 members. In this family, the girls were as tough, if not tougher, than the boys. It was strange, because Lisa Tyer was just plain beautiful. She had green eyes *before* color contacts were created. She talked in a slow, quiet tone, and everyone wanted to date her — or should I say something else other than 'date'? Her tiny little sister Angie was tougher than she was. There wasn't a fight in school that didn't involve one of these girls.

Their brothers, Jeffery and Timothy, were notorious and have their own stories in Detroit crime lore. I did not want to let Rodney ride Mark's bike, but I felt I had no choice. To my surprise, 30 minutes later Rodney returned to the playground and gave me back Mark's bike, saying, "Thanks. You are a good little dude, and tell Mark I said hi." Right then I realized that my brother and I had earned a level of respect in the neighborhood.

Jeffery was later charged with a murder and was on trial, and Timothy was jailed for making threatening gestures to witnesses. During his trial, Jeffery escaped from Detroit's County Jail and caused a few guards to be fired. Within a week, Timothy was found hanging in his cell and his death was called a suicide. No one in the neighborhood thought so, but it never came up again in the media. We suspected that the guards thought Timothy was Jeffery, or that it was in retaliation for the firings.

I was fortunate to have a bike returned in those days. It's ironic that little favors we may give at one point in our lives may cause us a little less drama at some other portion of them.

Going to school was an adventure in itself. It was akin to attending school on the set of *Saturday Night Live*. It's amazing that we learned anything at all. The teachers were as diverse as our neighborhood in its earlier years. I'm wondering if any of you had teachers that looked as if they should be in a group home. Either we were young, or they were as old as Methuselah. I had a teacher named Ms. Rose. She literally abused us. I must agree that we plucked her nerves and provoked most of it. She had a paddle that contained three drilled holes. When she hit us, the holes would suck our rear-ends directly into the paddle. We received this if we were late to class. I think her paddles were named Mr. Clean and Mrs. Clean. The two people who set her off each day were Pricilla Spikes and Alvin Vaughn. She tied Priscilla tightly to her chair with a clothesline, wrapping the line around her arms numerous times, and tied the ends into knots. Priscilla could not move until the class ended.

She also tried to put a full trashcan (pencil shavings included) over Alvin's head. Alvin was the Eddie Murphy of our class. Alvin had smarts, but refused to use them. He was known for his reading skills, or should I say his lack thereof. Ms. Rose would ask him to read a segment from a textbook and he would skip the words he didn't know and continue on with the paragraph. This was unique because Alvin would say, "My father drove me to (pause) I don't know that word, Amusement Park" or "I left my jacket at the (pause) I don't know that word, Street Library" or "I will clean the (pause) I don't know that word, and I don't know that one either, (pause) after school."

Alvin's skipping of the words and continuing on would drive Ms. Rose crazy. That's when she tried to put the trashcan over his head and he punched it to the floor. She ordered him to sit under her desk. He complied with this order, because anything to keep from doing work was fine with Alvin. She returned to her desk with him sitting under it. After class, Alvin told us that he saw more cobwebs under her dress than under her desk. I wonder if teachers of today could continue their careers after that move.

We had teachers who were so gorgeous that we purposely caused problems to get their attention. Ms. Mack would paddle our hands with a ruler if we were late. We had gym class prior to her math class and made it a point to be late. It was like we had a close-up of Halle Berry as she spanked our hands. After a few weeks she figured it out and stopped. We straightened up and arrived on time as well. It was just an older-women phase we were going through.

I can also remember parents spanking their children in front of the whole student body. We're talking about serious beat-downs. At least we didn't have to worry about that student acting out for the remainder of the school year. I can recall a kid named Eric getting a major beating from his father in the middle of the hallway. He never excelled in school after that. He's serving approximately 80 years now.

Recess had its own rewards if we could stand the weather or survive the outdoor activity that we played. The principal determined whether we played outdoors or indoors. We had to check a sign at the door leading to the playground that said, "Outdoors, Indoors, or Optional." If it was snow or just cold, we went outside. If it was a torrential rainstorm, we stayed inside.

If it was an earthquake, tornado, or typhoon, it was optional. We had a choice. Go figure. The playground was divided into The Girls' Side and The Boys' Side. Never did the two cross. I can't believe we obeyed this rule.

To say the least, we froze in the winter and burned in the summer. It was so crazy that we created two sick games, Bonny Door and Riding Edward. I'll discuss Riding Edward first. Edward had to have been six feet tall and at least 400 pounds in grade school. As many kids who could hold on would ride Edward like remoras as he ran around the playground for one hour straight. He didn't mind and we had a blast. He wasn't lemony fresh, but we didn't care. It was like hopping a train or the subway that Detroit never had.

Bonny Door was tackle tag on gravel. It started out with 50 guys racing from one end of the playground to the other. The last one to finish was *it*. As he stood alone, looking at 49 crazy-looking guys, we ran over him. If he tackled anyone, they became *it* as well, and it became two against 48, and so on. By the end of the recess hour, it would be 49 trying to catch and tackle the fastest, most elusive kid in the school. This game produced a number of pro football prospects, and a few quadriplegics as well. Nevertheless, we survived, were physically fit (except for Edward), and found ways to have fun on our own without modern electronics.

After our fair share of school, laughs, fun, and a few satisfied parents, it was time to head in because the streetlights were on. Television presented us a unique opportunity. We were allowed to venture into new worlds without leaving the space on the floor at the end of our parents' bed. How amazing was it to watch *Batman* and *Superman* in prime time. They'd never score on the Nielsen ratings today. We had to decide if the Hulk was better than the Green Hornet. I loved *Lost in Space*, *Batman*, and *Star Trek*. Who can't recall the words, "Crush, Kill, Destroy", "You bubble-headed booby", "POW! BAM! WHAM!" These were the sounds of our childhood. Each scene watched on a black-and-white 19-inch television which sat on top of a broken floor-model TV. A hanger replaced the broken antenna. We used a set of pliers to change the channel. The worst thing in the world was a running TV while we were watching *Green Acres* or *The Beverly*

Hillbillies. It is easy to see which shows were the most successful. They are still in syndication.

Chapter 5
How Could a Brother Can Kill a Tree?

-------------------☼-------------------

The demise of a neighborhood comes in many forms. The so-called white flight after the riots was the starting point, but white flight wasn't the only reason. For some reason, my brethren kill their own neighborhoods. To this day, this is one of the biggest mysteries in the African American community. It's still happening. Do you recall Rodney King? I truly think it has something to do with either a renter's mentality or pure laziness. I'm not saying that all renters destroy their property. What I'm saying is that some renters don't take care of items in or around their homes because the landlord is suppose to fix everything. It's terrible when folks call the landlord at midnight to change a light bulb, or won't buy a lawnmower to take care of the front of their home.

It's a mentality that says, "If it isn't mine, I'm not responsible for it." This mindset is the reason why trash permeates certain areas today. No one feels responsible for it, and therefore no one feels they have a reason to pick it up. This is why I pick up every piece of paper or shard of glass on or near my yard. I have driven past glass in the neighborhood and returned with a broom, dust pan, and box to put it in. Why should I get a flat tire a block away just because the broken glass is not in front of my house?

Public Works for the City of Detroit, aka "The City," planted trees along the curb on our entire block. These trees took hold and bloomed beautifully. These trees survived for a couple of years until the brothers began to pull the bark off of them strip by strip. The new trees started to die. We had no idea what they were doing with the strips of bark. I actually thought they were smoking it. When all of the new trees died, these lunatics moved on to the 100-year-old trees. Since stripping bark from them didn't cause immediate death, they carved them to death. You know: TM + WP, and so on.

The best thing that happened to the City of Detroit (or at least until they build a subway) was the adoption of bottle recycling. It wasn't a great idea for people who had roaches. We received a whole 10¢ for each bottle. Before recycling, I suspected that brothers chewed glass and spit it in the street. I felt this way because I never saw anyone break a bottle, but there were tiny shards of glass everywhere.

Speaking of roaches, I saw roaches in my neighborhood so big that they could go to the store to redeem their own bottles. They should have filmed *Mimic* in my neighborhood. How can a person sit in a living room with a group of people and not see a roach or mouse run by, especially when it runs across the TV screen during *Julia*? It never fails that the people with the most roaches were the first hosts to offer food. In most cases, the food smelled tremendous and looked even better.

I suspect they knew what was going on when we said, "I've already eaten."

It's even tougher when they said, "Well, take a plate with you."

I hoped they didn't follow me home and see the trail of food, like in Hansel and Gretel.

Roaches are not the only residents of Detroit. It has at least three species of rats. It has the alley rats that run amuck in the trashcans. It has the ones that walked us to school in the morning and back home at the end of the day. They think they're dogs. Last but not least, it has the little brown furry ones that we *thought* were mice, the kind that crawled up the curtain during my girlfriend's visit. These also had a jungle gym in the stove. They hung out around the food until we came in, then they ran down inside one of the burners.

I can't lie. We had this type for a couple of months one year. They were aggressive as hell. We'd hoped they were better trained and didn't come out during company, but not this type. They *only* came out during company. If we didn't have guests, we didn't have mice (or baby rats in this case). If we had guests, we inherited more rodent *guests*. I was glad my father found a way to kill this batch. I don't know which pets (I mean pests) I hated the most. I'll take one mouse without a nest over a wall-based roach any day. There is no telling just how many roaches are camped in the crawl spaces of a home.

The partial demise of Lemay came in the destruction of vacant homes. There was a home that was vacated and no one else wanted to move there. It was the house next door to Hot Dog's, where the father went crazy and shot his wife nine times with a rifle while he laughed throughout the whole ordeal. I didn't see it because it happened after the streetlights came on and we were all in the house. We did hear the shots. That house went vacant for at least three years after the shooting. It was basically a hangout for everyone. It had concrete stairs that were perfect for Home Run Derby. I think we literally broke that house apart, piece by piece.

That house was destroyed from the outside in. Remember, no one had the nerve to go inside. We pulled the thin brick siding off of the wall and stacked them together for the Bruce Lee chop. We discovered breaking bricks from watching old karate movies. This was crucial for the karate school in the Lewis" backyard. We would pull off as many as we could carry and take them across the street, then the chopping would commence. It wasn't long before the city demolished our hangout. They didn't have to do much; it basically fell to the ground as soon as the bulldozer pushed it. I forgot to mention that the lady who was shot nine times lived after her ordeal. They moved and we never knew what happened to them.

Not only did we play games, we participated in rituals as well. In Detroit, the night before Halloween is known as Devil's Night. When I was a kid, it was the day to knock over someone's trashcan, write on their car window with soap, hit someone with a water balloon, or toss a raw egg into a crowd on a playground. You know, little stuff. Before long, Devil's Night turned into a reason for slumlords or crazy homeowners to burn down their homes, garages, or both to take out insurance claims. I'm sure some young people chose this night to take out gripes with enemies, but for the most part, it was senseless. By the mid-90s, Devil's Night in Detroit produced hundreds of fires. On a few occasions, suburbanites were spotted and detained for towing cars into the city limits to set them on fire. Why couldn't they burn them in Auburn Hills, Grosse Point, or Bloomfield Hills?

In addition to the Devil's Night tradition, we searched vigorously for the *Pig Lady*. This was scary as hell. There was a rumor that during Halloween week a lady with a face that was half pig was killing kids and leaving them in vacant houses. We must have illegally entered 50 vacant houses looking for the Pig Lady. All it would take was someone to break a mirror or glass in these vacant houses and 20 kids would break their necks to get out. Each time, our hearts would literally beat out of our chests. We would search the gravel on the playground and say, "Look, a footprint." It could have been a dog's footprint but we didn't care – we took off running. It got so bad that the news would talk about the Pig Lady as well. I guess it was Detroit's version of Candyman.

We would enter these vacant homes at night and dare someone to look into the medicine cabinet mirror and say, "I'm not afraid of Mrs. Meriwether" three times. This was the mid-70s and we had the precursor to the *Candyman* movies. Candyman was based in Chicago, and the nearest major city to that is Detroit. Go figure. Wes Craven, I want my damn royalty check! For some reason, I still can't get my daughter to say the "Mrs. Meriwether" thing. I think we destroyed more stuff running from the Pig Lady and Mrs. Meriwether than we did while karate-chopping our neighbor's house to death.

Chapter 6
Motown Moved to California?
What Do We Do Now?

-------------------☼-------------------

E veryone received musical instruments for Christmas back in the day. Unfortunately for my house, they never lasted past 6:00 p.m. on Christmas day, especially the drum sets. I loved drum sets, but my cousins Frank and Don would bust them by 6:00 p.m. every single Christmas. I didn't want to be stingy, but I cringed every time one of my big cousins asked to play with a Christmas toy or instrument. I said, "Okay" unwillingly, then walked away saying, "Christmas is officially over." I would have nothing to play with for the remainder of the holiday season. I almost believed in Red Foxx's statement that, "We were so poor, that for Christmas, if I wasn't a little boy, I wouldn't have had anything to play with."

I'm glad to say that other families didn't experience our Christmas toy demise. Numerous music groups sprouted up around the neighborhood. Two of the most famous were Five Ounces of Soul and Al Hudson and the Soul Partners. They battled for hood supremacy at the neighborhood hole-in-the-walls. They were great. Five Ounces didn't have management behind them, but Al Hudson's group seemed to be headed in the right direction. Five young men from around the corner on Fairview Street started a singing group, and before long they were the lead singers for Al's group. These guys were amazing. They were a mix between the Jackson Five and the Dramatics, another Detroit icon.

Growing up in a house with three sisters was a benefit for my brother and me. There was always a group of older guys hanging around the house. I think initially they were all trying to tap my sisters, but eventually fell in love with our parents' open-door policy. My mother and father would allow young adults to hang around and maybe drink a beer or two. My mother always believed that it was better to allow these young adults to drink in the privacy of a home instead of hanging on a street corner. It may not be a Y2K PC thing to do, but back in the mid-70s, there was something to be said about this.

Hanging on a corner wasn't going to happen in my household. Hickey (Charles Franks) was a member of the Fairview Five, and was basically a big brother to my family. He was a handsome gentleman and the group's lead singer. As these groups developed, larger groups like Enchantment, Brainstorm, and members of Parliament/Funkadelic frequented these small clubs. I was tiny, agile, and a good dancer. Hickey and the other group members would come over my house to ask my parents if I could go with them to neighborhood house parties. After a short pause, they would say, "Yes." Little did they know that I was nowhere near any house party. I would be the dancer for these groups at small clubs all around the city. They would make sure I was home around 12-ish, and my parents wouldn't suspect anything unusual. Life was fun for a young kid from the block.

On one cold Saturday evening, we heard a loud knock at the door and someone rushed in and said, "Hickey was just shot at the store where he worked." We all rushed out of the house and to the corner store to find out that the storeowner's son was playing with the gun and pointing it at customers. Hickey told him to put it down and stop playing. The guy said, "I'll shoot you," and pointed the gun at Hickey. The gun went off and shot Hickey in the neck, killing him instantly.

That was one of the saddest days in my family's history. Many more incidents of this nature would happen over the years, but none seem to have the same impact on my family as this one. It was similar to the singer Aaliyah passing. You could see all of the talent blossoming around the neighborhood, and a tragic incident happening to one of these singing groups was heartbreaking. The other Fairview Five members disbanded and moved on with their lives. One member lives in the Baltimore/DC area, and I was fortunate to invite him to a high-level government Christmas party in Washington. I saw him again on TV shortly thereafter. He was the head FBI agent in charge of the DC sniper case.

Al Hudson and the Soul Partners dropped Red as their manager and were taken under the wing of The Perker – Al Perkins, a local morning radio DJ for WJLB. He was a rising star and the replacement for Donnie Simpson, who had taken a job at WKYS Radio in Washington, DC. Under The Perker, Al and the Soul Partners (who changed their name to One Way) took off. They cut a number of national hits, and it was amazing to see them on *Soul Train*. They made it. Unfortunately, The Perker was murdered shortly after taking over One Way's management. I never found out the details, or whether someone was convicted for that crime.

Another group, named Chapter 8, rose to the forefront in the late 70s. Michael Powell and David Washington originally formed the group after departing as backup musicians in the Detroit Emeralds. The Cabaret Lounge, located on Detroit's Eastside, was home to this group for a couple of years. Kids could enter this club despite our age if we were well-dressed. They didn't allow us to drink but we could watch the show. The group added a series of singers before releasing an album with Gerald Lyles and a woman with a unique singing style and extremely deep voice as their main vocalists. Her voice was a mixture of Ella Fitzgerald and Billie Holiday. She had tremendous range and a wonderful stage presence.

In 1979 they released an album titled *Chapter 8* and a hit song titled "Ready for Your Love." It featured both vocalists, but the woman's voice captivated the entire city. We rushed to buy this record to discover the singer's name, which was Anita Baker. I sensed early on that there would be problems with this group having longevity. Gerald commanded the stage, but Anita regularly stole the show. Long-term success would likely be difficult. They released a second cut from the album titled "I Just Want to Be Your Girl." This release showcased Anita Baker and it sealed the idea that she made the group. We could sense the tension between the lead vocalists during local performances.

The album sold well in and around Detroit, but national sales were not as steep. Varese/Ariola Records subsequently dropped them from the label. They also told Anita that she couldn't sing. The band continued on without Anita Baker and she returned to

31

office work. She later returned with a vengeance and released a series of Grammy winners as a solo artist. In addition, she displayed a captivating and extremely elegant stage performance. Her career is legendary.

Chapter 8 released a second album in 1985 for Beverly Glenn Records and a third album for Capitol Records. Neither developed into hits. The next most successful member of Chapter 8 was Michael Powell. He developed into a talented producer for Baker, Regina Belle, and James Ingraham. Mr. Lyles never developed into a national artist and I don't know if he's still in the music business. His claim to fame was the Jeffrey Osborn sound. Since Jeffrey is still touring, that can't be good for his career.

The current crop of Detroit acts were just as good as the groups Berry Gordy took to California with him. Subsequently, many of the individuals in Motown were not doing well. Florence Ballard of the Supremes had died, and the Temptations were passing one by one. The local Detroit groups were having trouble getting music contracts as well. Many branched out into solo production endeavors or left music altogether. When it was all said and done, we were proud of what Motown left behind.

Chapter 7
Who in the hell are the Turners?

--------------------☼-----------------

Dancing became the craze in our neighborhood and around the city. As a young kid, I won $5 at a Bump contest. Immediately after I won this contest, these two older guys who looked like twins approached me. They were also hanging around my sister Brenda. They looked sort of notorious, wearing big hats, baggy khakis, and suede Jingle boots. We called them Jingle Boots because they were the height of today's Timberlands, but were black and fairly flat, with metal buckles that these guys didn't desire to fasten, and they jingled or made loud noises when they walked or danced. Hell, it was easier to call them Jingle boots than to describe them. These guys introduced themselves as Biggy and Liddy Turner, who had just moved onto Fairview from the Harper and Gratiot area of Detroit's East Side, a well-known gang area. I suppose one was big and one was little at some point of their childhood.

The years were 1975-76. These guys were hard, and I could see that the other guys in the hall were leery to be around them. Since they'd taken a liking to my dance style, I didn't have a problem. Before long, they were hanging at the house, too. The same thing happened. They were trying to get some. I can't say if they did or didn't to be honest – I didn't see it. Within weeks, they'd taken a liking to our household as well, and had begun to teach me how to do dances that we'd never seen before. Most of these dances can be seen on hip-hop shows to this day.

They told us that they had 12 sisters and brothers, also living around the corner. Within two months of the Turners moving into the neighborhood, there was word of Turner family members picking fights all over the place. Pre-school kids were being beaten up by other pre-schoolers. Elementary school kids were coming home with black eyes. Middle schoolers suffered the same fate, and so did adults throughout the neighborhood. This was their way of letting you know that they were in the hood.

During this time the Johnsons were off-limits. They came from the neighborhood that housed the Chain Gang, a post-Black-Panther-era gang that may have developed from Chicago's Blackstone Rangers, aka EL Runkins. Various members were moving to Detroit to avoid legal cases and drama in Chicago.

A small gang from my neighborhood called the BAs developed in the early 70s. Their only claim to fame was charging kids to pass through Joy Junior High's humongous playground during snowstorms. If we didn't pay we had to walk outside the fence for nearly a mile. They never materialized as a force and were gone within a year.

Any time a gang arises, a rival gang is bound to follow. The Bishops were that rival gang. They warred with the Chains for years. These gangs went to Burroughs Junior High and Kettering High School, at least those who went to school. Both of these schools were off-limits to most sane students in Detroit. It was suicide to go to an away game at these schools. Our players had to fight their way onto the bus after games.

The Turners were a gang unto themselves. If one was in a fight, not only did the other 13 arrive, so did their mother. She was a large woman, and would arrive at her kids' fights wearing a sundress or a muumuu, with her hands in her pockets. We heard that she carried two .45 pistols in those pockets. She would begin to yell, "Who is messing with my babies?" Before long, everyone would scatter like roaches when the lights come on. She never shot anyone, but we were smart enough to not stay around to find out if she would.

Everyone in the hood had to deal with a Turner at some time in their adolescence. My encounter was with the worst one of them all. His name was Mark Twain and he stood about 4 feet 11 inches. He looked like a running back. He was called Mark Twain not because of his writing ability, but because his voice was so deep that when he told you his name, Turner sounded like Twain, so everyone called him Mark Twain.

Biggy warned me about Mark Twain. He said, "My brother is the same height as you, so he will try you." He was right.

I came out of my house on my birthday evening to sit on the Gardeners' porch. My future brother-in-law Bill was on the porch as well. He let me sip on a beer to celebrate my birthday. My parents were out of town and I was hanging. This was my first beer and I really wasn't feeling well. No excuse, but this little, hard-looking kid came up to the Gardeners' porch.

He looked at all of us and said to me, "I don't like you." His voice was so deep that I knew who he was immediately.

I said to myself, "Damn! Now I have to fight Mark Twain on my birthday while I'm buzzing."

He took a swing at me and I ducked. We tussled for about three minutes and no one was hit in the face or anything. Ironically, no one on the porch moved. They just sat there and watched us fight. It was just a wrestling match and nothing more. After that, we dusted ourselves off. I sat on the porch and Mark Twain walked down the street to pick another fight. Later that week, I heard that Liddy had confronted him at home for picking a fight with me.

Each time I saw Mark Twain after that, he would say, "Hey Tony, I just beat up Jonathan," or some other kid in the neighborhood.

I would say to him, "Mark Twain, why don't you stop fighting all of the guys in our own hood." He would just smile and ride away on his bike.

A month later, my brother Mark suffered the same fate with the Turner in his age group. Olla Turner approached Mark while a few of us were on our way to the corner store. Olla pushed my brother first and Mark grabbed him in a bear hug and bull rushed him into the plate glass window of the drycleaners. To our amazement, they both fell through the glass and Mark received cut his hand. Mark needed about 14 stitches and I don't recall Olla getting cut at all. Mark was considered the winner although he cut his hand. As far as the Turners were concerned, if kids fought back, they were respected and they would never mess with them again.

There were other brothers who fellow neighbors had to deal with as well. Tyrone was older than Mark Twain but not as feisty. Tyrone would shoot people instead. Ken-Tone was the toughest of the Turner boys. He didn't fight anyone in the neighborhood. No one messed with him and he messed with no one. Ken-Tone was cool with everybody. Ken-Tone had the idea that no one should come into our neighborhood who didn't belong and we shouldn't fight each other. The whole neighborhood respected Ken-Tone.

Ken-Tone wasn't around long. He was arrested at some point and received about 50 years in prison. I never knew exactly what he was charged with and never asked. We never knew exactly what level of crime this family was capable of committing. Frankly, no one wanted to know. There were incidents all over the neighborhood and I can't say who was responsible, but no one ruled them out. As long as we were not the target anymore, we moved on and let them be.

There was a large fire on Fairview on one weekend evening, and before long word had it that the Turners' house had been firebombed. Someone had firebombed the front of the house and had shot Tyrone in the leg as he ran out of the back. Rumor said that one of the Turners had had a run-in with another 14-person family in the neighborhood and the firebombing had been in retaliation.

Personally, my family had no issues with the Turners. We were fairly well liked, but I could sense a little relief from the other families in the neighborhood after they moved. They did leave a legacy; the idea that no one would come into our neighborhood and push us around had taken hold.

Chapter 8
BKs, Errol Flynns, and Borsalinos
-------------------☼-------------------

I f you have never attended an inner-city house party, it is likely
  that you have never partied. These aren't the usual stand-
around cocktail parties. They are dark, loud, and smoky. There is
something unsettling about people picking lint off of your
sweater when no lint actually exists. If you have never done this,
it's obvious that you have never been to a black-lights-in-the-
basement house party. Black light has a way of turning every
thread on a sweater into millions of minute pieces of lint. I guess
alcohol has a way of enhancing this effect, because the person
doing the picking always seemed to be wasted.

There were no DJs or MCs. There was only a component set,
which looked like a weird floor-model television. These were
nearly four to five feet wide, and a person could lift a wooden lid
to reach the record player inside. The speakers were hidden in the
front of the component and camouflaged with cloth and wood
trim. We could stack 25 45 rpm records on the record player and
they would drop one after another until the arm on the record
player stood too high to continue operation. If the stack got too
high, we had to place a nickel on the arm to keep it from slipping
off of the record.

The invitations to these parties were basic. They were created
on regular 3x5 white-lined index cards. We would keep it simple:
PLACE, DATE, RATE, PLATE, & MATE. This basic
information was enough to ensure that at least 75 people from all
over the city would attend a function. These five categories told
the location, the day and time of the event, what food would be

provided or sold, and whether the person invited should bring a date. No need to discuss music, because this was Motown.

There had been a time when parties were only attended by neighbors. This changed shortly after the Turners moved to our neighborhood and members of the Chain Gang came to visit them at our parties. They were extremely hard-core. The ladies in our neighborhood were intrigued with their toughness. It wasn't long before they started to flex their muscles towards the local guys. On more than one occasion, they groped a woman while provoking fights with the guys. On one occasion, the Chain Gang fired their guns in the basement windows of one of these parties. Fortunately, no one was hit in that incident.

A few days later, a meeting was held at the Brewer Recreation Center, adjacent to Joy Junior High School. The crux of this meeting was the decision not to let anyone from other neighborhoods attend the parties or have free rein in the area. At least 30 people, whose homes covered a four square mile area, attended this meeting. These representatives returned to their area and recruited, on average, five members each. Within a month of the meeting, the letters "BK" sprouted up on walls and vacant buildings around the neighborhood. It wasn't long before I found out that BK stood for Black Killers.

In a neighborhood that housed many individually tough teenagers, a gang was the last thing that we needed. We could feel the camaraderie developing in the air. We felt safe and free to go anywhere in this four mile area without trouble from someone outside of the hood. It was no longer called a neighborhood. I could also sense the development of gangs in school. Everyone seemed to go crazy all at once. I once saw a guy hanging upside down by one leg from the second floor of the school. His only saving grace was that the guy holding his leg didn't let him go. I saw one of my friends hit a guy in the forehead so hard that it caused a large black hickey with a slit in it. Ironically, it didn't bleed. When the guy looked in the mirror, he passed out.

A fat kid manhandled me in a pickup basketball game. I approached him after school about the court incident and he shoved me. Before I could throw the first punch, 10 people were stomping him. None of them were good friends of mine, but they felt a duty to defend me based on the guy not living in our neighborhood. A second rival to the Chain Gang was born.

Graffiti began to tarnish the entire city. BKs took a can of paint everywhere they went. The letters "BK's" were becoming well-known throughout the city.

On one occasion, one of the members observed a slow-moving police car driving down his street. He politely strolled to the middle of the street, turned in the direction of their car and fired a shotgun blast that shattered their back window. The cops never returned following that incident. Acts like that only solidified the reputation that was building city-wide.

Eventually, the police would find other methods to curtail gang participation. They would stop every young male or group of females on the street and jot their names onto a list. It didn't matter if we were a member, an affiliate, or just going to school or work. If a person was young and black, they were stopped, searched, and documented.

Along with the graffiti and the incidents of crime, the BKs began to establish themselves by name or nickname. Surprisingly, most members used their regular names, such as Sherman, Donnie, or Melvin. Nicknames such as Dollar Bill, Deckie, Big Bird, and Weasel were rare. Most of these guys were well-known by their birth names and could handle their own business when it came to fighting.

A gang in a hood with numerous households containing nine to 15 siblings would take things to another level. The one thing that always intrigued me was that this gang contained more individually hard-core members than tag-alongs and affiliates. Most gangs are made up of kids who are afraid to operate alone or are looking for protection. Not this gang. Many were boxers, and others were martial-arts experts. It seemed as if Mike Tyson had raised them. They could also handle weapons. On one occasion, they even possessed a box of dynamite and a Thompson sub-machine gun. Maybe they thought the dynamite sticks were Roman candles.

Formal leadership became an issue in our hood for the first time. This was my first real exposure to power and leadership. There were at least five separate sections of BKs in this four-mile radius. Each section had its own leaders rising to the forefront. East Warren Avenue was the main drag for the Black Killers. If you didn't live in this area, it was best that you avoid this stretch of street. The Southeast Section contained my block and the

Turner Family. With Turners in our section, we didn't need a leader. Nevertheless, Donnie rose to the forefront.

Donnie was basically a class clown during school, but he didn't take flack from anyone. He had charisma. Marvin and Bennie ran the Northeast Section. Although Bennie lived around the corner from me, he hung out mostly on Marvin's street. There was a section across the bridge that didn't really have a leader, but Johnny eventually rose to the forefront. They lived the closest to the Chain Gang, so they were on the front line. The Southeast Section was run by Michael, Dollar Bill, and Melvin. The Northwest Section's leaders were a set of twins who could easily have been successful businessmen. The overall leader of the BKs was Sherman, an older brother with tremendous leadership skills. Everyone listened to everything he said. If their efforts had been pointed in the right direction, all of these members could be CEOs in today's world.

Before long, the Black Killers grew to nearly 500 members, located mainly in our neighborhood. Of the 500 members, 50 were women – the Sister Ks. They were as hard-core as the guys. We had to be careful in our dealings with them because they carried a large portion of the weapons. They were always strapped. This was critical, since the guys were being thrown against the wall by John Law on a routine basis. They never searched the women. Fortunately for Lemay St., our women did not join. They were tough on their own.

On one occasion, two Sister Ks picked a fight with the two Lewis sisters, and before long, one of the gang members was picked up via the clean and jerk and tossed into a large rose bush. The other one received a pummeling about the head and face and asked repeatedly, "Are you coming back?"

The answer was an expected, "No."

Our girls handled their own work. After this fight, the Sister Ks were welcomed to visit our street at any time, as long as they came in peace. No hard feelings. The guys didn't have the same problem because most of them were already members.

On another occasion, while I was leaving school I saw at least 50 rival gang members standing in front of the school buses looking for someone to beat. I immediately turned around and reentered the school. Then I saw two Sister Ks, and all three of us walked through this crowd.

I heard the words, "We should take his jacket!"

Another guy said, "And then we have to fight 500 of them."

Needless to say, the two Sister Ks were both armed with 25-caliber pistols. We got on the bus and went home.

In my case, flipping the gang switch was a tough call. I never truly decided. I survived. While out of the neighborhood, I was a member. I usually dated girls from other hoods and I wanted to be safe while visiting them. As long as the guys in their hood thought I was a BK, they allowed me to come and go as I pleased – within reason, that is. I didn't disrespect anyone. I couldn't speak to them. I could bob my head in acknowledgment as I passed, but I didn't dare say a word. That would leave room for one of them to act like I'd said something derogatory. And I didn't go into the Chains' hood, period.

Although I was willing to hang with hard-core members and act accordingly, at some point someone usually asked me about my grades. I would tell them that I had "As and Bs", and they would make me walk home or pull the car over and say, "Get out." I would gripe and get out. I suppose they saw something in me that I didn't see in myself. Later that night or the next day, I would find out on the news that someone was shot or killed in another neighborhood. I never asked them if they had anything to do with these incidents. It was best left unsaid. What I didn't know wouldn't incriminate me.

Before long, I realized that the happy medium in which I found myself would keep me alive, out of jail, and – most importantly at this stage of my life – without a record. That is the difference between the old school crews and today's youth. Today's peer pressure is so staggering. The leaders feel that their lives are already hosed, so there is no reason to prevent someone else's mistake. In the 70s, the older guys did not let kids with potential ruin their lives unless it was absolutely self-defense.

Expansion occurred throughout the city as members moved into other neighborhoods. These gangs were developed mainly to protect home turf. There were no drug wars or financial reasons for these actions at this time. It was merely a safety net used to branch out of one's block or neighborhood. Jerome and Darryl moved to the 7-Mile Road area, taking Donnie with them most of the time. Before long, the 7-Mile BKs were established.

Billy Jack moved to the Bishops area, which was next to the Chains' hood. It was a fairly easy transition because Billy Jack had at least five extremely lovely sisters. Who wouldn't accept him? Billy Jack joined a group known as the East Hoods (an offshoot of the Bishops) and the BKs were allowed to enter and hang in this hood. This encircled the Chain Gang. Before long, the Chains' leader, Frog, was slain. The Chains began to slip.

My childhood strike-em-out buddy George moved to an area near the river and started the Black Gangsters. This allowed the BKs to venture into another portion of Detroit's East Side. Ironically, we had to be extra careful going to school because it cut right through a nice neighborhood that seemed to harbor resentment about our hood being known statewide.

While attending discos and high school dances, we noticed a group of well-dressed guys with finger-wave perms in their hair gathering on the dance floors and putting one of their hands in the air as if they had swords. It looked like a cool dance, but they yelled the words, "Errol Flynns!" I looked around for the TV. What in the hell were they doing? Who in the hell would yell out something from an old black-and-white movie? It wasn't long before we realized a new gang had arisen. The BKs had their personal rival. There were then four major gangs in Detroit.

We understood the Errol Flynns, but we didn't understand them. They lived in $60,000 suburban homes and wore $100 shoes and expensive clothes. We couldn't imagine someone wanting to fight while wearing expensive clothes. Then we realized that their game plan wasn't to fight. They shot.

By the summer of 1977, the city had erupted into a full-fledged gang war. The Bishops were fighting the Chains and the BKs were fighting the Errol Flynns. If the BKs shot or murdered someone on one evening, it was mandatory that we stay off of the street the next night, because there would be retaliation. This back-and-forth behavior continued for all of 1977 and the first half of 1978.

The Errol Flynns started to branch out as well. They established a large area near the Black Gangsters. They controlled Jefferson, Charlevoix, and Kerchaval Avenues. The expansion of the 7-Mile Road BKs caused the creation of the Latin Kings or LK/Skonies. Shortly after the LKs creation, the Strips started up and began controlling an area near East Grand Boulevard and

Mack Avenue. During this time, the West Side of Detroit remained mostly gang-free. The East Side was a war zone.

During a summer concert by the famous Average White Band, these gangs had a short truce. It lasted only long enough for them to go jointly onto the stage, take the instruments from the group, and attempt to play them for the audience. Before the night was out, they both raided every jewelry store in downtown Detroit. Ten to 15 gang members also entered clothing stores and shoe stores, tried on items, stood up, and walked out without paying.

The next morning Mayor Coleman Young placed the City of Detroit on a 10 p.m. curfew and created a task force headed by the infamous Sergeant Younger. He was a well-dressed plainclothes policeman. He talked in street lingo, so most members didn't realize they were dealing with a cop, and before long they were arrested. The next week the Detroit *News* released a front-page article listing every gang in the city and its members, based on the information compiled from previous police stops. I think this was a critical point in the start of the war on gangs that continued for the remainder of 1978.

It's an amazing thing to find out that parents grounded some of the hardest members after they read the article. It's tough to be a hard-core gangster while you're on a don't-leave-the-porch punishment. Although I had been stopped and questioned before, my name was not listed in the paper. Needless to say, the Average White Band promised never to come to Detroit again. As far as I know, they kept their promise.

There was a time when I thought my cross-hood dating would get me killed. I had asked my West Side girlfriend to meet me downtown so that we could hang out and window shop. I took the bus from the East Side and she arrived from the West. Everything was fine until I kept running into two known Errol Flynns from my school. Their names were Lamont and Little Hood. They were with 10 to 15 other gang members.

Detroit's downtown area seemed huge when I was a kid, but in retrospect it isn't large at all. I discovered this because I ran into this group about three times during that particular day. Each time, the other gang members looked at me as if they couldn't wait until I said something wrong.

The fourth time I ran into them they said, "If we see you again, we are going to whip your ass."

I was sort of ticked that Lamont and Little Hood didn't say that they knew me or that I was cool with them. I understood, because that is how it was in gang life. Nevertheless, I looked at my girlfriend and said, "Sweetheart, it's time for us to go. It's not worth it and I'll call you when I get home."

I mentioned the incident to some BKs when I got home and thought nothing of it. When I arrived at school on Monday, there was a ruckus going on in the main office. I heard that people were beating up two guys and they ran into the office to get away. I was told that the perpetrators jumped over the counter in the office to get to the two individuals. Little did I know that the perpetrators were BKs and the two people who were assaulted were Little Hood and Lamont.

It's amazing what happens when a person straddles the fence as a gang member. I didn't ask or expect something like this to happen because of that minor incident downtown. I suppose the guys in my hood didn't need much of an excuse to start a fight. Shortly after the incident, Little Hood and Lamont transferred to another school. To this day they probably don't know what triggered the fight. I never saw them again.

I was intrigued by the diversity in style found within the Detroit gangs. They had the usual khaki pants, jingle boots, and leather jacket-wearing members. They also had extremely well-dressed members. The signature item for Detroit gang members was hats. Initially, black curled-brim hats known as Godfather Hats were the norm. Within a year, a more expensive batch of hats arrived on the scene. These hats were known as Borsolinos and Barbiscos. They cost between $50 and $100 each and were made of beaver and other fine hat materials. Anyone wearing one of these hats who was not an old man was considered a gang member.

The Errol Flynns wore these as well, but they were also known for wearing a different style of hat known as the Sherlock. Go figure: they were named after a swashbuckler, but wore British hats. That should make it clear that TV had us all screwed up. I wonder exactly how much impact movies and media do have on the inception of gangs.

A shirt fetish also developed. A set of disco-style shirts named Roland and Nik Nik came into fashion. They were nylon with medium-sized open collars, and came in all sorts of colors or designs. Looking closely at the shirt, it was possible to see somewhere in tiny letters "Roland®" or "Nik Nik®." I liked Rolands, myself. Those shirts cost $30 apiece and my parents refused to buy them. A kid had to work somewhere or develop a legal (or not-so-legal) hustle to get them.

After a week of baby-sitting, I could afford only one shirt and put $15 in my pocket for the weekend, or the week, for that matter. People would pull my collar and look inside to see if I was wearing the real thing or if I had on a "Rolind" or a "Nic Nic." I couldn't wait to leave Detroit.

Another item that gained prominence in the late 70s was the Glass Heel shoe. Kousin's Shoes in Downtown Detroit introduced them and charged at least $100 per pair. They were extremely lovely Italian shoes, and the lower portion of their two-inch heels were completely transparent. That was just the beginning. Before long, they inserted things in these shoes. Kousin's inserted a gold-toned nude lady that looked like a museum sculpture. Whenever someone has a fast-selling, high-cost item, it doesn't take long before someone else bites it. Flagg Brothers Shoes created the first knockoffs for $50. What we *didn't* find in the Flagg Brothers' Glass Heel shoe was the question. They initially inserted a pair of dice in one pair and an ace of spades in another. I actually thought about buying those. The last and most famous insert was the fake goldfish. A person could actually walk around with an aquarium in his shoes. Sea World couldn't top that.

To this day, Detroit has a clothes fetish. On one visit in the mid-90s, I visited City Slickers, which is frequently advertised in GQ Magazine. On that particular cloudy November morning, a line was forming outside of the store. I didn't think I could afford anything in that store, but it was worth a look. The line had formed because some new pink suede and alligator shoes had arrived. Are you feeling me? They wore pink suede shoes in Detroit during the winter. I supposed they carried them with them to the club. Maybe they wore leg warmers and sneakers to the club and changed once inside. There was steam coming out of the manhole covers and it was bound to snow at least 10 inches in the next three minutes, or so it seemed, and these folks were getting their Gators on.

Since I wasn't well-dressed while shopping at 10 a.m. on a Saturday, the salespeople didn't help me. When they finally came by to see if I needed assistance, I was standing there in shock because the most expensive pair cost $1600.00. The cheapest pair was $450.00.

The salesperson saw this strange look on my face and asked me, "Can you handle this?"

The only words I could say were, "That's more than my mortgage." I walked out and never looked back.

If you visit Detroit, you will see three different types of attire. The younger folks are wearing the current hip-hop look. The second group (businesspersons, politicians, and local celebrities) wear traditional attire. They also hang out in a small downtown pub called Floods. I have to admit that I love Floods. It's consistent and I'm guaranteed to see high-school friends, relatives, and positive people. I can arrive in town, put on a decent suit, and walk right in. It doesn't have to be lime green.

The third group is in a category all by themselves. A person actually needs sun shades to look at them. Most of these brothers work in the factories and go all-out when they dress. I suppose if I wore blue collar clothing six days a week I might want to purchase a couple of orange-and-turquoise suits as well. There is an understanding why the loud clothing is a staple in Detroit. Steve Harvey tells all about it when he performs in Detroit. He will not go on stage without a pair of those shoes on his feet. How ironic is it for a stand-up comedian to avoid heckling? Detroiters will send people packing if their attire isn't tight.

Unfortunately, a new crisis is arising in Detroit. There is a severe shortage of knee-high stockings for the ladies to wear. Oh, my lord! Every color imaginable is sold out, because the brothers bought them all. How else does a man wear an orange suit with matching alligator shoes? There are no matching socks for men in orange. Being the creative geniuses they are, they decided to wear knee highs. Unfortunately for Detroit's women, they also have to wait in line every Saturday morning because the brothers have the manicurists' schedules on lock-down.

Clothing was a critical issue in gang life. For every young adult who could afford expensive hats, jackets, and shoes, there were 100 who couldn't. Unfortunately, the inclusion of $100 hats and $100 shoes in the gang wardrobe had a price. Detroit gangsters initiated the practice of taking clothing items from individuals. It started with the expensive hats. So many gang members and non-members lost their lives just for wearing a hat. Many young people walked home barefooted in the dead of winter because their shoes had been taken.

On many occasions, parents spent hard-earned money to give expensive Christmas gifts to their sons, only to have the presents taken or their sons killed before the new year arrived. This issue is an ongoing problem today. They no longer take glass-heel shoes and Borsolinos, but Air Jordans, Eddie Bauer jackets, and cars. A Detroit gang anomaly grew into a national epidemic.

Materialism can get a person killed.

My brother and I stumbled upon a family of beautiful girls. We dated two of them, and a few of our friends dated others in their circle. They came from the not-so-rich part of the Errol Flynns' hood. Everything was fine at first, but they decided to move right around the corner from us on Fairview. Needless to say, all of these girls had thin, flowing hair that reached their lower back. This could not be good in our neighborhood.

There are hair issues in the African American community that date back to the days of the Willie Lynch speech that encouraged slave owners to take advantage of the differences in the slaves. The old were pitted against the young. The house slave was pitted against the field slave, and so on. The old good hair/bad hair assessments continue today. My question has always been, "What makes it good or bad?" If I was in a fire, thin hair would be bad. If I was in Alaska, thick hair would be good. Who wins?

Shortly after quitting school, my brother got a job at Chrysler and was making good money for a teenager. My mother got him the job at the plant where she worked. He was able to buy a car and the latest fashions. Our girlfriends became infatuated with designer clothes and hanging out at clubs. I couldn't afford the same things and didn't desire to compete with my brother over their attention. I managed to dress fairly well by *coooorrrrdinating.* I could match anything and it would look unique. I babysat for my sister Andrea after school each day, and made $30-$45 a week. I would buy my own clothes to keep my parents from spending money. If they bought me something, it was either on Easter or

Christmas. Our girlfriends would look at the inside of our collars and tease us if we weren't wearing designer items, as if they were rich, but they weren't. They would wear a set of Chic jeans until the label fell off.

Let me tell about Chic jeans. They came out at the same time as Gloria Vanderbilts. Sisters wore Chics and non-blacks wore Vanderbilts. There were no jeans like them for African American women who wore jeans in the late 70s. I have no clue who Chic was, but I bet she was a Sister, or at least liked looking at them. These jeans had a way of instantly giving a woman a shape. Any woman familiar with these jeans will tell you that no jean company today can compare to them. If a woman had a shape, she was now a brickhouse. If she had no shape, now she had one.

It became extremely tough for me to keep up with pleasing my girlfriend with my attire off $35 a week, while my brother was making at least $16,000 a year. Before long, she no longer wanted to hang around the house with me, but ride with my brother and her sister.

Many times I was left behind because I wanted to be my own person, in my own relationship. This turned out to be a good thing. I stopped the relationship and returned to dating people outside of my immediate area.

I started dating the sister of Marvin, the BK section leader. It only lasted for a short time and all we did was sit on her sofa and kiss. We had one good summer together and then sort of drifted apart. This breakup was mainly due to distance. She lived six blocks away, and that was another world as far we were concerned. We departed on good terms. When school started, I heard that she was approached by my previous girlfriend and a fight broke out. During the fight, Marvin's sister's face was slashed. Later that night, my brother ran into our house in a rage saying that someone had firebombed the lady's home. Five minutes later the girls came to hide out in our house.

My household was in an uproar. My sisters were angry with us because our relationships had brought drama to the house. My father was standing watch with his rifle, and we stayed up all night long wondering if our home would be firebombed next. I told my brother that this is the reason I stopped dating them and that he should do the same. I felt it coming but couldn't figure out from what angle or how severe it would be when it reached us.

Two days later, 15 BKs approached our porch and we armed ourselves. My father opened the door as asked them what the problem was.

They said, "Mr. Johnson, we don't have a problem with your sons; we just want to talk."

My father said, "You don't come to someone's house with 15 people to talk."

They apologized and left our house. We didn't feel the sincerity in their apology and we stood watch for another two nights. We were so close to going to war in our own neighborhood over women, we could have wound up in jail for shooting someone. We chose the right switch on that occasion.

A few days later, someone came over to say that one of the members who led the march on our house had been shot in the face at a club and killed. He'd seen his ex-girlfriend in a club with another man and had slapped the man. The guy shot him in the face as soon as he walked out of the club. My brother and I attended the funeral as if nothing had previously happened. Nothing ever transpired after the bombing. I suppose the death overshadowed our potential conflict. I truly believe that they just forgot about it. The girls repaired and repainted their kitchen and life returned to normal. This was a wake-up call on how a relationship could get me killed by my own friends.

I hoped it was the beginning of the end – at least for me it was. The glamour was gone. I could only think about my mom feeding these guys. I could feel the gang life being chipped away from all of our lives. The hardcore members were shifting to the drug game and the rest pursued other positive options. I wanted to move on with my life as a teenager and break away from any serious relationships that could get me killed. I also wanted to save big bucks by not buying any more designer clothes.

Chapter 9
Too Many, Too Soon
-------------------☼------------------

Detroit has always been a rough place to grow up, but the inception of gangs took things to another level. Gang drive-by shootings became commonplace. They manifested into total chaos and began to affect the civilians as well. On one sunny summer Saturday my family was getting dressed to attend a wedding and reception. It was 4:30 p.m. and the neighborhood was full of kids playing and adults drinking on their porches. In other words, a typical hot summer day. The mothers of two teenage lovers had an argument over their role as expecting grandparents. They had been drinking together for most of the day. One of the parents left in anger, and with urging on by another woman, returned with a gun to confront the mother of the expecting teenager. While attempting to storm the porch, the woman with the gun tripped and the gun discharged. A second later, we all looked to see if someone on the porch had been shot. Fortunately, no one on the porch, including the pregnant teenager, had been injured.

To our dismay, though, another individual fell to the ground. The shooter's friend, who had instigated the confrontation, had been struck in the back of the head, having somehow got in the path of the bullet. I can recall her wearing a white blouse that immediately turned red with blood while she lay motionless in the walkway of my neighbor's home. The ambulance stayed an unusually long time. This was not a good sign. It was the first time I'd seen something of this magnitude. She was pronounced dead at the scene.

This shooting affected me for years, and my having to continue dressing to attend the wedding reception affected me more. This was one time I wanted to stay home in my room, but I had to attend this event. For some reason, parents at that time believed in moving forward despite tragic incidents. Today the whole block would receive counseling. There was no such thing in the mid-70s. Needless to say, I can't recall anything that happened at the wedding, and, to be honest, I'm glad I can't. I can only recall the most important thing that happened that day, and I know that is normal.

By the summer of 1978, and over the three-year gang period, I can honestly say that over 150 people in my hood were murdered. Not only were gang members murdered, but also victims of crimes perpetrated by our own neighbors. Another 100 or so were sent to prison for periods ranging from 18 months to 182 years. I can't recall any sentences of life imprisonment or life without the possibility of parole. Detroit courts just give out sentences of immeasurable time. They liked unbelievably high numbers because there is no death penalty.

There is one urban legend of a Detroit Recorder's Court Judge, Geraldine Ford, who would ask questions such as, "How many marbles are in this container?" Whatever the defendants said was the amount of years they would receive. I don't know if it was true, but I didn't break the law in order to find out.

It's tough to come home on vacation and find out that another acquaintance or friend has been murdered. This still happens today because the street gangs in Detroit turned into drug gangs in the 1980s. They initially gained financial success to the detriment of the neighborhood, then eventually imploded and attacked each other over MP&R (Money, Power and Respect). Today, most of the names are no more. If the gang life didn't get them, the drug life did.

I lost a particularly close friend and role model. Dale Cook, aka Boom, was an older brother in the BKs. He was by far the best-dressed gang member in the neighborhood. Although he was a member, I can't recall him fighting anyone. This didn't mean that he wouldn't shoot someone in the face. He had a business savvy about him that garnered respect from the entire neighborhood. As the gang life dwindled away, guys ventured out into other money-making schemes. Rumor had it that Boom was making large-scale drug deals with a few suburbanites. He was missing for 30 days or so before he was discovered in Lake Michigan, decomposing in a wire trash can, the type you see at the park. What a tragic way to leave this world.

The BKs spawned one of Detroit's largest and most profitable drug organizations, headed by two gentlemen known as the Twins, who spent time at our home in their earlier days. They treated everyone in the neighborhood with respect and showered us with money, transportation, or anything else we needed. This was a switch I never desired to flip. I could explain a lot of things to my parents, but that wasn't one of them. Their world caved in as well.

Today, groups known as East Warren are notorious throughout the Michigan prison system. There are ex-BKs who range in age from 38 to 50. They are just as ruthless in prison today as they were in 1977. I've learned from a friend who was paroled in the past few years that they control the ice industry in one particular prison. That's powerful on a hot summer day in a prison. On the other hand, it's pathetic when all you have is ice.

Some of these individuals are incarcerated today for incidents they were involved in on one given day in the 70s. Someone introduced PCP, aka angel dust, to a group of BKs standing nearby. The rest of us stood and watched, mainly because of the weird smell it produced. We didn't want any part of whatever it was.

Within minutes, these guys were doing weird things. One individual attempted to ride his bike at full speed through the side of a parked car and went airborne. Another guy saw a police car driving nearby. He took off running at full speed, right past them. The police were minding their own business and had no intentions of approaching him. When they saw this guy running they assumed that he'd done something wrong, so they gave chase and caught him. They ran his name through the system and discovered that he was an escapee from the youth home, so off to jail he went.

The incident that sticks with me the most happened later that afternoon. Two of the BKs who'd smoked the angel dust as well got into a car and drove off. On the 6:00 p.m. news we heard that two men walked onto a porch in a known Errol Flynn neighborhood and shot at least five people in broad daylight.

ANTHONY JOHNSON

Two of the five victims died. That was my first real view of the damage that drugs could bring on a community.

It's extremely sad that turf battles destroyed so many lives. Many of these individuals have children who are being raised by others, if not raising themselves. This false sense of security that started over conflicts at house parties has affected an entire community for a period of over 26 years. Since some of these members are serving sentences in excess of 50 years, the impact on my initial community is infinite. The majority of the hard-core BKs branched off into the drug business. Fortunately, I departed the city before the arrival of the cocaine industry that became responsible for the majority of the deaths after 1980.

Not all gang members are the terrible dregs of society that the media make them out to be. Unfortunately, gangs serve as surrogate parents and older siblings for members who don't receive love or attention at home. I truly believe there is a sanctioned undercover economy in America. How else can we explain the easy access to drugs and guns in the inner cities of this country? On any given day or night, we can see cars filled with suburbanites parked in areas of the city where I personally would not dare to stop. I doubt if they are asking for directions to a house party.

Only recently have I've seen a carload of suburbanites being arrested in one of these areas. I truly believe that coca leaves will rot on the vine in South America if Americans would stop or drastically reduce their consumption of cocaine and crack. As long as we can eliminate convicted felons from the voting process, issue mandatory prison sentences for possession of crack cocaine, and make possession of more substantial amounts of powdered cocaine misdemeanors, we can literally guarantee election results. American society must research the history of 1970s street gangs in order to deal with many of today's issues. As the youth aged, turf battles turned into drug wars. What was once fun in their eyes became business. Using the movies *Scarface*, *New Jack City*, and *Traffic* as boilerplates, the inner workings of the drug business are only a couple of DVDs away for most street gangs.

Chapter 10
It's Cool to be Smart
-------------------☼-------------------

Finney High School, located on the border of Detroit and the suburbs of Grosse Pointe Woods, was a unique experience. Due to cross-district bussing in 1975, the school had a rare racial makeup of nearly 50-45% between white and black students. The other 5% were made of Arabs and, off course, the Yees. Immediately upon arriving in 1976, we had skirmishes bordering on race riots. I cannot call them race riots because not everyone agreed with the confrontations and many chose not to participate. Moreover, after the fights ended, we went back to class with no hard feelings.

The inception of gang life into the high school scene drastically affected my sophomore grades. What had been As and Bs turned into Cs and Ds in the classes I didn't like. This phase lasted for one year and happened mainly because my school had a major infusion of BKs who had been kicked out of nearby Denby High School. Students kicked out of Finney were sent to Denby. Basically, it was a swap job by the Board of Education. Unfortunately for Finney, we lost gang affiliates and gained hard-core members. Unfortunately for me, most of these new students lived all around my home. We caught the bus together in the mornings and we rode home in the evenings. At times, the Twins drove us home in one of their new luxury cars. I didn't skip school completely, but I did miss a class here or there. School was too much fun to skip completely because of the comedians in class.

Detroit high school students do not take yellow buses to school. They have to take public transportation, which is subsidized for low-income students. The buses are extremely crowded each day, with students and workers using the same transportation system. Therefore, those wanting to have fun went to the back of the bus. It's ironic, because our parents fought with their lives to move to the front of the bus, but our generation returned to the back. The main reason for sitting in the back was to do whatever we wanted without the bus driver stopping us. If he heard something or, in most cases, smelled something, he didn't like, it was non-existent before he made it to the back. There were altar boys back there when he arrived.

The most well-known back-of-the-bus culprit was Chucky. Chucky was the one with the 40-oz. bottle of Colt 45 Malt Liquor and the bag of joints. He sold marijuana for the local drug gang and felt that he needed a kick each morning before class. By 6:30 a.m. Chucky had already smoked three joints and was about finished with the 40. He was known to hide his report card each marking period. We never really asked to see it because we felt he must have bombed all of his classes, but to our amazement Chucky maintained a 3.8 GPA throughout high school, or at least during the years he went. I'm not sure what happened to Chucky. I suspect that he's some college professor who is wasted out of his mind during his first lecture of the day, or a jailhouse lawyer.

Another reason to sit at the back of the bus was strictly for gossip purposes. We could see anyone who pulled the bell to get off the bus through the back door. We knew exactly where the most well-known students lived and what bus stops they took in the mornings. If for some reason a student rang the bell and departed at a certain stop, we knew the girl he was going to see, especially if she wasn't in school that day. It's unconvincing to say, "That's not my baby," when you get off at her bus stop at 6:45 a.m. every other day for three weeks. The worst part about these encounters was that they were gorgeous girls and everyone wanted to be that special someone at least once. It was a terrible thing when we *didn't* ring the bell and one of our friends stood up instead and exited the bus at an all-too-familiar spot, smiling all along the way. Well, all is fair …

The best thing that happened to me in school was the expulsion of the newly arrived BKs. I missed the laughter, but not the drama. They didn't last an entire school year. Unfortunately, my reputation was not totally untarnished. Some saw me as a gang member and others looked me at as the same person I had been prior to the arrival of my crew. The two Detroit policemen assigned to my school set up their office right across from my locker. I wondered why. I wasn't the leader, or so I thought. I had no choice but to keep my head straight and try to hit the books again. At the same time, an organization named Focus Hope arrived at our school. Their symbol was a white and black hand embracing. Focus Hope hosted most dances, field trips, and retreats.

During the fall of 1978 and during a lull in the gang violence, the Focus Hope instructors privately approached every student who they deemed a leader, contacting both positive and negative leaders. I was considered a negative leader at this time, a distinction that didn't sit well with me. They asked me if I would be willing to go on a retreat to a Northern Michigan campsite and act as a seminar leader for 100 other students. Any opportunity to get out of Detroit was fine with me. I jumped on the opportunity and enlisted about 20 to 30 other guys and girls.

When it was all said and done, we had four or five busloads of students attending the retreat, and it was a beautiful experience. We vented, and reestablished friendships that had been strained during the neighborhood gang wars. We interacted across racial, social, and economic lines. We flirted and coupled up with individuals who would not have given us the time of day previously. It was a life-changing event. When we returned to school things were noticeably different. Negative leadership turned into positive leadership literally overnight. We pressed on for the remainder of the school year without any major incidents and with zero gang violence or new members.

The name Fortuna struck unbelievable fear in kids who attended Finney High School from the late 60s through the 80s. Mr. Fortuna was Finney's premier history teacher and had the reputation of failing entire classes, dating back to the 60s. He failed all three of my sisters and all of their classmates. I fortunately had his course in the ninth grade and received a D. When I got home to show my report card to my family, my sister Brenda saw the D in Fortuna's class and said, "You did good!" I just looked at her. In retrospect I realize that to get a D in his class I actually had to earn a B. He didn't require the usual three-line answers on his tests. He wanted paragraphs for each answer.

I would have never thought that I would learn so much about Martin Luther and Charlemagne in my life. At first I thought he was talking about Martin Luther King and some girl named Charmaine.

I got his class again in my senior year. I thought someone was punishing me for my earlier indiscretions. This time my focus was different. I picked a seat in the front of the room next to the two smartest guys in the class, Tom Speilman and Scott Fallou. Tom was a huge football player and Scott was just plain smart. I wasn't alone. Some of the other brothers did the same thing. Lance, Shelby, Darryl, and Emanuel all joined me in stepping up our games and mastering our switches. We raised our hands for every question. Mr. Fortuna got so tired of the same 10 people always answering all of the questions that in most cases he ignored our raised hands. We all earned between Bs and Cs, and the confidence we earned in his class was enough to catapult us in other classes.

Along with other students who were not in Mr. Fortuna's class, we constituted the nucleus that endeavored to change our school. This nucleus came from all backgrounds and walks of life. John, Murphy, and I came from the Shoemaker area. Darryl came from the Parkside Projects. Lance and Emanuel had nice homes not far from the school. Shelby (RIP) had to commute from the other side of Detroit each day to attend Finney. He would have had to deal with additional gang warfare if he'd attended the school in his neighborhood, MLK High.

I can say this proudly: "We changed our school." We did whatever we could, legally, to assist our parents in buying our clothes. We flipped burgers, baby-sat, sold papers, and kept our noses clean.

I had another positive core group that I hung out with: Jonathan, Jerome, Lacy, Chris, and Ray. We were eye-catching, if I do say so myself. Each of us had his own style and manner of dress. We went to separate schools, but managed to get together every day after school. We recently lost Jonathan to an illness, but the remaining group will continue to love each other in a special way. We can go without seeing each other for years, but we pick up where we left off whenever we get together. Lacy is a member of the singing group Enchantment. It's a wonderful feeling to have this type of relationship among men. We had our notorious moments as well, but we were products of great mentors, such as Jerome's brother James. With the exception of my father and a few cousins, James was highly responsible for raising my class level. He basically taught me how to conduct myself with class. This lifestyle change would prove critical in adulthood. He taught me how to stand out without standing out, so to speak.

We competed in class to get As. It was an amazing turnaround for most of us. We had become the positive leaders in the school. Freshman students, both male and female, looked to us as mentors. They asked us to pick the proper locker location for them so they could make it to all their classes on time. There was not a time when someone wasn't asking us for direction on a multitude of topics. The police moved their office to another side of the building and sought us out any time a new student who looked like a gang member from another area arrived. We pulled these new students aside and kindly advised them that we had been through it before and that we were not going back, and we never had additional problems.

A number of social groups began sprouting up all over campus as we approached graduation. Some wise person thought of the name "Slick and Shady, Class of 80." I hated it. It sounded as if we were pimps on *Mister Rogers*. I joined a group of 15 guys who thought the title was corny. At the urging of the commercial foods instructor, Mr. Faustina, we created what we called *The Executive Board*. This group contained the most popular guys in the school, with the exception of Lance, Emanuel, and Darryl. They joined Slick and Shady. Both groups did wonderful things for the senior class. We raised a little money by putting on fashion shows at the famous Ten Gentlemen Social Club in Detroit. Slick and Shady sponsored the senior trip to Toronto, Ontario. The school prom was held in the Gold Room at the Hillcrest Country Club in Mt. Clemens, Michigan (rumored to be a mob haven). It was a diverse group of students and we had a wonderful time. There were no limos. Everyone borrowed a family car or was driven by a relative. We made it home safe – the next day, that is.

In 1980 there were 28 public high schools inside the Detroit city limits. Case Tech was historically the number one school academically. Renaissance High was the newest school; it was established by recruiting the top two students from all Detroit public, private, and parochial schools, and had become number one academically. Case was number two, and, after testing, Finney High had become number three. The entire school raised itself from fifteenth to third place, an amazing turnaround by any standard. We had regained our respect and our smarts.

Chapter 11
When I Turn 18

----------------------☼----------------------

After graduating in the summer of 1980 at the age of 17, I had neither the firm plans nor the strong financial backing to go directly to college. I didn't press my parents for funding, either. I had (and still have) this thing about taking care of my own business. I had excelled in typing and administrative skills during my senior year in high school. I tested and applied for jobs with the Federal Government, the Michigan Board of Education, and the Detroit City Government. These agencies told me that I had passed all tests and had tremendous potential, but, unfortunately, they couldn't offer me a job because they had to offer them to older people who had recently been laid off by the auto industry.

This was heartbreaking because I didn't want to work in a factory. I wanted to use my mind more than my hands to make a living. I had nothing against the auto industry because both of my parents were long-time Chrysler employees. What sealed my manual-labor fate was a field trip to an open house at Chrysler's Warren Stamping Plant. Stamping plants basically turn sheet metal into doors, hoods, and so forth. Workers are issued a rack of 500 or so sheets of metal and when the horn blows, they start stamping. When the horn blows again, I suppose they stop or move to another part of the plant. It was loud as hell in there and I think I saw a few people walking around with nubs. I guess the horn had blown and they'd forgotten to move their hands. All I can remember from that point on was the free candy. They gave out miniature Hershey candy bars and that's about all I could concentrate on while the tour was underway. I knew that I didn't want to work there. It was too dangerous and repetitive for me. My factory job prospects ended.

1980 was a long, hot summer in Detroit. I was tired of baby-sitting and didn't want to work in the fast-food industry. At one point I didn't feel that I had a choice. I applied to work at a Burger King restaurant near downtown Detroit. I was told that I had to go to the offices of Mr. Brady Keys. Mr. Keys owned a number of fast-food restaurants in Detroit and is one of the richest African American businessmen in the nation. During my interview with them, his management staff told me that I was an excellent candidate and directed me back to the Burger King that had sent me to his office.

The next day I asked my sister Brenda to drive me to work. I gave the manager the paperwork from Mr. Key's office. He wasn't really paying attention because he was trying to talk to my sister. When she didn't give him the time of day, he told me that I wasn't hired. I left there mad, but not exactly crushed, because I really didn't want to work there, anyway. At that time I thought of the fast-food industry as a job for high school students. On the next business day, I decided to take the test for the U.S. Coast Guard.

I took the Warren Through bus downtown to meet Petty Officer Bert Stillman. I did not discuss my plans with my parents or anyone else. I'd always had an interest in the Coast Guard because their boats were white and didn't look like the drab gray Navy boats. Their members looked more like police or firefighters and not like the other services. I also could swim like a fish, a rarity in most parts of the country for African Americans.

I was somewhat nervous while taking the test, but I did well and passed it with flying colors. Moreover, my score was high enough for me to pursue the job that involved working in offices, yeoman. I was, in the words of Mike Tyson, ecstatic. They asked me if I wanted to get the physical out of the way as well. I said yes, and found myself in a van headed for Plymouth, Michigan. I knew I'd passed the physical before it was over because I heard the dogs barking in the alley while in the soundproof booth taking my hearing test. I felt that if I could hear those dogs I should be able to hear these beeps.

I passed my test and the recruiter drove me home. He came into my home with me to give my parents the good news.

Unfortunately, they were not pleased because I hadn't consulted with them about my plans. I didn't understand because they never seriously discussed college with me. I'd taken both the SAT & ACT, but that was as far as it went. I'd assumed that money was not available and I never pressed the issue.

I was an independent kid growing up. I was the youngest of five and the second boy. After three sisters, my brother Mark was the first boy. I always felt that he had a special place in my parent's heart, which was understandable for being the first boy. I had no problem with that because I wanted to make my own way. I spent most of my childhood out of the house playing sports, riding bikes, and just hanging out with kids in or out of my neighborhood. Plus, I didn't want to be the spoiled brat that most people assumed I would be as the baby of the family. That's why I could understand the distance my parents felt on this decision; they didn't really know what made me tick or in what direction I was heading. All I knew was that I was tired of the temptations of drinking, drugs, and the oncoming cocaine world that was seething in my neighborhood. Temptation and severe boredom had knocked on my door while they'd worked.

It's a feeling of hopelessness that set in when I didn't have a clue about my future. I dealt with life in a day-to-day manner, and if I hadn't changed my environment I'd have been bound to do something negative. I felt it coming. It was as if I couldn't breathe in my neighborhood any longer. I stopped walking to the store. I only walked around at night when I couldn't be seen as much. I no longer wanted to live in a *hood*. I wanted a *neighborhood* again. My sister Andrea had recently moved to a house on the Northeast side of the city and I wanted to live in that environment. It was peaceful and there were no shootouts. I hated for my parents to ask me to pick up a pack of cigarettes or a lottery ticket. I was becoming embarrassed and somewhat afraid to live in this neighborhood that was falling apart before my eyes.

Although Lemay and Fairview continued to prosper and had a minimal amount of vacant homes, the nearby streets looked like ghost towns. French Road is two blocks away and had more vacant lots than homes. It was becoming depressing because I was spending lots of time in other environments and wanted to be a part of that lifestyle. It was selfish, but I all I wanted was something better for my family and me. I wasn't afraid of others in my neighborhood, but after the firebombing of my ex-girlfriend's house I knew potential problems with others existed. I never knew when I would be the focus of an argument or somebody's beef, and these guys were no longer fighting with their hands.

After the Coast Guard recruiter left my home, my parents told me that they were not signing for me to go into the military. I tried to explain the Coast Guard missions and describe what made this service different. They were not hearing it.

I gave up and said the words, "That's fine. When I turn 18 in October, I'll sign for myself!"

That was the last time we discussed it. Two months later, I signed for myself and was put on a four-month waiting list. On 21 January 1981 I received a call from Petty Officer Stillman and he gave me a 9 February departure date for Coast Guard boot camp on the East Coast.

Chapter 12
Sunny Cape May

-------------------☼-------------------

It was so cold outside that I couldn't get my borrowed car to start. All I wanted was to go over my girlfriend's house and say goodbye before I flew to New Jersey in the morning. It was 16 degrees below zero, with three inches of snow on top of one inch of ice. I finally got my future brother-in-law Bill's Deuce and a Quarter to start. Oh, I forgot to break it down – Buick Electra 225.

Dee Dee lived in one of those nice Errol Flynn neighborhoods. I was a glutton for punishment. I continued to date women in the enemy's land. The gangs had ceased by this time. I said my goodbyes, cried a little, and got ready to hit the road and the world. My mom accompanied me to the recruiting office that morning. That day was a complete blur. I can't remember anything except that I wore a thick bright-orange down-filled coat. I suppose I was getting ready for the Coast Guard orange I would soon wear.

Another guy departed Detroit with me. His name was Ricky Bird. He was extremely cut and muscular. His only fear was the swimming he would have to perform. I figured that I would help him out with the swimming and benefit from his size in case we ran into trouble during training. I possessed those thoughts because I'd listened too much to the Vietnam vets in my neighborhood prior to departing. They'd told me every horror story imaginable. The best one was about gambling. They'd told me that I would lose every paycheck because I hadn't shot dice while I was growing up. That was all fine and dandy, because Bo won all of their paychecks each week, anyway. So gambling in boot camp would be the least of my problems.

They treated us nicely at the USO office at Philadelphia International Airport and during the bus ride from Philly to Cape May I thought, "This will be a piece of cake; they are so nice."

I arrived at Cape May, New Jersey for eight weeks of Coast Guard boot camp around 1500 (3 p.m.). It was 53 degrees and the grass was green. The trees still had leaves on them. I never knew a place north of Florida existed like this in February. When they entered the bus, the shouting began. It scared the living daylights out of us.

It was two busloads of recruits, or approximately 100 men and women. The busses pulled up in front of a building called Munro Hall. The first thing I thought was that Alvin Vaughn must have spelled Munro for them. As a fairly laid-back child, I'd learned to think and keep things to myself. It seemed that those who thought aloud were the first ones to get hollered at. They told us that we had 15 seconds to get into that building.

After 100 people took off running, someone screamed, "But you better not run!"

It was like 100 Wildebeest stopped in their tracks and started to walk. It was hilarious, but we didn't want them to see us laughing, I think.

The called us Forming Company. I suspected that they were forming us into something, but by the looks of this pre-haircut group, I couldn't imagine what. As a product of cross-district bussing, this was my second exposure to many cultures and races. We were placed in a large room with tall wooden tables that reminded me of art class, except these were old and Christmas-tree green. They gave us stencil kits to put our names on all belongings. I screwed that up. I still have the laundry bags with my messed-up stencil job on the cloth tab that distinguished me from the other recruits.

They asked us to put all contraband in the Amnesty Box. I didn't know what in the hell they were saying. I thought I had joined Amnesty International and they were going to ship my ass off to some screwed-up part of Europe. I assumed that they were talking about my Certs and the book I'd been conned into buying from a Hari Krishna at Philly International. When I looked in the Amnesty Box, I saw four bags of marijuana, some pills, candy, condoms, and some golf balls. Rumor had it that the golf clubs were on the back of the bus. Some recruiter had told this applicant that we could play golf. It probably wasn't a brother. Needless to say, I took my Certs back and left the book that I'd wasted $5 buying.

For the next hour, all we heard was that they were going to split us up into two companies, and that Tango Company *(as they laughed)* was going to get Ishman. Whoever or whatever Ishman was didn't seem good. They performed the good old odd-even count off; I ended up in the company that was getting Ishman.

An hour later we were placed in another room in Munro Hall, and all we could hear was this clicking coming down the hallway and getting louder. Then this six-foot-five brother walked into the room. He had metal taps on his shoes and they were extremely intimidating. He wore a police-type of hat on his head, but he was also wearing this chinstrap thingy. He looked like a Terminator, but that movie hadn't been released yet.

His name was Storekeeper First Class (SK1) Frank Ishman. We were told that he was the worst company commander (CC) that we could get, and he was all ours. He started yelling at us with a voice that cut directly to our hearts. It was a mixture of Charlie Brown's teacher and Larry Blackmon of the singing group Cameo – it was indescribable.

He told us to form it up outside in 20 seconds, and we took off. He yelled behind us, "But you better not run!"

Again, we came to this weird screeching walk as if someone had inserted corncobs in our rears while we ran. It was crazy. He told us to form four lines with the tallest people in front. Thank God, I was second to last. At 5-foot-four I was close, but not the winner.

We arrived at this thing called the galley. I didn't know what it was but I thought I saw people eating inside, so it was cool with me. SK1 Ishman walked around our four squads looking at us from about four inches from our faces. Some of us burst out in laughter because it was hilarious. He told us that the first and last words out of our mouths should be Sir or Ma'am. When he approached me, I didn't know whether to look at him or look ahead. Not knowing what to do, I looked at him.

He yelled, "Don't look at me, Numbnut! Keep your damn eyes in the boat!"

Hell, I started looking around for the boat.

He yelled again, "That means straight ahead, fool!"

So I just looked at the back of the neck of the person in front of me.

He said, "Where are you from?"

I said, "Sir, Detroit, sir."

He yelled, "I knew it! I knew it! It's one of those Detroit gangsters!" Then he said, "I want you to run your ass up to that hatch (I guessed it was the door to the galley) and say, 'Tango Company reporting for chow.'"

I took off running at full speed. I got to the door and opened it and forgot every damn thing he'd just told me. I turned around and looked at him and the other 100 people in total silence.

He said, "Get your ass down here!" Then, when I had, "What is your name?"

I replied, "Sir, Johnson, sir."

He started to lean down and look me in the face. It took about an hour for him to get there. When he was eye level, he said, "Johnson, you're dumb, Johnson. You're plain dumb."

I didn't know whether to laugh or cry so I just stood still. He assigned someone else to that task and we were allowed to eat supper.

No one could sleep that night. Some guy ran in there and said that he was going to make us run the grinder if we didn't shut up and go to sleep. We didn't and he didn't, either. We were stupid, because the grinder didn't sound like something we would want to run at 0300, or 3 a.m. in civilian time.

The next day they issued us uniforms and cut our heads. We marched to some far end of the base to meet Max the Ax. Max was a huge German barber. We'd say, "Just a little off of the top and sides," and Max would say, "Yaw, Yaw." I suspected that was yes or yeah.

Max then took his clippers and started at the backs of our necks and ended at our foreheads. In about five swoops we were completely bald. Some of us had gashes and cuts. As we departed the barbershop/uniform center, some guy in uniform yelled from across the street, "Now you look like a bunch of fucking Americans instead of a bunch of dorks!"

We thought that was a good thing. I was more surprised that the first word out of most mouths was a curse word. I knew that they beat people up in boot camp during Vietnam, so I was bracing for the beat down. It never came, but they said everything under the sun to us.

Ishman approached me again and said, "Hey Detroit Thug, get up here." Since it was two of us from Detroit, I didn't move. He yelled my last name. First names were never used there. I ran up to the front. He said, "I'm going to make you my right guide." I was a little shaken because I thought it was another way of saying "right guard" and I didn't want to be in a head lock under his armpit. He said, "Right guide stands in front of the fourth squad and he paces the group when we march. He also keeps the Guidon (flag holder) in step and in the right position." This seemed like a promotion to me since I was "Dumb Johnson" the night before. Before long, we began to master this marching thing.

We were told that Ishman used to be in the Honor Guard and had marched for the President. He had us experimenting on moves, and on one occasion he had us embarrass the graduating company in front of their parents. In our first two weeks we were doing things that the senior companies couldn't do. The graduating company was marching to the gym for their ceremony and we were coming from the galley. It didn't look like either company was budging and that we were on a collision course.

When we got within 25 feet of them, Ishman yelled, "Split Squad, March!"

Our group commenced to split into separate squads with two on each side of the other company. Once the last person passed them, we returned to four squads and kept on marching. The families started to clap and the CC for the graduating company made them do pushups on their graduation day for looking around at us and getting embarrassed. We had some fun with it and our reputation was developing.

Coast Guard boot camp was a unique experience. It was a combination of classroom, physical fitness, first aid, and head games. We were told repeatedly that we had the toughest mental challenges of all the armed services. They wanted us to be able to handle pulling a body out of the water. It didn't matter if the recruit was a man or woman. We were all dogged, and now I can understand why.

During one class they told us that only the commandant writes with red ink. Since I didn't have red pens, I kept quiet. Not Seaman Recruit Trohau. This nutcase stood up and said, "Sir, Seaman Recruit Trohau here, Sir. I have a red pen that writes blue. Can I use it?"

People could hear the rolling laughter all the way up the Garden State Parkway to Atlantic City. The instructor said, "Sit your dumb ass down."

Later that day, another rocket scientist who asked tons of questions each day said, "Sir, Seaman Recruit Bentley, Sir. [pause] Sir, I seem to have forgotten the question, Sir."

This instructor said to the classroom, "At Ease! Laugh! Now, everyone shut up and get back to work."

This type of stuff happened every day. We had one gentleman named Stecker. Stecker could not keep his hand out of his pocket or his finger out of his nose. He had to walk around all day with his left index finger in his nose and his right hand in his pocket. Unfortunately for him, our days were from 0530 to 2100. Eventually, he had to insert beach sand in his pockets and sew all of his pockets shut. He was somewhat overweight and reminded me of the guy in *Full Metal Jacket* who couldn't get anything right.

My biggest challenge in boot camp was passing the swimming test. Don't get me wrong, I could swim, but I soon realized that I could do the individual medley, but only for 50 meters. I had every stroke known to mankind, but I couldn't make it all the way around the pool without pooping out. In Detroit, most high schools had pools, but it was so many people in the pool that I couldn't build up endurance. I passed every session except the endurance test.

When I finally passed the test, Ishman yelled out, "Johnson, you're a fucking fish!"

I took that as a compliment. Those who didn't pass the test had to leave their current company and join Swim Hole Element, which didn't sound too wonderful to me. I didn't want to be in anyone's hole element. All I knew was that the women in Swim Hole Element looked terrible. They swam for eight hours a day and couldn't take care of their hair. The guys were all ashy. I wanted no parts of that, so I prayed hard and practiced at night.

I was becoming an important member of Tango Company as its right guide. The right guide determines the entire pace and style of marching formations. I didn't call out the commands, but I was the silent person who walked off the required steps, with everyone else following suit. I eventually passed the endurance test on the Friday of my third week and remained with my company as right guide. If I'd failed they would have reverted me to Swim Hole Element on Monday morning and I would have graduated boot camp with another company.

Inspections were an experience. They would look us up and down and find the smallest discrepancy on our uniforms. They called the tiny shreds on new clothes *Irish pennants*. I guessed this is derogatory to the Irish because pennants were the American battle attachments that hung on the flags we used for marching. The more we had the better. If the Irish pennants were that small, they couldn't be a good thing. We had to ensure that our *gig lines* were intact. This is the edge of the shirt on the outside of the buttons. That edge must line up with the edge of the zipper flap on the trousers. If they were not lined up, someone would yank the shirt directly out of the pants and say, "Fix your gig line!"

At inspection, we did not want to be asked a question and not know the answer. On one occasion, they asked one of our ladies, "How long is a 44-Footer?"

She said, "Sir, I don't know, sir."

That cost the entire company 50 pushups.

The next week they asked the same girl, "What's your CC's paygrade?"

He happened to be an E-6, but she said "Sir, 3,800, sir."

Another 50.

Getting cranked was another word for getting punished with physical fitness. One payday we messed up outside the exchange and we were cranked right in the parking lot as shoppers rolled their carts past our heads. I can recall personally looking up at one mother with the look of "Help us!" on my face. She just looked at me, laughed, and continued to push her cart.

One of my shipmates was from Puerto Rico and his English was a bit suspect. He ticked Ishman off during one of the evening training sessions and he was given *puda*. Puda is a punishment in which we had to hold our rifles out in front of us until our arms could not take it anymore. Seaman Recruit White's veins were popping out of his head and down his forehead. Ishman kept asking him if he was cool.

White kept saying, "Yes, I'm cool."

After 15 minutes of this, we realized that White was saying that he was okay. Ishman thought he was being sarcastic and saying that he was cool in style. After persuading Ishman that White was misunderstanding him because of the dialect, Ishman ended the cranking. I think he felt terrible about that one.

On another occasion, we were cranked in the shower, fully dressed I must add. One of us had on a dirty t-shirt during inspection and he made us scrub our bodies with small push brooms and repeat, "Rubadub dub, many fools in a tub." It was terrible, but extremely funny. If we messed up during marching, we were embarrassed in front of the entire training center. On many occasions we were forced to yell, "We are Dumb and We Don't Care," for about an hour.

These little stupid things built character because we didn't want to be singled out or bring shame on our company or CC. Whenever we messed up while marching, Ishman would yell, "No Pride! No Snap! Get Down!" He didn't want to hear a ripple effect when we stopped or did a maneuver. Therefore, we had to have *snap*. Snap caused most of the cranking. We would find ourselves doing close to 100 pushups. Doing jumping jacks was the easiest of all exercises, but caused us the most heartache. He would give us a set number to perform, and Stecker or some other idiot would do an extra one. Ishman would then scream, "OK, Stecker wants to do 51, so start together, stay together, begin." Needless to say, Stecker would do 52. We would end up completing 350 jumping jacks when we were only ordered to do 50.

It was also better for those who had simple names. Ishman would completely embarrass anyone with a strange name or something with a ring to it. Unfortunately, we had a guy with the last name of Munn. I can't recall what he did, but it was major. I can recall Ishman screaming at the top of his lungs, "It's Munn! It's Munn! Dumb Munn! Munn's Dumb!" When you are in a controlled environment, the little things generate more laughter than what you may think.

The one phrase no one wanted to hear was, "You're in a World of Shit." That meant that life would soon become a lot harder. Whenever this was said, we braced for the impact. It was usually major. The first time we entered the world of shit, Ishman marched us directly into the Atlantic Ocean. Since the guidon and right guide were in front, we got it first. It was an extremely cold March day and I was up to my chin in ocean because we had caused ourselves to be in the world of shit. Considering that March is worst than February on the East Coast at times, ocean marching was extreme punishment.

During our fifth week we had to cook for the entire base. This was called Galley Week. This is now contracted out. New recruits don't have to endure Galley Week any more. We had to wake up at 0400 and return to the barracks at 2200. We prepared three meals a day for everyone assigned to the base. This was grueling work, but a lot of fun and a break from the normal boot camp grind. During Galley Week it was impossible to keep our lockers or the barracks clean. We wore colored belts around our uniforms that distinguished how long we had been in training. Prior to Galley Week, we were all green belts. Green belts were not allowed to do anything fun. We couldn't go to the gym or base movie theater after training. We weren't allowed to use the phone booth, and we weren't allowed to walk anywhere. We had to run any time we transited the base alone.

SK1 Ishman decided to have an impromptu locker inspection during Galley Week. When a person other than a shipmate enters the sleeping area of the barracks, known as the squad bay, the first person to see them is suppose to yell out, "Attention in the squad bay!" My locker was the closest to door. I thought I saw someone enter, but my head was nearly inside my locker. It was too late for me to yell it without his wrath coming down on me. I had a selfish moment, but I'd been taught to CYOA (cover your own ass) at times.

Ishman was halfway down the squad bay before someone saw him and yelled, "Attention!"

He was furious. He began to look in lockers and throw everyone's belongings on the floor. He yelled, "Just because this is Galley Week doesn't mean you don't have to try to keep your stuff squared away!"

When he got to my locker I was petrified because I had thrown all of my dirty clothes into my mesh laundry bag. For the most part, however, my locker remained intact.

After the inspection he yelled, "One guy! One damn guy has his shit together!" Then he said, "Johnson! Only Johnson has his shit together! Johnson, report to my office to pick up your blue belt!"

As Mikey T. would have said, I was ecstatic. I did feel bad for not calling, "Attention in the squad bay," but I didn't feel bad because I'd worked just as hard as everyone else in my company during that trying week.

My first treat as a blue belt was a phone-booth call home to brag, "Hey Momma, I got my blue belt," not thinking that she didn't have a damn clue what I was talking about.

She said what every mother would say, "That's nice, Baby."

No longer was I required to run everywhere when alone. I could walk like a normal human. I could also go to the gym or movies at night.

After a week of this and the preferential treatment it allowed me, I felt a sense of jealousy in the company, and I didn't want it to end in a blanket party for me. A blanket party is when shipmates sneak up on their victim's rack in the middle of the night and throw a blanket over him. Four guys hold the edges down, trapping him to his rack while the rest of the company begin to beat him with bars of soap, or even padlocks inside socks. Not a good thing. I personally asked SK1 Ishman to promote the rest of the company to being blue belts. A week later he did, and all was normal on the Eastern Front.

It was eventually time to pick billets. Billets are the job assignments that recruits want to pursue after boot camp. Most go to ships or to small boat stations. Small boat stations operate like police or fire stations near the water. I was excited. During the previous seven weeks, Ishman had asked me sometimes what I wanted to be, and I always said, "A yeoman." I wanted to type, file, and work in an office. This goes back to my thinking after touring the auto plant.

Ishman would then say, "You don't want to be no damn yo-yo."

I thought long and hard, because they treated our company yeoman like crap. I thought that it had to be different in the field.

We picked billets academically and I was ranked to pick third out of the 100 people in both Sierra and Tango Companies. Our recruit commander, Martin, was scheduled to pick first, and

Seaman Recruit Bentley from Sierra Company would pick second. Martin picked a ship out of South Florida and Bentley went to the Northeast.

As I stood up to pick a unit in the Michigan area, Ishman shouted, "Johnson, get your ass up to the squad bay." I was floored. I did not know what I'd done or why he'd done this to me on our most important day.

I returned to the squad bay and observed as each person came in to say that they were headed to this or that unit. All recruits returned to the squad bay, some happy, others not so happy. Many ships were assigned. One recruit received orders to Loran Station, Kargabarun, Turkey, and another to Loran Station, Carabou, Maine. I thought, well, maybe getting into trouble for some unknown reason isn't all that bad.

SK1 Ishman returned to the squad bay and the whole company stood around my locker because they were as confused as I was. They also wanted to know what happened.

He said with that unique voice, "Johnnnsun."

Since I was a Blue Belt, sir or ma'am no longer had to be the first and last word out of my mouth. I said, "Yes, SK1."

He looked at me, smiled, and said, "I'm sending your ass directly to Yeoman School in Petaluma, California."

I just looked at him in amazement with my mouth hanging open. He walked out the same way that the chief walked out of the courtroom in the movie *Men of Honor* after Cuba Gooding, Jr. passed his diving suit test. He knew that he had done something wonderful for me and he was happy within.

I am forever grateful to SK1 Ishman for what he did for me. He flipped the switch for me the same way the OGs used to. The assignment directly to a school would ensure that I didn't have to report to a Coast Guard unit as unskilled labor. No matter what the location, I had guaranteed office work. Another lifetime goal attained. No painting, scraping, or climbing on or off boats. In other words, I started out with a briefcase.

As I learned the Coast Guard and became aware that it wasn't the most diverse agency in the government, I thanked SK1 Frank Ishman more. I began to ask the question, "Where is Petaluma?"

The answer I received was to watch the movie *The Birds*. They said Bodega Bay was the town next to Petaluma. Hell, I was actually a little scared after learning that. I thought that I would be the only brother in the town. Another individual said, "You'll like it – it's 48 miles north of San Francisco and Oakland." I was ecstatic again.

Graduation was a blur. I do recall marching in our dress uniforms and putting on an Ishman-like display. In other words, we turned it out. My parents, my sister Andrea, and her husband Jasper arrived late, as usual. If any readers know me, they are aware that my mother and father arrive everywhere late. I think they were messing around in Atlantic City and misjudged the time. That was okay, because this was a long way from the days of BKs and Lemay Street and I just wanted them to get a glance at this new environment.

After the ceremony, I introduced them to SK1 Ishman. I thanked him again as well. That was the last time I saw SK1 Ishman, but I talked to him once on the phone just to let him know that I was doing fine. He treated me like any veteran treats a rookie. They sound harder than what they are feeling inside. His words remained stern, but I could feel he was pleased with my accomplishments.

My parents asked me if I wanted to go to Atlantic City with them and I emphatically declined. I had been in New Jersey for the previous eight weeks and wanted no parts of it. I immediately flew back to Detroit to spend 10 days before my trip to California – and to get some. From whom, I didn't know. I sort of lost my desire for my girlfriend somewhere on the grinder. They were right when they said you forget about high school folks and things shortly after graduating.

Chapter 13
Golden Gates and Making Rate

-------------------☼-------------------

San Francisco International Airport is colossal. I had to lug a large, green sea bag from one end of it to the other for a taxi. I'd never dreamed that I would ride across the Golden Gate Bridge. Nevertheless, there I was, riding through towns that I'd heard of as a teenager listening to jazz artists such as Michael Franks or Grover Washington, Jr. It was invigorating to ride through Sausilito and Marin County, which was the most expensive county in America, to see places named Union City, Hayward, and Berkeley, and to hear terms like Embarcadero, Mission District, and Haight-Ashbury thrown around with great frequency.

I didn't have a clue what everyone was talking about. I quickly learned and used the word, *eclectic*. That was the best way to describe the Bay Area. The rolling hills were astounding; they looked just like the background scenes in *The Birds*. The mountainsides appear as a wall of corrugated grass, because the faces of the hills curve in and out.

I recall the taxicab driver asking me if I loved cows.

I said, "I love to eat them, but I don't know any personally."

He said, "You'll learn to love them."

As we entered Napa Valley, Sonoma County, and approached Petaluma, I knew why he said that. It wasn't the Grapes of Wrath that I smelled. I'd thought riding through Ohio had been a treat. Cattle surrounded us. I later learned that Petaluma was known for its dairy products, deer, and for being the hand-wrestling capital of the world. How exciting. There were towns directly out of the 70s. Cotati is a town due north of Petaluma, and it seems to be a

77

haven for both ex- and current hippies. They wore headbands, tie-dyed shirts, and everything in between. They must have migrated there from Haight-Ashbury – the famous hippie haven from the 60s. Northern Californians don't live large or small, they just live. This is a lesson the East Coast can learn while driving at 70mph to the 7/11 on a Sunday morning.

I arrived at Coast Guard Training Center Petaluma at around 1600 on a warm April day. This was where I would hone the military administrative skills that would sustain me in my Coast Guard career. The base sits in the middle of vast farmland. There was no point in thinking about walking anywhere – there was nowhere to go, at least on foot. I could see deer grazing everywhere and smell the cattle, or at least their manure. There were no liquor or lottery stores. No one loitered on corners. Most importantly, no one got shot each night.

It was an amazing place, not like boot camp at all. I could wear my regular clothing, or *civvies* as they are called in military life, after class. When I wasn't in training or having extra duty I was allowed to do my own thing. No more double-timing it around the base. Considering where I had been 10 days before, it was a drastic change for me. I still had a boot-camp style haircut; most trainees had grown their hair back. We stayed in a college-style dormitory, with three or four people to a room. When I arrived my room had two other guys in it, but one would graduate by the end of the week.

Later that day I decided to get a bite to eat. When I returned, there were bags on my bed. Being the street thug that I was, I yelled, "Who's stuff is this on my rack?"

This short, stocky guy came out of the bathroom and said, "It's mine."

I felt a bit bad because of how I'd approached the situation. I immediately calmed down and we introduced ourselves. His name was Mike Macon and he had just reported from a ship in Cleveland. He'd had more time in the Coast Guard than I had, and, more importantly, operational experience. He knew what it was really like.

The negative part about going straight from boot camp to school was my lack of realistic experience. I could only guess what life would be like; he knew. Mike also had a car, a 1974 yellow Volvo sedan that he'd driven across the country. I recall

Mike saying that he'd picked up a hitch-hiker along the way and dropped him off in San Francisco. That should tell you that times were different in more ways than one. Mike and I became great friends and continue this friendship today.

We had other roommates – Steve and Mack. Steve was from Boston and was as crazy as a box of rocks. I doubt that he was sober during much of the training. He was extremely funny and liked to party. He'd pay me to do the Moonwalk. This was in 1981 and Michael Jackson hadn't begun to moonwalk yet. It lights my fire to see that the world thinks he created it. I would give credit to the brothers from the movie *Breakin* before I'd give it to him. He rode the popularity of this dance, but it was going hot and heavy in 1980 prior to my departure from Detroit. Steve would say, "Look at his feet," and another five bucks for me. I can't recall where Mack was from, but I know he was a surfer from somewhere that didn't have access to water. He kept his huge surfboard in the corner on his side of the room.

One good thing about going to Yeoman School was the number of women who attended as well. We didn't have to keep our eyes in the boat in Petaluma. Couples were developing daily. A few were married shortly after leaving the school. We marched together to and from class each day, but we clowned the whole way. No one cared if we bounced or had snap. Unfortunately, Yeoman School was at the top of the hill and required the longest transit to class.

There were other schools at Petaluma. Radiomen had to attend at least 20 weeks of training. Storekeepers attended for 10 weeks, the same as yeomen. Subsistence Specialists (cooks) attended for 10 weeks as well. There were also advanced schools located on base. Petaluma was basically a college campus for military personnel. Since the radiomen were there the longest, they seemed to have a free rein of the place. They were somewhat different to me, so different that if they'd been attending public school, it's possible that they would have used the short yellow buses. To be honest, they had the toughest school on base and had to learn Morse code. It wasn't strange to see them walking around saying, "Dit Dit Dash" or "Dash Dit Dash Dash." Their behavior became understandable because they couldn't graduate unless they passed the Morse-code portion, and they didn't want to be there past 20 weeks.

On one early Saturday, around 0300, and after a severe round of drinking, someone pulled the base fire alarm. The Bay Area can be extremely cold at night. When we came outside, there was a radioman standing on a table holding his arms in the air. He yelled, "Can you count, Suckerssss!"

Even though we were sleepy, or should I say drunk, we burst into laughter. He had just reenacted the opening scene from the movie *The Warriors*, a well-known gang movie in which the leader, Cyrus, yelled those same words while trying to unite 100 New York City street gangs.

I don't recall the student receiving any punishment. That was how it was back then. He may have received a strong talking-to from the master chief, but they didn't end his career, as they would now. If he'd done that now he'd find himself in the brig for at least a year. Unfunny how time changes.

During the second weekend, Mike called the guy he'd picked up hitchhiking to ask if we could stay at his place when we arrived San Francisco. He replied that he wouldn't be there for most weekends and that the key was under the mat. How amazing. When we arrived we found the key and had a warm place to stay. No need to waste money on a hotel. Our only mission was to ensure that his cat ate well. We partied in San Francisco or Oakland basically every other weekend. We needed no hotels during this 10-week period, and we never saw the hitchhiker again. By the way, his cat ate well during the weekends and we didn't trash the place.

The one thing I noticed first-hand about San Francisco was its laid-back attitude. Even though there was traffic, no one drove aggressively except us; we made a U-turn on the Golden Gate Bridge. We were probably the only ones to ever do that. Well, it's better than jumping off of it like other emotionally challenged visitors. In the Bay Area no one rushes to do anything. It was such a stress-free environment, unlike the East Coast, where the calendar directs everyone to accomplish something before the weather breaks.

I did notice the openness of the gay relationships, but I also realized early on that I was the only one looking. I quickly dropped that habit and maintain the same attitude today. A person is likely to see anything in San Francisco. There are street performers, skateboarders, and tons of tourists at Fisherman's

Wharf. The exploding punk scene was also prevalent. On one occasion we met four ladies with numerous facial piercings and other punk attire outside of a disco named Studio West. At first glance we assumed that they were down on their luck. After observing them closely, though, we soon realized that they were wearing obviously expensive torn clothing. Even their dental work was noticeable. I quickly learned that I shouldn't assume anything, especially in this environment. We thought they were rich, rebellious youths.

San Francisco immediately taught me that not all seafood is fried, which wasn't the case in Detroit, where even today the majority of seafood is fried. The first time I saw baked or broiled fish was in San Francisco. Prior to 1981 I'd never eaten spiced shrimp or shrimp cocktail, two of my favorites today. Fortunately, I observed others in action before asking the waiter to take my shrimp back to fry them. People who are not exposed to other cultures, dialects, or cuisine have severely hindered growth.

This may be the main reason that some individuals refuse to travel. There is a legitimate fear of not knowing something. If we don't venture out of our boxes we're safe. I'm wondering if I'm the only person in America who is tired of traditional holiday meals and most soul foods. At this point, they are a bit boring. How many types of macaroni and cheese are there? It is amazing how many meals we have eaten that have been exactly the same. I am fortunate to have had the opportunity to see places such as San Francisco before I became set in my ways.

Most of us would prefer if certain individuals prepared their specialty, and the experimenters stick to condiments and paper plates. I would enjoy it immensely if I could have my Aunt Bertha's potato salad, and Bill's stuffing and so on, but no – that doesn't happen. The crack-head in the family wants to cook the desserts. The cousin who works on engines wants to cook the turkey. How in the hell can he prepare the main dish with black grease lines still around his fingernails? Can he get the napkins, please? By the way, he could use a few when he finishes washing his hands.

Oakland was fun, but we didn't spend as much time there as I would've liked. It hadn't dawned on me previously that these folks'd had to migrate to the far West Coast. Mike and I visited an Oakland barbershop one Saturday and had the time of our lives talking to the guys. I discovered that they said some of the same slang as the Lewis' in my neighborhood. Today, this particular dialect has been made famous by the rapper Snoop Dogg. Snoop adds "sss" and "zzz" to certain words. For example, the most utilized four-letter-s-word is called *shiznit*. Television is called *televizzal*, and so on. All of the Lewis boys talked like this in the 70s.

Director/rapper Ice Cube's dialect is straight out of Kansas. Car is pronounced *cor*. Park is pronounced *pork*. We used to tease my Kansas City cousins Carlos, Cameron, and Carmelita about their *-or* words, while they teased us about our *-ar* words. I also discovered that a major portion of the brothers from Chicago, Cleveland, and Detroit migrated to California after the fall of the Black Panthers. Many were escaping legal cases and others were looking for a new way of life. Mass migration changes culture and creates slang and dialect for years to come.

One of the best Oakland sites was Lake Merritt Park. In Detroit, it's tough going to the park without a fight or some type of drama developing. Lake Merritt was exclusively African American, and I can't recall one single incident. Frankly, it was just friendly. I didn't see the type of gang violence that plagued Southern California. The guys would give us specific directions to barbers or the hottest nightclub. The ladies – well, I should probably stop here. I saw my first burgundy-hair girl in Oakland. Northern California women are extremely loyal. I never saw anything like this in the Midwest or East Coast.

On one occasion in Oakland I met a lady just as my friend asked if I was ready to go. To be honest, I wasn't. He asked me to drop him off at a friend's house and I could keep the car. I asked her to wait for me to return to the club, and she said, "Yes, I'll wait."

This was one of those extremely foggy Bay Area nights and visibility was a mere 25 feet. I left the club at 11 p.m. and didn't return until 1:50 a.m., 10 minutes before closing time. As I approached the door the bouncer said, "Are you the one that the lady sitting next to the stage is waiting for?"

I looked over his shoulder and I saw her sitting and looking sort of sad, as if I wasn't going to return.

I said, "Yes, I am."

He said, "She's right there waiting for you."

In the Midwest, one of two things would have happened. Either she would have been gone, or some other brother would have had her head on *his* shoulder. On the East Coast, one thing would have happened. She would have cursed me out in front of the entire establishment for leaving her too long and preventing her from getting her favorite table at IHoP.

The Bay Area is my favorite stateside spot, followed by Connecticut, New Orleans, Rhode Island, Savannah, and Boston. You perhaps noticed that I picked places that are not the usual urban hangouts – other than NOLA. It's the food, baby!

The San Francisco architecture forces a person to ask the question, "How did they *do* that?" How can they build a tall building on such a steep street? How do they drive on these roads and not hit a cable car? How did they build Lombard Street, known as the world's crookedest street? Lombard Street runs parallel to San Francisco Bay and is extremely steep. From the apex it immediately zig-zags down a cobblestone street with million-dollar homes on each side. It's an amazing experience. My next challenge is to drive a five-speed sports car in San Francisco. If and when I accomplish that, look out Manhattan! Until then, it's the train to Penn Station and I'll hoof it from there.

After 10 weeks of learning, partying, networking, and growing, it was time to pick billets again. I didn't want to leave California, but there were only two positions available. One guy had a serious car accident out there and he received one of the positions because of his therapy needs. I think one of the students had caught the eye of one of our instructors, and that individual received the other position. We had two ships available. Our class leader took one of the ships and the other was reserved for a women. Our classmate Linda took that ship. It was located in Honolulu. The only remaining position that caught my eye was Headquarters, Washington, DC.

Coming from the North, I didn't want to go to the South. Since I couldn't stay out West, I didn't want to go back to the Midwest. Mike and I selected DC, as did many others at the school. Prior to leaving, we were called into the master chief's office and offered positions in New Orleans. I thought about it for about 2.5 seconds and quickly declined. Mike did as well. This was a flip of the switch that would likely alter my entire life. I didn't think of it that way. I just thought that I didn't join the Coast Guard to go to the Deep South. I hadn't even heard of Mardi Gras at that time. We never thought about it again and prepared ourselves for a long journey across country in Mike's 1974 Volvo. He wanted to visit his family in Jacksonville, Florida prior to arriving DC and I would tag along.

We graduated Yeoman Class "A" School on June 6, 1981. They gave us $1000 each and 18 days to get to Washington, DC by car. We said a few goodbyes, packed up the Volvo, and headed down to *Soul Train*. We planned to get a hotel in Los Angeles and hang out for the weekend, but we never accomplished that mission. We scraped the bottom of the car after filling up at an East Los Angeles gas station. We couldn't figure out where the gas smell was coming from, but we soon noticed that the meter was slowly heading towards empty. This couldn't be; we'd just filled up. It couldn't have been gas because drivers were flicking lit cigarettes out of their car windows right next to us. We crept into another gas station, looked under the car, and saw gas pouring out as if we were pumping it directly onto the ground. Our *Soul Train* dreams had come to a screeching halt.

The kind gentleman at the gas station, who spoke little English, agreed to fix our car on Monday. He also drove us around to a number of hotels. We felt that the $2000 we had between us would help immensely, especially since all of the hotels had "Vacancy" signs flashing in broad daylight on a Friday Afternoon. Were we wrong. This was the first time I experienced racism by someone other than a Caucasian or one of the Middle Eastern storeowners in Detroit. Mike and I asked, "May we rent a room please?", and the uniform response was "No Vacanceee!" In each case, we looked outside and discovered that the vacancy sign had been turned off.

Eventually, the mechanic helped us locate a sleazebag hotel that was happy to take our money. It was a drab, damp, dark-green room with one large area and one closet (which housed my bed). Mike began showing symptoms of tonsillitis and developed a high temperature. I was sick to my stomach because of the stench in our room, or it may have been the white port I'd drunk. I don't think we left that room for three days. They fixed the car on Monday and gave Mike a homemade concoction for his throat. We never looked back. No Hollywood sign, no *Soul Train*, and definitely no women.

Mike started out the drive east until he could go no further. I took over just west of the Arizona border. We decided to stop in Flagstaff to sleep for the night. The next morning we ventured out bright and early. This was a weird drive. We found ourselves in the deserts of New Mexico. It was at least 98°, and somewhere along the way the Volvo's windshield cracked. We didn't see or hear it happen. We could only guess that the heat was the culprit.

Eastern Arizona and New Mexico were beautiful. Every aspect of old western movies came to mind. We saw stretches of desert with nothing but tumbleweeds and the red clay mountain ranges, each one shaped differently. Since we'd lost three days in L.A., we decided to go as far as we could before getting another room. As nightfall arrived, we found ourselves in the Panhandle city of Amarillo, Texas. It was around 3 a.m. and it didn't take a rocket scientist to know that we were the only brothers in the truck stop. It didn't take long before some guy who looked like Ernie from *My Three Sons* told us, "Ya'll don't want to be in here!"

Being the rocket scientists we were, or had to be in this case, we said, "We know."

At the same time, we saw a huge African American truck driver with his family. We acknowledged each other, and when he walked out of the door we were right behind him like two puppies. I haven't been back to Texas since.

Mike was still under the weather and I was doing a major portion of the driving. We were literally humping across country. Our next encounter happened a day or so later in Oklahoma. It was dusk and Mike was asleep. There was no one on I-10 but us, or at least so I thought. Out of nowhere, I saw two ladies waving at me from their car in the fast lane. I was leery and I wasn't about to stop and assist anyone in the middle of Tumbleweed City, Oklahoma.

They began to speed up past me, which was fine by me. To my surprise, they then veered in front of me and hit their brakes. I swerved to avoid colliding with them, regained my control, and hauled more than my rear end.

Mike woke up and yelled, "What's going on?"

I told him what happened. We didn't see them again and were glad that we didn't. A few years later I saw the movie *Thelma and Louise*. I wonder if that movie was a true story.

We arrived in Tupelo, Mississippi, the Birthplace of Elvis, roughly three days after our West Coast departure. This was unique. No sooner did we enter the city limits than a police car was behind us. They didn't stop us. They just followed us everywhere we went. They followed us to Burger King and during our quest for a motel.

I was naïve and had never experienced blatant profiling. I recall telling Mike, "We are in the Coast Guard, and if something happens to us, there will be a thorough investigation."

Mike, coming from Jacksonville, said, "Yeah, right!"

I had to think about where I was and immediately thought of the civil rights workers who were found buried in a ravine.

Needless to say, I didn't sleep well that night and was glad that Mike was feeling better. We were out of there in the morning. Our next stops were Little Rock, Arkansas and Memphis, Tennessee. Little Rock was uneventful. I purchased the loudest clock in history from Radio Shack. I feared being AWOL because of all of the California partying; I knew Headquarters would be different. That clock never died. It just stopped showing all of the digits, but it was good for a 5 a.m. wake-up even if I couldn't see the numbers.

Memphis and Atlanta were a breath of fresh air. We saw people everywhere, mainly ladies. We didn't spend enough time in Memphis and were tired when we arrived Atlanta. We enjoyed eating at Church's Chicken and watching all of the African Americans walking around. I wanted to stay the night, but Mike was anxious to get home since he was so close. He hadn't gone home prior to leaving the ship in Cleveland for California. I was tired from the drive, so we pressed on to Florida.

We arrived at Mike's family home in Jacksonville, Florida on Wednesday. Mike's family was extremely hospitable and down-to-earth. They made me feel right at home and fed us well. We had a wonderful time and managed to get out on the town a couple of times. Who would have thought that we could travel from the West Coast to the East in three to four days? Anything could have happened to us, and almost did; we could have exploded or been lynched, kidnapped, or shot. In that exact order. It never happened, and we made it. I wasn't too concerned, because no matter what anyone says, I was in the United States Coast Guard and there would have been a thorough investigation. It's funny how indestructible we feel when we're youths.

Chapter 14
Nine to One?

------------------------☼------------------------

If I never see the sign "South of the Border" again, it will be too soon. There were tons of billboards in the Carolinas saying, "South of the Border Just Ahead." After experiencing the most boring part of I-95, we were excited to finally reach South of the Border. What I'd envisioned was a place similar to the "Titty Twister" in the movie *From Dusk to Dawn*. I was thinking strip clubs, bar brawls, and great food. When we reached this place we discovered that it was a dingy truck stop that looked like a fake Hollywood set for a Mexican movie. It sucked. They sold souvenirs and fireworks, and that's it.

I was so disappointed that I forgot to get food. We gassed up and got out of there. Needless to say, I haven't driven to the Carolinas since. Every time I hear someone say that they are going to South of the Border, or see a bumper sticker, I just laugh to myself. I'm sure it has changed, but not enough for me to spend a few bucks there.

We arrived in Washington, DC at 6:00 a.m. on a weekday. I immediately noticed two things: guys waiting for the liquor stores to open and ladies at the bus stop or subway on their way to work. I thought it had to be something wrong with this picture. The first street we drove down was 14th Street. This was the street that displayed all of the prostitutes, or at least the more flamboyant ones. I'd never seen anything like that in my life. In Detroit, Mack Avenue ladies of the night looked like they were straight out of a refugee camp. In DC, they looked like Halle Berry and Pam Grier, the only difference being their lack of clothing. I think they were wearing the first phase thongs. At least

I hope they were thongs. They walked directly down the middle of the street. If I'd stuck my hand out of the window I could have literally smacked them on the rear. I thought about it. Didn't do it.

We drove all morning trying to find Coast Guard Headquarters. I'd been told not to expect it to be in a prime location. The Coast Guard is frugal when it comes to personnel matters or facilities. We're likely to have a beautiful ship assigned to a dump of a station. We wound up crossing the Woodrow Wilson Bridge into Virginia trying to find our new job in DC.

I had heard that a person could look at something in DC for 30 minutes before figuring out how to get to it, which was right. If you ever see the Washington Monument or the Capitol, try to drive to it and you'll hit one of DC's famous circles. Geico must have created these things to ensure unlimited claims. They involve at least five streets leading into an area that looks like a small park with streetlights all the way around it. Venture into it and all hell breaks loose, with people driving in every direction trying to circumvent and exit the contraption.

We located Bolling Air Force Base in Southwest Washington. We thought that we could ask a military person how to find our building. Most Air Force personnel didn't know where it was. The Coast Guard has a sponsor program that is designed to alleviate the burden on relocated personnel. Our sponsor evidently wasn't on the case. Fortunately, we were able to recognize someone in a Coast Guard uniform at a base bus stop. We gave him a lift to our building and he directed us to our sponsor. Our sponsor directed us to the housing office and I haven't seen him since.

We had no idea where we were going to live. Our take-home pay was approximately $236 every two weeks. We could make more if we decided to go out on the economy and locate our own apartment. We were given the option of obtaining Government Leased Housing. Since the Coast Guard didn't have a local base in Washington, it set up private leases in local housing complexes. This program would cause us to forfeit nearly an additional $200 per month. This was fine because we would not be responsible for paying the bill each month. Moreover, the apartments were furnished. This was an excellent idea to assist young, lower-level military personnel to get by in a high-cost area. They assigned two Coast Guard members to an apartment. In some cases, they assigned three members to a three-bedroom apartment.

I noticed an immediate eyesore in and around DC; families were constantly evicted, their personal belongings being strewn on curbs in both DC and suburban Maryland. I guess landlords had no qualms about setting someone out. This made our government lease decision a great one. I knew that it wouldn't be my stuff in front whenever I arrived home. If it was, there would be a thorough investigation.

The housing office, headed by Ms. Crishman and Ms. Brody, advised us that they needed about a week to organize housing for us. They put us in the Best Western closest to the job for six days. I saw a couple of pet roaches in our room. I thought I was back at home. Mike and I decided to drive around the city and see the sights. As usual, we found ourselves smack in the middle of the hood. It doesn't take long to locate it. All you have to do is look for Martin Luther King Avenue.

We found a Church's Chicken on the corner of Martin Luther King Avenue and Portland Street. We were in the Southeast portion of the city and a half a mile from St. Elizabeth's Hospital. Do you know John Hinkley? We thought this would be comical. We began to eat our chicken and watch the sights. There was a liquor store on one corner and a large bus stop on the other.

Within minutes, a drunk sat next to us and said, "What's your MOS?"

We said, "We don't know; we don't have an MOS."

He said, "You are in the military, aren't you?"

We said, "Yes."

He said, "Then you gotta to have a fucking MOS."

Mike and I just looked at each other and said with our eyes, "Four years of this shit?"

The Army, Marines, and Air Force call their job specialties MOSs and the Navy and Coast Guard call them Rates. We didn't get into all of that and just let him talk trash to us. He did say one thing that made us think. It wasn't the first time we heard it, but it was great to hear it from someone in the city. He said, "Ya'll know there be nine women to every man here?"

I didn't care how he said it, but it stuck in my mind.

After the sixth day, we were given keys to two apartments in Lanham, Maryland, about half-way between Washington and Baltimore, in a nice garden apartment complex about a mile from the NASA Goddard Space Flight Center. It was not in the hood. We'd hit the jackpot with this Coast Guard stuff. Mike and I were not able to room together, which was a bummer, but we did live directly across the street from one another. Mike's roommate eventually transferred within the first week; leaving Mike with an apartment to himself. Another person immediately moved in with him. I was housed with Yeoman Second Class Steve Mayer. He was in his mid to late 20s and well-established. He had been in the Coast Guard for six or seven years, a lifetime to two guys who planned to serve four years and get out.

I began to look around my new crib. It was nice, and, more importantly, furnished. I had my own queen-size bedroom set, a decent living and dining room set, and the kitchen had a dishwasher. In my homes, *we* were the dishwashers. Steve was out of the house when I arrived and I looked forward to meeting him. It couldn't be as bad as a 50-person squad bay or a room of four as in Petaluma. Mike was checking out his crib as well. We decided to go to the nearest mall and pick up a few items, like towels, pots and pans, and such. You see, Wendy's barely existed and McDonald's wasn't within walking distance to me. I couldn't afford to eat out and I didn't have the transportation to get there. I was forced to cook. There was a grocery store nearby called Basics. That was fine, because I needed something fairly close or within a short cab ride. I still own the cast-iron skillet and thin pot that I bought that day. I still have the towels from that apartment – for washing my car.

My roommate Steve returned later in the weekend and we hit it off okay. He was a jazz music buff and an avid bike rider. He had a nice Datsun B210. It was a late model, small, white hatchback. He had so many girls running in and out of the apartment that I knew *he* had his nine. The apartment had an entire glass front with sliding doors. We didn't have the usual curtain set up, but rather a bamboo screen that we could roll up and tie off.

On one occasion, Steve was waiting on a date and I heard a knock at the door. I looked out of the peephole and saw a very tall woman at the door. Initially thinking it was Steve's date, I opened it and found a transvestite standing there. Within a matter of two seconds I'd looked at his face, hands, and feet and slammed the door.

Steve asked, "What happened?"

I said, "You don't want to know," and pulled down the bamboo screen.

Steve had relatives living in the area and spent a large portion of his time with them. I spent most of my time alone, either studying for the next pay grade or trying to get to the city.

I'd never foreseen myself living anywhere but in a hood. I expected to see liquor stores and bums on one corner and prostitutes or gang members on the other. I'd never thought that I'd be able to sit on a third floor balcony looking down on my neighbors. Many of them were looking at me because I was to damn young to have my own apartment, especially since most of my peer group in this complex lived with their parents. I quickly noticed that most of the guys in the complex had nice cars, but lived at home. Most were close to 30 years old. It was strange to me that they would prefer a huge stereo system and a nice car to living on their own. It just didn't make sense to me.

It didn't take long for me to notice what type of neighbors I had. The complex was mainly African American and covered every age group, except women in the 18-22 age group. They were either in their late 20s or under 17. The scary part was that the older women didn't speak to me and 15-year-olds flirted hard. This couldn't be good. It's funny that a guy can be two to three years older than a girl, but if they are under 18 they're extremely too young. I retained those beliefs and stuck to my guns.

I did meet a lady who lived in the building directly in front of us named Stephanie Curtis. She was beautiful and tall. Everyone is tall to me. She was an Air Force Staff Sergeant who worked at the hospital on Andrews Air Force Base. She was funny as hell. I liked her but I sensed she liked Steve. Well, that led to us entering the Brother/Sister Zone. A person never gets out of the Brother/Sister Zone. Rod Serling actually introduces you before you enter it. There can be two people in the entire world, but if you are in the Zone, it ain't happening. We became close while sitting on the stoop with others from the neighborhood.

She would always ask, "Where's your roommate?"

I basically told her, "You don't want to know!" because, as usual, he wasn't alone.

We kept in touch with each other, but at some point I lost contact with her.

Before long, two guys befriended Mike and me. One was named Antwon and another called himself Q. They were street-smart guys and a few years older. Antwon's family was nice; his father was an educator at nearby Morgan State University. I never visited Q's home. On one occasion, Antwon and Q asked Mike and me if we wanted to go to a club in DC. It was fine with us because we hadn't experienced anything in the city since arriving, and since I didn't have a car anywhere was fine with me. They took us to a hole in the wall called A Touch of Class, a strip club on Georgia Avenue. Antwon and Q said that they were going across the street to another club called Macombo's.

A Touch of Class was dingy, smelly, and had one dancer on a small stage. Someone told us, "You guys should go upstairs," and not knowing any better, we went upstairs, where they were butterball naked and giving lap dances. This could have been fun, but they were all at least 200 pounds. I was only 130 at the time and they were crushing me. In addition, I felt as if I'd just finished working at Fisherman's Wharf when they finished.

We decided to go across the street to Macombo's and tell the guys that we were ready to go home. To our amazement, they were gone. They'd left us in Northwest DC. We were furious, and as far as I was concerned war was imminent. My thoughts had returned to my gang days in Detroit. I thought about what I was going to do to them for the entire $15 cab ride home. The closer we got to home, the more my thoughts went to just leaving them alone and cutting ties. I had come too far to revert back to the street life over a couple of jealous knuckleheads. This was a switch that I nearly flipped which could have landed me in jail, dead, kicked out of the Coast Guard, and, subsequently, back home.

Seeking friendship can be a dangerous thing in a new city, especially for a person who doesn't have transportation or much of a social life. This situation made me more apt to befriend and surround myself with the wrong element, something that was true for women as well. I eventually became friends with Antwon's younger brother and sister, and she informed me that he had always been jealous of my military career and my apartment. I wondered how that could be when he had a nice sports car and could do whatever he liked.

To my surprise, his sister said, "And that's all he has. What you have is a future!"

That young lady opened my eyes to something that will carry me for the rest of my life. I buckled down with my promotion books and saved $110 a month. In nine months I was the proud owner of a 1977 Toyota Celica. I can vividly recall that day.

When I arrived back at my apartment Steve was on the balcony and quickly yelled, "My son, you are now a man!"

From then on I could get to work on my own and do whatever I pleased.

Chapter 15
Plastic Briefcases and Salami Sandwiches

---------------------☼----------------

Coast Guard Headquarters is a six-story office building in the Buzzards Point area of the Southwest section of the city. It's not easy to locate and people have to pass through the projects to get to it. At least 2000 people work in the building. How in the world could I survive working in a building every day while properly greeting and saluting 1000 officers? I knew I would be in a world of shit at some point, but at last I'd have my own desk, typewriter, and copier. I'd tried hard to get there when I'd taken the business classes in high school. I'd tried to pursue jobs in the federal, state, and local governments in my home town of Detroit, only to be told that I'd have to step aside while they took care of a recently laid-off autoworker. Finally, I could try to prove myself in an office environment.

We were assigned to work as military administrative assistants to senior Coast Guard officers and civilians. I knew that I had died and gone to heaven. Our working hours were 0600-1630 from Monday through Thursday. That's correct, we had every Friday off. For an 18-year-old, this was great. Government office buildings are filled with women. The ratio wasn't nine to one in my building. It was more like 20 to one. Yes, it was heaven. I wasn't fortunate enough to get my nine. The ladies took care of that for me. They told me two things: "You are too young for me" and "I'm not driving all the way out to no damn Lanham." That nine-to-one thing quickly dwindled down to one – *me*.

In order to advance in the Coast Guard as an enlisted man, I had to take a series of correspondence courses, on the job training, and a service-wide examination. The first two evaluations were fairly easy, but the service wide examination was a different ballgame. Every person in my specialty and at my level took the same test. I could earn 100% on my test, but my time in service, evaluations, and medals were calculated into the mix and a list was generated. It wasn't strange for a highly senior person to take a test and bomb it - only to find out that his or her length of service and awards had moved him or her up a number of slots. Although an individual may score higher and be a better technician, other factors determine who gets promoted or not. The final list may have 300 people on it, but the Coast Guard can determine that they only need the top 20. The other 280 have to retest within six or 12 months, along with newly eligible personnel. For those who do not study it can take years to move up one pay grade. It is not unusual for someone to retire at the E-5 level. An E-5, or second class petty officer, who retires can honestly say that he or she has passed one service-wide exam in an entire 20-year career.

I do not knock anyone for the level of success they have attained in a career. Who's to say that the person didn't set out to be the best second class petty officer in the Coast Guard? Who are we to judge? Each individual's view of success is personal. I hope and pray that one day we can stop measuring a person's current status by pay grade, but by that person's starting point.

One example was a situation I came across in Petaluma. Headquarters received a number of congressional letters for a petty officer who was appealing a possible discharge. He was in his late 50s and was serving as a third class yeoman in the Personnel Reporting Unit. His peers were between the ages of 18 and 23. They couldn't imagine themselves working with someone who they considered to be too old for the rank. They gave him a hard time and made it extremely uncomfortable for him. What they didn't know was that his dream was to serve in every armed service in the United States. He had completed tours of duty in the Army, Navy, Air Force, and Marines. He'd joined the Coast Guard Reserves and had jumped on the opportunity to go on active duty and complete his five-service odyssey. How could we hate him?

I had the opportunity to meet him at a later date and found a tiny, energetic professional with a smile a mile wide. He ran around the office at 100 mph and did all of the dirty work. He dumped the trash cans, rolled up his sleeves and fixed copiers and fax machines, and made the runs with the vehicles to get lunch for his shipmates. He was a fireball of energy. Eventually, his discharge was overturned and he continued to serve our nation proudly. It's not good to judge folks or to second-guess their potential or perceived lack of motivation.

Not only was I learning my administrative and military craft, I was learning how to be a man. I had to learn responsibility and how to get to work on time. Getting to work had been easy when I rode with Mike. I could also take a bus to the Metro station. The hardest part was getting to work *after* I got my car, after trying to hang out all night. There were times when I returned home at 4:30 a.m. and had to be at my desk by 6:00 a.m. I didn't go to sleep on those occasions, but I managed to put in a decent day's work, anyway. It was easy because my bosses were like big brothers.

My captain, Robert Vanpelt, was an aviator. He lived on a houseboat directly behind Hogates, one of the nicest nightclubs on the Washington waterfront. Captain Vanpelt's family remained in Virginia Beach while he worked in Washington during the week. He would leave work for the week on Wednesday or Thursday. Since Friday was an off day, he only worked three to four days a week. He would pay me $50 a week to look after his houseboat. This was great because I frequented Hogates, anyway. Hogates had a deck area on the rear and many patrons loved to sit out there instead of inside the crowded club.

On many occasions, I left the deck, walked 15 feet, and entered the houseboat. I could see the jaws drop as I opened the hatch and entered. It confused them because I was a teenager and I acted as if it was mine. I knew that if they thought I was rich or someone special I wouldn't encounter any problems. After Capt Vanpelt retired it was somewhat hard trying to explain where the houseboat had gone, but I just said it had a leak and I sold it.

I had many role models. Guys like Steve, Boyce, Tony, and Cooley showed me the ropes. They taught me how to carry myself.

Carrying yourself is a term that is only used in the African American community. It refers to how a person should walk into a room and how to introduce himself to people. It establishes a person as a class act. They taught me how to fill out my taxes and military paperwork. They showed me how to start an allotment to pay my car note or send money home. I did nothing alone. Someone had the information because they had recently been there.

I can vividly recall walking down a hallway once when a young lady stuck her head outside an office and yelled, "Hey you – I want to talk to you. Can you meet me at the Quonset Lounge next weekend?"

I was startled, but professional, carrying my plastic GSA Store briefcase. I didn't know what to do or say. I just looked at her mean. Her name was NeNe. I was slightly intimidated by her straightforwardness, which was normal for some DC women. The guys were a bit raw and so were some of the women. I would only talk to the quiet, prissy women. I never dated her, but we talked on the phone often. She wasn't coming all the way to Lanham, either. We remained friends until I lost contact with her.

I did gain a batch of new friends. The older gentlemen at that club taught me how to get around DC and deal with the people. They showed me that if I treated everyone with respect and love, respect and love would come back to me, which was no different than my upbringing in Detroit. They taught me which women were trouble or wanted me for my money. I didn't have much, but suppose I looked like it. I had benefits and that was enough. I give special thanks to Harry, Marlon, Damian, Bobby B., and at least 10 Tuskegee airmen. They served as my big brothers, even though they probably don't realize their role in my adult life.

There were other role models, both good and bad. Mark and Mack were the most famous petty officers in Headquarters – tall, handsome young men who had the most fun. They came from the same small town in Alabama, but claimed Atlanta as their home. They were the class clowns of Coast Guard Headquarters. They had lots of lady friends, but they were not the most responsible guys in the building. They didn't own cars, but they were able to get around. They rode to work with others, usually paying about $10 bi-weekly. They didn't care, because the women came to see them and the rest of us would help them get back and forth to work. They actually had it made. Mark visited me in my office in 2001 and was doing well in New Orleans. Mack James died, along with his new bride, in an automobile accident in 2001. I've recently talked to my ex-roommate Steve and he's doing fine in the DC area as well.

I would suppose that the lounge we had in the building didn't help our maturity much. The infamous Icebreaker Lounge will go down in Coast Guard history as the place that destroyed our service, but this could not be further from the truth. The Icebreaker Lounge was a small, dark mini-restaurant on the ground floor of our building. It had the reputation of a city bar. People who didn't work in Coast Guard Headquarters created this reputation. It's not acceptable by today's standards to have a restaurant-bar in an office building, but it was in the early 80s, especially since we worked at Buzzards Point and had no way of leaving the area for lunch other than via a shuttle bus. Moreover, the cafeteria food was bland and predictable.

We treated the lounge as a military Non-Commissioned Officers (NCO) Club. No one complained about the Navy Yard's club, and they had strippers perform at lunchtime. The lounge served as a place for the senior-most enlisted person in the service, the Master Chief of the Coast Guard, to use as a gathering place for his motivational speeches to us. We used it as a meeting place for groups who wanted to go out together on Friday afternoons. It's almost unheard of for 20 to 30 people – women and men, black and white – to go out together after work. This camaraderie and networking was critical to the morale of our building. Out of the 2000 people in Headquarters, 1000 were officers, 700 were civilian administrators, and the remaining 300 were enlisted members or lower-level civilians. We did whatever we could to learn our craft, have fun, and, most importantly, to respect each other. If we didn't do it, no one would.

One incident may have nailed the coffin in the Icebreaker Lounge's door. Petty Officer Dooley was a photojournalist, following in Alex Haley's (author of *Roots*) footsteps. Alex Haley was critical in the creation of Coast Guard photojournalists. He'd written love letters for his shipmates to mail home. Their wives had assumed that their husbands and boyfriends had written them. Alex Haley became the Coast Guard's first chief journalist. Dooley was no Alex Haley. He was more like Richard Pryor. He was a clown. During one of our group gatherings we misplaced Dooley, then found him out in the street with his Coast Guard service coat in his hands and his garrison cap turned sideways like a Matador. He was using bullfighting techniques to let the cars down the street one at a time. We literally captured him and drove him home before he could lose a stripe, especially since the Commandant would be leaving the building shortly.

My position in Governmental Affairs was abolished in 1983. I was recruited and assigned to the Enlisted Assignments Branch. This is the office responsible for transferring all enlisted personnel worldwide. There were only two locations at Headquarters that customers considered places for *real* yeomen, the Administrative Support Branch and Enlisted Assignments. These offices had large staffs and worked directly in our specialty. Their yeomen were not administrative assistants per se, but pay and benefit technicians as well as experts in Coast Guard policy. It was an honor to work in one of these offices.

I was assigned the job of yeoman for the aviation, medical, navigation, and engineering details, which included nearly 4000 of the 30,000 enlisted members. There were no high-tech phones. I had a black dial phone with six lines. I answered the phone at least 80 times a day by saying, "Enlisted Assignments, please hold; Enlisted Assignments, please hold; Enlisted Assignments, may I help you?" After I completed the last call I'd go back and pick up the others. There was no call-waiting or voice mail. Initially, we had IBM Selectric typewriters for each yeoman and a Wang Computer for six or so to share.

After a couple of years we all had our own Wang, but the typewriter was still king. We used it to produce documents called the ETOs, or Enlisted Transfer Orders. ETOs were compiled for each specialty and cut and pasted on the original documents, which were hand carried to the Department of Transportation Printing Office and mass-produced. They would return on either Thursday or Friday of each week. We printed out hundreds of mailing labels to send this document to every unit in the Coast Guard. We could not leave for the weekend without the ETO departing our office. When we were not creating the ETO, we were releasing teletype messages individually to transfer the remaining personnel who were not included on the ETO.

Another task we were in charge of was monitoring and filing Assignment Data Forms, also known as *dream sheets*. These documents stated the duty stations that each individual requested. The assignment officers used them to make their determinations.

For some reason, I could not stay on top of filing my dream sheets. I would take them home and still remain behind. I worked late one evening and counted the workforce numbers for all enlisted specialties. I realized that I and one other yeoman were managing 4000 member accounts apiece and that the other personnel averaged 2000 in their accounts. I brought this information to the attention of the office manager and we reorganized the accounts fairly. I could finally keep my filing up-to-date and manage my position better.

A member's attitude can dictate assignments. Those with no operational experience, such as a ship or air station, were unlikely to receive an office job in Honolulu. Those with numerous years of ops experience were likely to go wherever they liked if it was available. Two phone calls stick out in my mind. On one occasion, an irate sailor called and cursed me out because my boss hadn't returned his call. I advised him that the detailer was extremely busy and would call as soon as he could.

The gentleman said, "Wrong answer. Both you and the detailer can kiss my ass!"

I said, O.K. and hung up the phone.

I informed the detailer about what had happened and he said, "Pull his dream sheet."

We noticed that the gentleman asked for air stations in the Southeast sector or Puerto Rico. The detailer said, "Cut him orders to Sitka, Alaska."

Case closed.

On another case, the gentleman called from the icebreaking ship *Westwind.* He said, with a strong southern accent, "Man, get me off this *Westwind.* We be here in the yards in New Orleans and we ain't gone nowhere. I joined the Coast Guard to see the world and we ain't done squat. Morale be low!"

No matter how he said it, I felt for him. I advised the detailer what the member said and we pulled his dream sheet. We sent him to the Coast Guard Cutter *Mallow* in Honolulu. Another case closed. I quickly got the swing of how powerful my office was.

Five or six yeoman showed me the ropes in this office. Without their help I would not be where I am today. The senior enlisted personnel were First Class Petty Officers Mike Ouellete and Joe Steele. My peers were Alex Borden, Brian Brigeman, and Matt Kingsley. They were pros, no doubt about it. Chief Warrant

Officer Lee Kean ran the entire administrative section. He was old school and no nonsense. He never yelled or raised his voice. No one messed with him and everyone wanted to please him with our smarts and work ethic. Before he transferred, he called me into his office to tell me that I was number 23 on the E5/Second Class Yeoman advancement list of nearly 200 members. I'd nearly aced the service-wide examination. That was one of the best days in my life.

Another leader in the office in a non-supervisory role was Master Chief Leamington. Where can I start? Master Chief Leamington was an avid coffee drinker and chain smoker. Smokers could then smoke right at their desks without having to go outside or find a smoking spot. The entire building was open game. He looked at least 65, but he was in his mid-40s. He was bald and extremely skinny. He was single and had no kids. He would walk around the office saying, "Yes sir, yes sir, yes sir" at 100 miles per hour. We thought it was a tick of some kind, no more, no less. I thought of him as a loner, since he was the only master chief in the building who didn't get visits from other master chiefs.

We were responsible for keeping a five-gallon jug of water filled for him. If we forgot, we would soon know it, because the master chief would launch it into the nearest wall. Never mind that the commander would come out of his office to see what happened, notice it was the master chief, and return to his desk saying nothing. He would berate us for not being on our game. None of the yeomen drank coffee, but it was our duty to fill it twice a day. He was completely out of control. At some point they put Master Chief Leamington in charge of the yeomen. This lasted maybe six months, and I may have been a contributing factor.

It was the week before Christmas 1984 and the yeomen were trying to get the ETO out before attending our Christmas party at an offsite location. I had been promoted to team leader and was responsible for getting the document mailed and the yeomen across town afterwards. We finished our mass mailing and arrived the party at 1245. Everyone had eaten and were having cocktails. The admiral asked me where had we been. I advised him that we were getting the ETO out and came as soon as we could.

He said, "Fine, you and your guys can take the rest of the afternoon off."

We were pleased and began to enjoy our holiday party. I told the master chief that the admiral had told us to stay and enjoy the party.

He said, "You don't work for the admiral. Get your ass back to the office."

I said, "But the admiral said ..."

He replied, "I don't care."

I was furious and I noticed my peers having a great time. Since it was 1430 and we only had an hour left at work, and a 20-minute ride back to the office, I made the call for everyone to stay. I felt that I should listen to the senior person, who happened to be a two-star admiral. I had recently worked with this admiral on a major project in the Pentagon and felt that a rapport existed between us.

Monday morning was uneventful. In the afternoon, the master chief called me into his office and commenced to call me every name under the sun. I just looked straight ahead, but I could feel the tears welling up on my eyes. One of the yeomen heard him and came in to say that it wasn't entirely my fault. Actually, it had been my call and I was taking what I expected to take. At one point he put his finger in my face. That's when I walked out of the office and left two hours early for home. I went AWOL. I didn't care anymore. I would deal with it in the morning.

The next morning I visited the admiral to verify that he in fact had wanted us to stay.

He said, actually "I ordered you to stay."

I said "Thanks," and he said he would take care of the master chief.

The next morning was uneventful as well. At 1530 (my shutdown time), the admiral, the captain, the commander, and lieutenant all entered the master chief's office and shut the door behind them. I left the office smiling. Within weeks the master chief had orders to St. Louis, Missouri. I didn't realize I was that well-liked or respected by management. For that matter, maybe they just didn't like Master Chief Livingston for throwing the coffee bucket every day, or his antics in regard to the yeomen.

The master chief's replacement was Chief Hopwell, who treated everyone with respect. We continued to get the job done.

Mike eventually moved from Lanham to Temple Hills, Maryland. His new roommate got out of the Coast Guard and left a vacant bedroom at that apartment. I was able to move in with Mike and we set up a great little home. We were closer to work and also to Virginia, where most of the Coast Guard people lived at the time. Temple Hills was a nice area. We had a two-bedroom, two-bath ground-floor garden apartment. The neighbors were more our age, early 20s. Steve eventually transferred to Cleveland and I lost touch with him. I could literally eat lunch at home. This apartment was also furnished, but within six months everyone E-5 and above had to forfeit their furniture. That was fine for us because we had begun buying our own. I didn't want my stereo or TV on cinder blocks. It was about priorities.

We had a lot of fun in this apartment. Mack, Mark, and Leroy lived in the same complex. We never lacked comic relief, especially during the well-known Washington snow days. We had an 18-inch snowfall and were completely trapped inside our complex. We had to negotiate a steep hill to leave the complex, and for a few days no one could enter or leave. We had food, beer, and a football. That's all we needed. Mack and Mark made it seem as if we were living near Chris Rock and Bernie Mack. Mike had a new girlfriend, and she had a couple of sisters and many friends. Our apartment became a small hangout. It was a nice atmosphere in which to watch the Redskins. The ladies could cook as well. Even though I wasn't fortunate enough to date any of them, I ate well. Mike eventually married his sweetheart and moved out.

Another Mike moved in directly behind him. Mike Gannon was a Coast Guard storekeeper (budget and supply person) and a native Washingtonian. This was one reality about government-leased apartments. As soon as someone moved out, someone else immediately moved in. The complex would not paint the place because there wasn't a break between tenants. We would have had to do it ourselves, and it's nearly impossible to get any young coasties to paint something around their home. After painting ships and other Coast Guard property, we have this thing against painting. At least I do. Our apartment walls were tart, to say the least.

Mike Gannon and I decided to buy new cars on the same weekend. He received a great trade-in deal with an older car. I felt that I'd do well with my Celica. He returned with a five-speed candy-apple red Celica. I bought a five-speed Honda Accord hatchback. We looked great, but neither one of us could drive a darn stickshift. Why did we do that to ourselves? I guess it was a phase. I can't begin to recall how I got the car home. I know it was a Saturday and I had to work a normal schedule the next week. I drove the car down to the job and practiced around Buzzards Point. There were cops nearby, but they understood what I was doing.

Buzzards Point is a ghost town in the evenings and on the weekend, the perfect place to learn to drive a stick, or for the Mayor of DC to have an illegal rendezvous. I don't recall what Mike did for practice. I do know that on Monday afternoon his car rolled nose-first into the Anacostia River and rested in about 10 inches of water. It had been parked on a small cliff around the corner from our job. I suppose he'd tried to put it in gear, but it keep rolling forward. I can recall people coming into the Icebreaker Lounge saying that Mike's new red car was in the river. They were laughing profusely. I wanted to laugh, but I knew if I laughed at the club, I would laugh at the apartment, so I maintained a look of concern. On the inside, though, I was glad it wasn't me. Since it had gone in nose first he had no major damage, just a bent spoiler.

Within two weeks I had completely learned the hang of manual transmissions.

I received another warm surprise during this time. I can vividly recall walking down the third floor hallway at work and seeing a lovely woman in a blue uniform walking in my direction. I couldn't make out her face from a distance, but the walk, hairstyle, and height were familiar. As we approached each other and our eyes met, I suddenly dropped everything I was carrying on the floor. It was my "sister" Stephanie. I quickly noticed she wasn't in Air Force Blue, but Coast Guard Blue. She'd got out of the Air Force and joined the Coast Guard. I was surprised. These types of experiences make people religious in a heartbeat. My best woman friend was now one of us and in the same building. I later asked her why.

Her response was, "All you guys did was sit on the porch and drink beer; why wouldn't I want to change services?"

She was right. Now she was in the house as well. To this day, she is one of my best friends in the entire world. I love her dearly.

We enjoyed the remainder of the summer of 1984. On Labor Day, we decided to go to a nearby club called the Classics, the stuffiest place in the Washington area. The guys hung on the walls like portraits and looked at the women. It was still nine to one, but they were too cool to notice. I did notice someone in particular. She was short, with a light complexion. She was wearing red, with a small red hat. She wasn't alone and I made the tragic mistake of asking if one of the ladies was her mother. She said it was one of her younger sisters. That was a life-long lesson. The lady I met's nickname was Lady. Her real name was Sherri. She was beautiful and well-dressed. We danced and talked all night.

The next day I couldn't wait to call her, but she called me first. I was tired of bouncing from person to person. Chasing nine wasn't working. She was older than me and had a son. That was fine by me because I thought I was grown at that time and could handle anything. Little did I know how tough it would be to share her and raise a kid when I was still a kid myself. We dated continuously for six months or so and then we parted ways. We kept in touch. She was coming out of a relationship and I was still young and enjoying the single life.

My time at Headquarters was quickly coming to an end. I had arrived there an 18-year-old kid and was then 22. I didn't know exactly what duty station I wanted to pursue. My bosses always told me that I needed to go to sea or get operational experience. They advised that the ships would become plentiful in the late 80s or early 90s and that everyone would have to go sooner or later. They warned me that I shouldn't wait until I was in my mid-30s or 40. The wear and tear on the body is terrible at that age. I believed them. I initially put in to return to Memphis.

There was a vacancy at an operational shore station called Group Lower Mississippi River. Mike Macon had recently transferred to a ship that maintained buoys in St. Petersburg, Florida. He ran the ship's office and only answered to the ship's captain and executive officer. I thought about it for a while, but I was afraid to go to sea. I changed my mind about the Group and decided to pursue the Coast Guard Cutter *Bramble* in Port Huron, Michigan, up the road from my home. This idea was fine until I saw a picture of her covered in ice. The crew was breaking ice off of the railings with baseball bats.

I said, "Hell No!"

While attending one of the famous Headquarters Christmas parties, I was approached by one of my bosses, who at the time was the yeoman assignment officer-detailer. He said that he had a vacancy that he couldn't fill in Guam. The ship was called the *Basswood* and it was a 180-foot-long buoy tender. It was an old black ship with a large crane on the bow, responsible for traveling throughout the Pacific fixing navigational aids and performing law enforcement and search and rescue. This sounded interesting, but the only problem was Guam. It was 10,000 miles away. The damn country is only 3000 miles wide. Where would I be? I looked at a map and realized that Guam was closer to Japan, Hawaii, and the Philippines than it was to L.A. I thought long and hard on this. Moreover, I had reestablished my relationship with Lady and didn't want to leave her and her son Gregory.

I had major decisions to make. We were in love and didn't want this assignment to come between us. One positive aspect of this assignment was the 18-month duration. The Memphis assignment was for four years and the *Bramble* tour would have been three years. I determined that 18 months in the tropics was better than three years in the snow. She promised to be there when I returned. So we went to the County Courthouse and got married. We didn't tell anyone other than her best friend and Gregory. It wasn't the best way to do this, but we were only thinking of ourselves. Six months later I was on my way to Guam. After saying my goodbyes in Detroit and Washington, DC, I flew to Chicago and connected with a non-stop 14-hour flight to Honolulu, Hawaii.

Chapter 16
Go West Young Man
-------------------☼-------------------

The Coast Guard usually sends individuals to advance training prior to taking an arduous assignment. Unfortunately, they canceled the advanced school in Petaluma that I was scheduled to take. To make up for the additional training they sent me to the Fourteenth Coast Guard District Office in downtown Honolulu for eight days. I was sent to train in the personnel office prior to continuing on to Guam. Unfortunately, no one could train me in eight days to assist in the personnel unit. To get me out of their way, I was sent to the recruiting branch. To my amazement I knew the recruiter, Chief Charlie Tocci, who had been the assistant to the Master Chief of the Coast Guard who had sponsored the meetings at the Icebreaker Lounge.

Three close friends from Headquarters, Alex, Matt, and Leroy, were also assigned to District Fourteen. Matt and Alex had worked with me in the detailer's office and Leroy had been Mark and Mack's roommate. I had also trained on the new Coast Guard computer in Leroy's office. His chief, Garcia Graves, was also an ex-HQ manager. To be honest, this was the best eight-day vacation I've ever had. I didn't need a hotel at all. It couldn't get any better than that. It was tough leaving the States and a new family, but I had to get this ship thing over and done with. I stayed with Leroy and Matt for four days each. Leroy lived one block from the ocean and in the heart of the hotel district.

I didn't have much money to spend because I was continuing on to Guam. I don't think Leroy had much money either. His apartment had to be expensive. I discovered Cup-of-Soups and Oodles of Noodles. In Hawaii they doctored their noodles up, adding chicken breasts, green peppers, and onions, making them mini meals. This freed up dollars for the important things: beer and sightseeing. Leroy had a part-time job and he wasn't home until 9 p.m. I couldn't wait for Leroy to come home to experience Honolulu. He lived directly in front of Hamburger Mary's, a restaurant with many Christmas lights on the outer walls, known as a hangout for cross-dressers.

I walked directly past it and frequented a place call the Shore Bird East, which had the first open-air bar I'd ever seen. It was amazing to see total darkness at 5:30 p.m. and torches burning all over the beach. It was nothing for an exotic bird to fly in and sit on a table next to me. I met a few Australian Marines, who introduced me to Fosters Lager Beer. The one thing that I learned from them was a firm handshake. Aussies squeeze the blood out of a person's hand. The only thing I could think of was, "You're not going to get any milk out of it." Since they were marines, I shook their hands just as hard. When in Rome.

Alex had developed Bell's palsy and wasn't able to see me. He had some facial paralysis and didn't feel up to visitors. I hated not getting to see him because we were close. He had personally trained me in the Assignments Branch. Matt was stationed at the Omega Navigation Station on the north side of the island, in a town called Kaneohe. The Omega station housed the islands' largest radio tower. This is the antenna tower that is seen frequently on the *Magnum P.I.* television show. Matt's townhouse was definitely expensive, which was understandable because Matt dated a comfortably well-off lady from the DC area. I didn't expect anything less.

That side of Honolulu was completely different from the downtown area. It possessed the most beautiful hillsides that I've ever seen. The rolling hills were similar to the farmland in Sonoma County. Matt was on vacation at the time and we were able to do just about anything. I snorkeled, rode bikes, and saw the land. We ate squid and drank sake. Actually, after the sake, I couldn't taste the squid. On one occasion, Matt, Leroy, and I hit the town. We visited one of Leroy's hangouts and it was extreme fun. Lots of reggae. We also visited Rene's, in Pearl City. Many sailors from Pearl Harbor frequented this club. It was owned by Roger E. Moseley from *Magnum P.I.* It was a luxurious establishment.

After eight days of fun in the sun it was time to head over to the island of Guam and meet the ship. I flew via Continental Airlines' island hopper for 12 hours. The funniest part of the island hopper was the appearance of the new passengers. As we flew further and further from Hawaii, the people became darker and the afros became larger. I can recall the stopovers vividly and have subsequently researched each location if I didn't visit it on other occasions.

Our first stop was Johnston Island. We were not allowed to depart the plane during any of these stops. We added passengers, instead. [1]Johnston Island is a low sand and coral island, 717 miles WSW of Honolulu. It is 1,000 yards long and about 200 yards wide. In 1941 the Japanese shelled Johnston Island after attacking Pearl Harbor. In 1948 it was placed under the control of the US Air Force. During the 1950s and 1960s the Air Force conducted numerous nuclear-test launchings there. Two of these missiles exploded directly over the Johnston Island runway. Since then the Government has spent decades gathering the radioactive contaminants that the tests spewed over the Island. In 1971 the Army started to stockpile its chemical weapons on Johnston Atoll, moving them from Okinawa. In 1985, Congress ordered the disposal of all stockpiled chemical agents and munitions, and construction began on an incineration plant. Destruction of the weapons began in 1990. In November 2000 the destruction operation was completed. I suppose these are the reasons why they wouldn't let us get off of the plane.

The next island stop was Kwajalein Atoll. It is the world's largest coral atoll, and includes 97 islands, with a total land mass of just 6.5 square miles, surrounding a huge 1,100-square-mile lagoon. The lagoon, sometimes called "the catcher's mitt," is the target for intercontinental ballistic missiles (ICBMs) fired from Vandenburg Air Force Base in California, a measly 4,200 miles away. The tests generally occur at night, lighting up the sky with explosions, debris, and sonic booms. About 3,000 American contract workers and their families live on Kwajalein. Another fine place for me *not* to exit an aircraft.

The next stop was Majuro Atoll. It is the political and economic hub of the Marshall Islands and the home of most of

---

[1] Johnson Island History/Togography – www.janesesture.com/johnston

its population. The atoll has 57 small islands connected by a single 35-mile stretch of paved road, making Majuro look like one long island from the air. Robert Louis Stevenson called the atoll the "Pearl of the Pacific." It's not the same quiet place today. Majuro is the most Westernized of the Marshall Islands. These new passengers had huge afros. I thought I was on a time machine.

Our next stop was Kosrae Island and the start of the Micronesian island chain. Kosrae's greatest feature is the clear, immaculate ocean and living coral reefs that completely encircle it. The island is nearly triangular and great dive spots are located on all three sides. The locals believe that in ancient times the gods became angry with Kosrae and laid her on her back where she became an island. I suppose she has big *breastasis*. It is also called the *land of the sleeping lady*. You can still see her head, hair, stomach, and breasts outlined against the sky. Legend has it that a king of Micronesia ruled from Kosrae and that the first settlers arrived by canoes from East Asia and other islands in the South Pacific. In 1776, whalers and missionaries arrived from Boston and educated the people, producing the first written version of the local language. In 1874, the pirate William 'Bully' Hayes wrecked his ship the *Leonora* in Utwe Harbor during a storm. He supposedly buried his treasure after his ship sank. The ship still lies in the harbor mud, but the treasure has never been recovered. This is the easternmost worksite for the *Basswood*.

The next stop was luxurious Pohnpei (Ponapé); one of my favorites. This is the largest island in the Eastern Caroline group and the capital of the Federated States of Micronesia (FSM). It fits the typical South Sea island image with its lush vegetation and abundant rainfall washing into streams, rivers and tumbling waterfalls. Unlike other Micronesian islands it has tropical jungles, mist-covered mountains, swamps, and exotic plants. [2]Situated in the Western Pacific, it is 2,900 feet high, 13 miles wide, and shaped somewhat like a circular tent. Its best-known landmark is Sokehs Rock, a steep cliff. The first European to visit the island group was Spaniard Diego de Rocha. The islands were originally called the New Philippines until 1696 when they were renamed the Caroline Islands. Occupied by Spain, Germany,

[2] Pohnpei History/Topography – www.visit-fsm.org/pohnpei/sights.html.

Japan, and the USA, Pohnpei experienced 100 years of foreign rule because it proved to be an excellent supply stop for Pacific expeditions. English is the predominant language spoken. Pohnpei is also known for its fresh black pepper. If you visit Pohnpei and don't return with pepper, no one will believe you've been there. They are also known for woodcarvings. I want another carved hammerhead shark. The shippers broke it during my return to the States.

The next stop on my western excursion was Truk Atoll in the Caroline Islands. The Japanese fleet maintained a forward port in Truk. After the attack on Pearl Harbor, America sank the Japanese fleet stationed in Truk. Today Truk serves as one of the most popular dive spots in the entire would; mainly because of the underwater Japanese ships. [3]Truk Atoll encompasses 15 large islands, 192 outer islands, and 80 small islands and has one of the largest lagoons in the world. It measures 56 miles at its widest point and encloses an area of 822 square miles. Beneath the water is a submerged museum containing more than sixty ships of the Japanese wartime fleet lying at various depths and covered with coral. On them are fighter planes, trucks still connected to the decks of freighters, and china and utensils with brand names still visible. The lagoon has been declared a monument, and law prohibits salvage and the taking of relics as souvenirs. Divers must obtain a permit before venturing around the ships.

The next stop, Guam!

----

[3] Truk topography - www.visit-fsm.org/chuuk/index.html

Chapter 17
The Wood

-------------------☼-------------------

I arrived Guam International Airport at approximately 9 p.m. I was picked up by a Coast Guard petty officer. Her name was Susan and she was African American. I knew at that point that I wouldn't be the only person of color in the Coast Guard on the island. She worked at the Marianas Section Office (Marsec), which was the shore facility in charge of Coast Guard units from Guam to Japan.

It was extremely weird to be in the *real* tropics. It had to be at least 85 degrees and at least 98% humidity. The air was salty and I could taste it on my lips and feel it on my arms. Palm trees were everywhere. The roads were paved, but looked slick. I later found out that they were made from crushed coral, which is unbelievably slippery when wet. Susan was driving the small government pickup truck like a champ. She handled every curve. We arrived at the main gate at Naval Station Guam at 9:30 p.m. I would finally get to see my new home, the Coast Guard Cutter *Basswood* (WLB-388), a seagoing buoy tender built in 1944. it was a 180-foot-long black-hulled ship that looked more like a construction boat than one of the pretty white ships I'd expected to sail when I'd joined the service. Our job was to fix the red and green floating buoys that can be seen floating in the water. To my surprise, Susan said, "Oh, I thought you were going to the *Cape George*," which was another cutter stationed in Guam.

I said that I was assigned to the *Basswood*. She told me that the *Basswood* was in Japan and that I had to fly to meet the ship.

That was extremely cool to me because I was already 9000 miles from home and I was ready to see Hawaii, multiple islands, and Japan all in the same week. I was hyped for this adventure.

She got me checked in to Base Administration and I was issued a key to the barracks. The *Cape George* and Marsec personnel lived on the ground floor of the two-story building and the *Basswood* had the top floor. Since they were gone, I had the entire floor to myself. For three days, I hung out on the Rec (Recreation) Deck shooting pool and meeting the guys from the other ships.

Naval Station Guam has large vessels assigned there. There were the *Proteus*, the *San Jose*, the *Haliakala*, and the *White Plains*. They were all supply vessels or submarine tenders. Thousands of sailors and families lived on that base. Since I didn't know anyone, I literally walked around the base. I didn't realize how large it was or how intense tropical heat can be if I was just hanging out in it, fully clothed. My car wouldn't arrive on Guam for another 45 days.

Guam was uneventful, except for the sticky heat, without the ship or anyone to talk to. I quickly learned from disgruntled sailors that they had a definition for the word Guam: Give Up And Masturbate. I guess I can say that they kept their hands to themselves. It seemed to explain the attitude of the other coasties stationed at Marsec. They seemed to have cabin fever. Most never left the island or experienced any of the exotic locales within a decent plane ride away.

Three days after arriving on Guam I flew on All Nippon Airlines to Narita International Airport, near Tokyo. All I could think of was Godzilla movies. I imagined him destroying the buildings. Stereotypes were setting in.

Again, I traveled in full military uniform, which was a mistake. I could feel the eyes of the old WWII veterans staring at me. The men were extremely well-dressed, with their white socks and loafers. The ladies looked like supermodels. Nevertheless, I was well on my way to seeing the Far East. I couldn't speak or read a lick of Japanese. I was afraid that I would end up in China trying to make it to Japan.

I arrived Narita Airport and I noticed how high-tech things were. They had vending machines for everything: lotion, meals, and anything else a person could want to buy. There happened to be a car show underway at the airport. I noticed that the Japanese cars I was accustomed to in America were only taxis here. Lexus didn't exist because they were also Toyotas. Infinitis didn't exist either; they were Nissans. Acuras were non-existent; they were Hondas. It dawned on me that I would probably see these new models when I returned to America.

Knowing what I know now, Americans had the oakey-doak run on them. They created Acuras, Infinitis and Lexuses from previous Hondas, Nissans, and Toyotas. They just added gold lettering on the trunk and raised the price $20k-$30k each. I have proof. I have a picture of a 1986 Integra with an H on the grill. As a Motor City kid, this car situation started the wheels turning in my head. Would these cars change my hometown? If you drop an A-bomb on a race of people, you will pay one day.

I discovered I had to take a bus ride to another airport to fly to Nagasaki. From Nagasaki, I would be driven to the ship in Sasebo. In a 10-day period, I would have traveled from Washington, D.C. to the place that was the recipient of the second atomic bomb used on people. I flew from Tokyo to Nagasaki on a huge plane. It had three aisles and a large TV screen mounted on the forward wall for all to see. They were not showing a movie, but displayed what the pilots were seeing while flying. Unfortunately for me, it was storming like cats and dogs. This flight was going downhill fast.

It seemed that we hit turbulence every two minutes. When we were close to landing, I could hear the pilot making announcements, but couldn't understand a thing that he said. I tried to judge what he was saying by looking at the other passengers. Since no one had their head between their knees, I felt we were fine. Was I wrong! They were just cool. As we approached the runway, the pilot started to yell, "So me kan, ab let tong," or whatever the hell he said. We slammed the runway with a loud "Bam". I could feel the wheels run on the grass and back onto the runway. The only thing I could think of was, "Get me off this damn plane before Godzilla comes!"

After I picked up my luggage, I noticed a Japanese man holding a sign that said, "Basswood." He drove me an additional 40 miles from Nagasaki to the Naval Station at Sasebo. The *Basswood* was in the yards for annual repair. It was fun to ride on the wrong side of the street. I wondered throughout the entire ride whether I could drive here. It was raining continuously and that guy drove like a maniac. He didn't say anything and I couldn't speak the language, either.

I arrived my ship at approximately 2300. The first person I met was the officer of the day, Lieutenant Junior Grade Coyle. He'd reported from Coast Guard Headquarters a couple of months earlier. I didn't recognize him from the building, but I knew I wouldn't be the only green person on the ship. He fed me some leftover meatloaf that the crew had eaten for supper, gave me linen, and took me down to the tombs known as *after berthing* – the sleeping area under the waterline at the back of the ship. I wondered what was down there because it sounded like "afterbirth." It was at least 25 to 30 people sleeping there. It was the smelliest place I've ever entered. He told me that I could sleep in the bed of another person who was away on leave. He also informed me that the guy I was replacing had returned to Guam and would not be coming back. This was bad. I knew nothing about ship life or how to run a ship's office.

At 2200 (10 p.m.), ships render taps, or lights out. We crept around the berthing area until we found the rack to which I was assigned. It was a top bunk in a corner. There were pipes directly above my face. This sleep lasted for two hours and I couldn't take it. I returned to the galley and sat there for the rest of the night. I'd had my first bout with claustrophobia. I also wanted more of that dried-up meatloaf that I'd eaten earlier. I had the opportunity to meet a few of the engineers and others standing watch. One guy was an African American named James. He was from Compton, California and was a second class machinist mate. He sat with me for a couple of hours and we hit it off well. He was expecting a child back in Guam and was scheduled to return to Guam whenever he received the call. I mustered up enough nerve to go back to bed.

The next morning, I reported to the quarterdeck for morning muster, or head count. The quarterdeck is the area of the ship where visitors are greeted. Someone stands watch there 24 hours a day. No one is supposed to lollygag or horse around on the quarterdeck. Most announcements are made there and it's the location where shipmates call if they are looking for another person onboard.

Early that morning a crew member asked me if I was a

"cherry boy." He said it in a joking fashion.

I smiled and said, "No."

He walked away laughing.

I was introduced to the crew at muster in a unique way. To my surprise, Headquarters had forwarded a thank-you letter to the ship for my services in Washington, DC's Cherry Blossom Parade. A few months earlier, I'd ridden on a USO float and waved at thousands of citizens. When Captain Petworth began to read, "For participating in the Cherry Blossom Festival," the crew began to laugh uncontrollably. I couldn't figure out what everyone was laughing at. The captain was laughing while reading the letter. It was so funny that I began to laugh. There were 60 people laughing.

Afterwards, someone told me that being a cherry boy was an inside joke on the ship. It meant someone who had never slept with a Filipino or had wild excursions in the Philippines. Now I understood why the shipmate had asked me if I was a cherry boy. What a way to introduce myself to the ship! Many crew members introduced themselves by wanting to meet the cherry-blossom king.

Many crew members asked me another question: if I was going to say that I loved the XO. I didn't know what they were talking about, but I didn't want to play into it. "XO" was short for executive officer.

I said, "Hell, no."

Most replied, "Good!"

I later found out that the previous yeoman, while dangerously drunk, had looked up at the XO and said, "I love you, XO."

Later that day, one of the boatswain's mates, who were the saltiest guys on the entire ship, asked me to ask the XO if he had the keys to the sea chest. I did, and the XO just looked at me and laughed. I'd been scammed again. You see, the sea chest is not a chest, but a mechanical piece in the bowels of the ship that received salt water for cooling the engines.

Another scam that I witnessed, but which didn't happen to me, was radar calibration. They would dress a sailor out in a suit of aluminum foil and send him out on the pier. He would move his arms and twist and turn while someone yelled from the bridge, "A little to the left." I saw other scams perpetrated on new people. One gentleman was asked to get a bucket of prop wash and wash the ship's propeller. Someone gave him a bucket of soapy water that he believed was prop wash. He tossed it over the focsle (front of the ship, or forecastle) and ran as fast as he could to the back. He saw the churning turquoise water and yelled, "It's working! It's working!" I'm glad I didn't have to experience anything other than the keys to the sea chest.

Once I made it through the first phase, getting to know the guys, it was time to learn my office duties. I didn't realize how lucky I was to have a personal work location on a ship. Most crew members worked on a specific piece of equipment or in the engine room. They didn't have a place for solitude. I opened the door to my office and saw boxes everywhere. I shared the office with Storekeeper First Class Cliff Meeks. He was on a 96-hour vacation back to Guam to see his family. He was the only one who could open boxes in order to account for the shipping paperwork, so all of the boxes and mail piled up in the office while he was gone.

The commanding officer, also known as the captain or the CO, came into the office, and his first order was, "Learn the C3." It was a BTOS computer with the green letters on the screen. I also had the everlasting IBM Selectric III, the best typewriter of all time.

The office was cool. I had two portholes on the bulkhead (wall). I could also open them on sunny days and air out the office. Cliff had a stereo set mounted in the office. That's correct: mounted. Everything in the office was welded, strapped, or taped down. That's how to prevent things from flying around underway, from becoming missile hazards. Even the typewriter had duct tape around the edges to secure it to the typing tray on the metal desk. I had one of those money-green metal and Formica desks. I couldn't complain. Our office was approximately 10x18 and my bed was only 2.5x6, with a curtain.

The office had a glass opening to the passageway, which had mail slots. If someone didn't want to come in, he could open the glass and put something in one of the boxes. This independent duty assignment would be interesting. There was no one to do my specific job but me. I worked for three people: The CO, the XO and the operations officer, the lieutenant who'd welcomed me aboard. I didn't have to answer officially to anyone else. My job was to take care of them. I was responsible for their transfers, pay problems, training opportunities, and vacations. I had their service records. There are three people on a ship that crew members do not mess with – the yeoman who handles their business, the storekeeper who handles their checks and supplies, and the cook. Everyone looked alike on the *Basswood*. At least 80% had beards, including the CO and XO. After I'd quickly learned a good portion of their names, the Commandant of the Coast Guard ordered everyone who didn't have a medical condition to cut off their beards. Damn. I had to learn all of their names and faces again.

What impressed me most about the crew's makeup was the amount of people of color. There were four African Americans, two Guamanians, two Filipinos, four Mexicans, four Puerto Ricans, and two native Hawaiians. That's pretty good diversity for a crew of 60.

Moreover, most were petty officers or chiefs. The chiefs were a group all to themselves. The chiefs' mess was next door to my office. Mainly they played cribbage all day. We had excellent first-class petty officers onboard and they ran the ship. The chiefs only ventured out of their mess if there were issues or during major evolutions (seamanship activities). Each one of them was salty and highly respected. There were two warrant officers on board; Mr. McDougal was the engineering officer and Mr. Kelly was the first lieutenant in charge of deck force. He had the most folks working for him. Deck force worked the buoy deck and kept the ship painted. They also drove the small boats. The engineers ran the engine room and kept the small boats running.

I was in the operations division. We ran the ship's bridge, medical unit, radio room, electronics, and office. While deck force and engineering wore coveralls or working blue uniforms, operations wore the traditional light-blue Coast Guard short-sleeve shirts. They weren't as starched and stiff as those worn at shore stations. On warm days we had blue shorts to wear. Now that I think of it, they must have been hot pants compared to the length of today's shorts.

I quickly learned the shipboard routine and was assigned to stand fire watch. This didn't mean that I was watching over my shipmates to wake them in case of a fire. I was tasked with standing on the other side of a bulkhead to see if the sparks from the Japanese workers' torches were causing a hazard. This was as boring as it could get. I had at least a four-hour watch. I sort of wished they'd burn something to make it more exciting.

The most exciting thing that happened was catching the Japanese workers teasing American culture. Eddie Murphy has a joke in which a Japanese McDonald's worker teased Americans by holding his eyes wide open with his fingers and saying, "BIG MAC, SMALL FRY, SHAKE." I thought that was just a joke until I saw the workers pointing at items in our galley. I literally died when I heard one point to the labeled sugar container and laugh uncontrollably while saying, "SOOGAR." I couldn't help but laugh as well. Since we couldn't understand what each other was saying, we used the international language – laughter.

Ships have their own unique quirks. I'm not trying say that I'm the strongest person around, but it takes a special breed to have a successful tour onboard ship. Basically, they are floating jails without fences, gates, or locked doors. From what I hear, the similarities are astounding. They wake crew members up in the morning with a loudspeaker that says the same thing each day: "Reveille! Reveille! Reveille! Up! Up! All hands. Heave out. Trice up. The smoking lamp is lit in all authorized spaces. Now 0600, Reveille!" People never forget words like that. Meals are piped over the loudspeakers as well. They announce taps each night at 2200, or 10 p.m. It's whispered into the loudspeaker. After taps, we closed doors lightly, and, if we were working late, had to walk down a ladder in the dark, open a locker, and get undressed and in bed without making a peep.

We performed these silent evolutions nightly to the best of our ability, all in the name of not waking a shipmate who may have to stand a midnight to 0900 watch. I once fell down the steep ladder. Since I landed on my feet, there was no problem, and I just walked away without stumbling. I haven't been to jail but it has to have similarities in its logic and operating procedures. Where else can you eat Thanksgiving dinner on metal trays?

Having arrived at night, I was anxious to see the town. Sasebo is a port city on Japan's southwestern coast. The city of Sasebo, which is now the second-largest city in Nagasaki Prefecture, was once a small village of only 800 houses. A naval dockyard was built in 1886, and the population grew tremendously. Trains arrived in 1902 and it became a city rather

124

than a town. The shipbuilding industry grew as a result of World War II and the population grew to 300,000. After the war, the port city was the center for receiving people who returned to Japan from various battlefields. The U.S. Navy and the Japanese Self-Defense Force still use these ports.

I ventured out to the mall and didn't find one. I found instead a seven-block-long shopping tunnel. This stretch of establishments, known as an arcade, contained department stores, boutiques, restaurants, and gift shops. Can you imagine walking through a covered strip mall and crossing streets? Each section is about a block long. People can cross the street and the mall continues.

If you go there, though, just don't buy anything. You probably can't afford it. When I was in Japan, the yen rate was 129 to the dollar. That meant ¥3900 would cost you about $30, which would buy you one cheap steak dinner, two drinks with tips, nine cans of Budweiser, a decent T-shirt, and one cheap pair of plastic sunglasses. It was better to shop on base or in the red-light district and just take pictures off base. That's what I did.

The only place that I could afford to have fun was the red-light district. It was a block away from the base; no surprise there. One of the boatswains took me out one night. He told me that I would get a kick out of this small bar. He also warned me to avoid going upstairs unless I had to use the restroom. The highlight of this bar was the small paper plates all over the walls. The mamasan (house lady) would allow patrons to fill out their name, ship, and date on a paper plate and staple it to the wall. Somewhere in Japan my information is on a wall in plain sight. I'm sure one of my buddies has seen it.

I noticed a few sailors go upstairs and never come down. After a few Kirin beers, I had to use the rest room. It never dawned on me why a lady would periodically come downstairs and rinse out her mouth in the small sink behind the bar. While walking through a dark series of booths to get to the rest room, I could here smacking sounds. The best way I could describe it would be to build up spit in my cheeks and pull them with my index finger and thumb rapidly. It makes a nasty, smacking sound. I looked in one of the cubes and a Japanese lady was masturbating (and other things) sailors. Then I knew why there was lotion in the vending machines. I nearly ran through the booths to get to the restroom. It was the grossest thing I had seen since leaving home.

When I returned downstairs, the mamasan said, "You don't want hand job?"

I said, "You can *hand* me my damn bill and I'll go back to *my job*!"

I never made it back to that place, but it was cool as long as I stayed downstairs and didn't need servicing. I would love to see my plate on the wall one day. I'll plug my ears when I go to the restroom.

Chapter 18
Waiting for the Next Train. Not!

------------------☼------------------

It came time to leave Sasebo. We were headed to Yokosuka (Ya-kus-ka) Naval Station, which was just outside of Tokyo. Yokosuka has a population of 433,358. In addition to numerous shipyards, it is a major fishing and trade port. It is also known for the tomb of William Adams, the first Englishman to visit Japan. It would take us a couple of days to get there through the South China Sea. I was told that it could be a rough ride. A funny thing happened after we left Sasebo Harbor. Someone played the American National Anthem on a loudspeaker as we passed their home. We never knew anything about the family or whether or not they were Americans living in Japan. It was always a proud moment.

This was my first underway experience. Office work wasn't my only assignment aboard ship. Each person was assigned watches or other collateral duties. My assignment was to be the main communications person on the bridge, which was known as *conn.* I relayed information from other parts of the ship to the captain via a sound-powered phone. This was a tough assignment because I wasn't familiar with shipboard terminology. Initially, someone else on the bridge actually handled the phones while I observed. We set the special sea detail, an evolution to get the ship underway. Since my predecessor wasn't there, I really didn't have anyone to show me the intricacies of my phone duties. I noticed immediately that crew members' overall respect was directly tied our performance of extra duties. The crew assumed that everyone knew his primary task and took notice if someone couldn't handle the military-type duties.

The *Basswood* had a round hull and bobbed like a cork in the water. The transit between Sasebo and Yokosuka was tough on me. We pitched up and down the entire way. Lieutenant Coleman, the XO and my boss at this time, was scheduled to transfer as soon as we returned to Guam. He seemed to be a no-nonsense person. I suppose he was ready to get off of the ship. I tried to work in my office, but I felt queasy. We hit a large swell and I immediately puked on the wall behind my typewriter. All I could do was push the trashcan up against the wall and hope most of it rolled into it. After I cleaned up my mess, the ship's hospital corpsman (Doc) asked the XO if I could hit the rack.

He emphatically said, "No, I need to get some things done before we reach Guam."

I didn't say anything because that's the way it was. I sucked it up and continued to work. Dinner didn't help; it was greasy chili and grilled cheese sandwiches. Unless people are extremely salty, their stomachs can't retain a meal of that nature. It was a rough two-day trip for me. I couldn't wait to touch land.

We arrived Yokosuka to attend firefighting and damage control training. We would stay there for one month before returning to Guam. Yokosuka was a beautiful port town only a short distance from Tokyo. The naval base was the largest facility I'd ever seen. It was totally self-sufficient and the home port for a number of naval vessels, including the aircraft carrier *Midway*. Unfortunately, the *Midway* was in dire straits. While in the yards, they'd added some stabilizers to it and ruined it. It sat at the pier listing to one side. We couldn't poke too much fun at it. The Navy sailors teased us for bringing what they called our black tugboat to their base. That's exactly what we looked like, moored next to a carrier. At least ours moved.

On one occasion I saw a sailor who I recognized from the base exchange in Guam. His ship, the *White Plains*, had arrived earlier in the week. He said, "How long did it take you guys to get to Japan from Guam?"

I said, "eight days."

He laughed profusely. He told me it took their ship three. It didn't matter to me because I was still in Japan. It was good to have a rapport with other sailors. No matter how small our ship was, we arrived at the same Western Pacific (WESTPAC) ports of call.

Firefighting and damage control school was a blast. We had two Navy hull technicians (HTs) as instructors. They were salty, yet hilarious. During class, one of our know-it-all petty officers ticked one of the instructors off. The instructor eventually asked him if he had a security clearance.

The sailor said, "Yes."

With a surly voice, the HT said, "Then here – hold this!" He gave him a cigar that he had been chewing on for a couple of days. It was dripping with spit. That was the last time our shipmate played Mr. Know-it-all.

We were beginning to develop a reputation on base as experts on our small ship. During our practical exam we were tasked with stopping flooding in a small room. They gave us patches, stakes, and rope. The room contained a number of pipes that had holes in them.

We said, "This is a piece of cake."

Before we could revel in our confidence, they turned the water on full blast. Within five minutes we were up to our waists in water. We failed that day. The next day, one of our resident geniuses decided that we would clog exposed pipes with rags. They allowed us to patch the holes first and they turned the water on after we finished. Not a drop. We received accolades from everyone on the base. Unfortunately, we'd cheated. We had the same test again a week later. Not a drop. We decided to play by the book and were just as successful. That was a learning experience by any standard.

I eventually made it to the NCO Club. It was a five-story establishment. The first level housed the main party room, which was extremely high-tech. It was like dancing in Studio 54. The second level had a large video screen and everyone danced off of the videos they played. The third level was a Country and Western room. I ventured into this room to get a break from the smoke. Before I could put my foot down, I heard, "Yeee-Haa!" I don't recall my foot hitting the ground. I do recall doing an about-face and getting the hell out of there. The fourth level contained at least 25 private phone booths for sailors to call the States. The fifth level was a full sit-down restaurant. What an amazing place!

I also made it to a town called Shinjuku. This major city was located approximately 40 miles from Tokyo by subway and housed many of Japan's skyscrapers. My shipmate Les and I found a jazz club. It had pictures of Miles Davis and other jazz greats on the wall. We entered this dark club at 4 p.m. There were no tables, only wooden school desks. Each person had his or her own eighth-grade, early-twentieth-century desk. It was weird. The desks were not the only weird thing about that place. In most countries, listeners are allowed to clap during jazz performances. In Japan they only clap at the end. We clapped loudly and yelled "Yes!" to acknowledge a nice solo, and the entire club turned around and looked at us as if we had cursed the band. We wanted to hide under our desks, as we'd done during the bomb drills of the 50s and 60s. At that point, a waiter arrived with our drinks. To our dismay, he had charged us the equivalent of $20 for each drink, a $10 overcharge. We refused to pay that amount and produced a card from a Japanese bank that explained the yen rate. They purposely made us uncomfortable and we left shortly thereafter.

Unfortunately, Les and I got lost trying to negotiate the Shinjuku subway station. He'd been stationed in Japan before and thought he knew how to get back to the city. It was intimidating. We wanted to ask for directions, but stood there looking stupid instead.

The one person we were scared to ask actually helped us. He was distinguished looking and he politely walked over to us and said in a soft voice, "You need to take the Number 8 train and transfer to the 15. It will take you back to the base. You are trying to get back to Yokosuka?"

We said, "Yes, sir, and thank you very much!"

We can get help from the least likely person. Another lesson learned.

There were a million people commuting. There is no such thing as waiting for a less crowded train. I tried to do that and the crowd surge forced me onto the next train. I could see old ladies with their faces literally plastered against the glass on the doors. I heard that Shinjuku has subway workers with large foam sticks that they use to push as many people as possible onto the trains. The guys would not give up their seat for even the oldest women commuter. They just looked up at them and continued reading their bondage magazines. They seem to have a fetish for girls in school uniforms.

While standing and holding the hand ring on the train, I

glanced down at a multitude of X-rated books. It was a porn fest. We noticed quickly that they were looking at us as much as we were looking at them reading magazines. It didn't dawn on me that I was different – as in African American. While glancing up at the advertising that was displayed on the hand-ring mechanism, I noticed advertising for dolls that looked like Aunt Jemima with interchangeable lip sizes. I suppose they only know what America allows them to know.

Nightlife in Yokosuka was exciting in comparison with Sasebo's. Everything was located within two blocks of the base. I was amazed to see a nightclub with a mural of a black man and woman. They had huge afros and were wearing loud colors and platform shoes. It was the "Jambo Desco." That's how they spelled it, and the mural said, "Get Down, Get Funky." It was the most buffoonish thing I've ever seen. I was told that Americans were not allowed to enter that club, but that couldn't have been the case. It looked like an advertisement for African Americans to patronize their establishment, but I didn't like the tone of the mural, especially for 1986. I never visited the place.

A block away was every type of clothing store a person could imagine. It was like today's outlet malls, and the items were unique and reasonably priced. I think my ship bought out that entire street.

One night after leaving the base club, a sailor told me to go to a particular establishment off base, saying that it closed at dawn. I couldn't believe it so I had to find out for myself. To my amazement, he'd been right. They stopped serving drinks at 3 a.m., but continued to serve food and coffee. What was most unique about this place was its music collection. It had walls and walls of primarily R&B and soul albums. There were so many albums there that the DJ used a brass library ladder to maneuver around the room. What was even more breathtaking was how intense this record collection was. Customers could ask the DJ to play a song right off the top of their head. He'd then move his ladder, and before long the requested record would play. It was amazing to be in a foreign country and watch that happen. He had every Parliament, Ohio Players, and Isley Brothers album ever made. He had Average White Band, Run DMC, and even Eric B. and Rakim. I couldn't believe it. Before I knew it I was walking out of that place at dawn. Fortunately, liberty had been granted for that day. Otherwise I would have been late or AWOL.

I firmly believe that the *Basswood*'s sailors had too much time on their hands. Even though I was busy every day, others may not have been. On one workday, the base military police arrived and asked to speak to the commanding officer. We sought out the officer of the deck (OOD). The MP advised the OOD that we had defaced government property. After hearing that, we sent for the commanding officer. When the CO arrived, the MP told him that one of our guys had added an F and an L to the back license plate of a government truck with electrical tape. Instead of the truck displaying the word IZUZU, it had become a FIZUZUL. The CO had to laugh at that one.

We were considered clowns in every port. I don't know what it was. Maybe it was the asbestos on a 1944 ship. Those guys were comedians. I suppose it had something to do with being the most distant Coast Guard ship from the U.S. We could have issues and handle them internally before word made it to Honolulu, San Francisco, or Washington. This attitude was responsible for creating what we called the *Bitch Log*. The *Bitch Log* was a green ledger book that remained on one of the galley tables, in which anyone with a complaint or gripe could write in their problem. Not only did they complain, they drew cartoons of the various complaints or situations. These are a few of the entries:

The captain wanted to head to Korea instead of heading home. The crew was burned out and didn't want to go to Korea. Someone drew the captain in the *Bitch Log* riding on a donkey, which was labeled "Crew." The captain had a fishing rod with a carrot hanging in front of the donkey's mouth labeled, "KOREA." I was told that we had promises of parties and other morale activities. I don't think the ward room liked that one much.

Once, at a remote island, the crew was asked to perform an early-morning boat-lowering operation to impress a Navy chaplain. The captain didn't know that most of the boat crew had just arrived from a night of partying. While lowering the small boat in the water, we heard screams and a loud splash. Someone had screwed up and the entire small boat fell about

10 feet into the water. No one was hurt, including the boat, because they'd all been holding onto knots in the safety ropes. They looked like Tarzans swinging through the jungle. It was a riot. The captain seemed more pissed off than concerned. We'd messed up this evolution and had embarrassed him in front of a naval officer. Our guys didn't care. Within minutes the whole evolution was in the *Bitch Log* in dark blue pen, complete with one of the boat crew members asking the famous question, "Hey, what's this clove hitch for?"

The best drawing was of a guy named Dave Slade and a local called Crazy Rose. Dave was an engineer with ears that stuck out like a monkey's, and since he also chewed dip in his upper lip, he looked even more like a monkey. That was fine with Crazy Rose. She was a Yapese who hung out wherever sailors were; she was a bit touched in the head. If you asked Rose, "Let me see your breasts," there they were. It was sick. Someone once found them in the woods having sex, and the only thing they could see were his ears and the multitude of flies flying around their rear ends. The observer took time to color this entry in the *Bitch Log* to highlight the flies. Someone then asked Dave if he had slept with Crazy Rose, and Dave said, "No, I was wide awake when I waxed that ass!"

One of the funniest editorials wasn't in the *Bitch Log*. The *Pacific Stars and Stripes* newspaper routinely published pictures of all new babies born to military families in WESTPAC. One of our guys picked out a series of babies who looked exactly like our officers might have looked like if they were newborn. Titled: Basswood Babies, he wrote captions of what the particular officer might say next to the baby that most resembled him.

Two babies off to the side were designated for the two salty warrant officers. The caption had one saying, "Hey Mac, number one engine is down."

Mac replied, "Fuck it, let's go get a beer."

They even found a redheaded kid for Ensign Scott, and had him saying, "Yes Sir, Yes Sir, Yes Sir." The ones writing the captions considered him to be a suck-up, but he was cool with me – always professional. I felt slightly bad for that one.

Our new XO was a stickler for neatness. His baby's caption said, "Why is that damn buoy dirty?" with someone replying,

"Because we just took it out of the damn water!" We never got to read the rest because someone from the Wardroom tore it down.

Then it was time to leave Japan. I looked forward to returning the following spring.

Chapter 19
Iwo Jima Memorial – The Real Thing.

-------------------☼-------------------

It was time for me to stand my own underway evolutions. No more help. We departed Yokosuka for the eight-day sail back to Guam. My job was to follow the person with the conn. This was the person assigned to command the bridge at any particular time. I had to repeat his commands into the sound-powered phone. The only problem was that I didn't understand the terminology or know exactly what he said. My task was over as soon as we hit open sea, but I was nervous and concerned about my next time on the bridge.

After three days I heard an announcement ordering, "Set the anchor detail."

I figured out that we were dropping anchor, but where? When I reached the bridge, I quickly realized that we were sitting off the coast of Iwo Jima, the famous island full of WWII tales and Marine escapades.

The captain said, "Johnson, I want you to follow the XO around and say exactly what he says."

I could see that the captain was nervous. He established a forward lookout to watch for coral reefs to keep the ship from running aground. This was the real deal.

The XO's first command was, "HEAVE AROUND TO SHORT STAY."

I yelled into the phone, "HEAVE AROUND TILL IT STAYS."

The Captain lost it. He yelled for me to get my ass right under the XO's and listen! I butchered every command he gave. I hated my job and anchor detail.

Well, no use crying over spilled beer. I was in Iwo Jima. Who would have thunk it. I figured that I'd better enjoy it until it was time to pull up that damn anchor. We stopped at Iwo Jima to see the 26 coasties who were stationed at the Long Range Aids to Navigation (LORAN) Station. This station was responsible for producing radio signals to assist planes and ships to navigate in that portion of the Pacific. Its main feature was a slender tower that rose hundreds of feet into the air. Electronic technicians and engineers were responsible for climbing it daily to make adjustments or repair things. These poor bastards were assigned to this remote island in the middle of the Pacific for one-year stints. They were allowed one 30-day vacation home and had to return to complete their tour of duty. Thirty or so Japanese aviators were stationed there as well. Approximately 60 people were on the island, and none were women.

We took the rigid hull inflatable (RHI) boat and the motor lifeboat (MCB), that we would eventually drop into the water, to go back and forth between the ship and the shore. The boatswains made runs all day long. The duty section wasn't allowed to go ashore. They set up a barbecue on the buoy deck for the folks who stayed onboard. We had a full-fledged picnic and sports day on the island. Iwo Jima had black sand beaches. I could see bursts of steam rising from spots all over the island. They were sulfur pits. I do regret not taking a bottle of the black sand. When we are young, we develop this travel arrogance that gives us the sense that we will visit again at another portion of our lives. This is a prime example of why we should not only smell the roses along the way, we should take some, too.

The men on this island lived and ate like kings. I guess that made up for the location. Their weather was tropical; they didn't have to worry about winter. Each room was huge and contained booming entertainment systems. We literally had a blast. The Japanese aviators were cool, too. They were friendly and had a sense of humor. We played softball in 95 degree heat. I didn't think brothers could get sunburned. I was wrong. My forehead began to sting, and by the next day the first layer of skin peeled completely off. Never again!

After eating, drinking, and playing ball, it was time to tour the island. We piled into the backs of pickup trunks and found ourselves on top of Mount Suribachi. This was where the marines placed the American flag in the famous photo, which is also the design for the Marine Corps Memorial at the entrance of Arlington National Cemetery.

How lucky was I? I read the placard on the top of the mountain. I was so stunned to be there that I can't recall what it said. I took a look over the backside of the mountain, and it was at least 200 feet high, if not more. We were told that a large portion of the marines scaled this mountain face to surprise the Japanese who were waiting on them to invade the beach. I couldn't imagine how they scaled that wall without the first few hundred being wasted. A look at the numbers related to this battle shows that, I suppose, they were.

Here is a short history of that battle:

Iwo Jima sits halfway between Japan and the Marianas Islands that housed American bombers. The U.S. Air Force pounded Iwo in the longest aerial offensive of the war. Amazingly, the bombardment had little effect. Hardly any of the Japanese underground fortresses were harmed. Twenty-one thousand Japanese soldiers burrowed into the volcanic rock and waited for the Americans to invade. The United States sent more marines to Iwo Jima than to any other battle, 110,000 marines in 880 ships. The convoy of ships sailed from Hawaii to Iwo in 40 days. On February 19, 1945, the Navy bombarded the island again with big guns. After an hour of non-stop pounding, the island was in flames.

One hundred and ten bombers streaked through the sky and dropped more bombs. At 8:30 a.m. the historic order, "Land the Landing Force" sent the first wave of marines towards the dangerous shores. When they landed, they had trouble digging foxholes in the volcanic ash and were sitting ducks. It was a nightmare. When it was all said and done, 100,000 men waged war on this postage stamp of an island that's the size of a large city neighborhood. The Americans fought above ground and the Japanese lived below it or in caves. In 36 days of fighting there were 25,000 U.S. casualties, and 6,825 of them died. Nearly the entire Japanese force of 22,000 perished.

Today, Iwo Jima is one of the greenest places on Earth. I have the photos to prove it. The grass just blows in the wind, along with the smell of barbecue and the thud of volleyballs. Loran Station Iwo Jima was decommissioned in the late 80s and all Coast Guard personnel were assigned to stateside locations, or wherever they desired, receiving the first pick out of all positions. This was the most arduous duty in the Coast Guard. The service took care of those who went to one of these stations.

Chapter 20
Now Can I See Guam?

----------------------☼-----------------

When I got back to the ship's office from my Iwo excursion, I took out a small green memo book and wrote every seagoing evolution in it. I listed the parts of the ship I would be communicating with for each evolution. You see, some evolutions didn't require certain parts of the ship. If we were doing anchor detail, we didn't need the people on the fantail (back of the ship). If we were setting the special sea detail, everyone would be online, and so on. I began to pull this book out every time we had an emergency drill or shipboard operation. It helped me understand who was handling what or what part of the ship was in play during the evolution. I would have been lost if I'd misplaced my little green book. It also showed my professionalism. It showed them that I was serious about my job and I was more than the ship's yo-yo. I wanted to be an integral part of the functioning of this cutter. I wanted to make a mark, both administratively and militarily.

We had an uneventful four-day sail back to Guam from Iwo Jima. It was time to set the special sea detail and pull in the ship. I could see families on the pier pacing and looking for their loved ones. Everyone was excited. We felt like heroes returning from war. I noticed a few sad faces as well. They were on the single guys who didn't have anyone waiting for them on the pier (me included).

We worked hard, but we played harder. It was time to get to know my roommates and my land-based job while in Guam. I had a good indoctrination about life underway, but life ashore assigned to a ship was different. It wasn't DC. It was a constant

85° to 96° environment in the daytime, and a toasty 69° minimum at night. I must say it was heaven.

Daryl Harrell and Tom McCloud were my roommates. Daryl was a handsome exercise buff. He had a few ladies on the island already lined up when he returned. Todd was a typical New Yorker, with jokes. Todd was known for disobeying the CO's order not to drink before getting underway. He was scheduled for discharge from the service as soon as we hit the pier, so he didn't pay the drinking rule any attention.

The CO told Todd to shoot navigational angles on the bridge wing.

Todd shot a few angles and then said, "You *don't* want me to do this!"

The CO yelled at him and thought that he could at least do his normal task of monitoring the radar. Todd was an electronics technician, so it shouldn't have been a problem.

Todd looked down at the radar and said, "I *know* you don't want me to do this."

The entire bridge burst into laughter. The CO shook his head and ordered him to the mess deck. What could he do? The guy would be discharged as soon as we put over line four. I couldn't understand why so many people avoided sea duty. It was akin to living with the crew from *Saturday Night Live*.

Our housing unit was directly next door to the women's barracks. The NCO club, the package store, and the mini-mart/barbershop surrounded us. We didn't have to drive anywhere unless we were going to McDonald's or the theater near the entrance of the base. In addition, the pool and barbecue area was just outside our rear door. We had prime real estate on the base. I was able to pick up the car that I'd shipped from Baltimore. Life would become a lot easier. A man could lose his mind on this small island without transportation. I was pretty well off with my 1985 Honda Accord hatchback because most people drove Guam bombs. These were a series of used cars that had been eaten away by the salt air. They are not worth sending back to the U.S. after a tour is complete, and are passed on to anyone on the island who will buy them or take them off of the owners' hands for free.

My car made me able to get off of the huge base. Those who

couldn't depart the base still had plenty of things to do. Overseas military bases are fully self-sufficient. We had our own private beach, known as Gab Gab Beach, and a number of swimming pools. The so-called Beach-Pool was an intricately designed fishing pier that led directly into the ocean. We could literally swim out to sea if not for the safety net. On the bright side, it kept the sharks out as well. Technically, it was a pool that used ocean water, with the bottom dredged flat to resemble a normal pool. It was much more fun to swim in this contraption than a pool with 50 kids tinkling in it. In addition, it was the number one outdoor party site on the base.

Naval Station Guam is located on the west-central part of the island, with Andersen Air Force Base utilizing the north end. We could leave the Naval Base and drive directly to the Air Force base without changing roads. The Air Force base was extremely beautiful in comparison to the Naval base. I was told that the Air Force's Tarague Beach would be breathtaking. I first visited this place on the Fourth of July in 1986. I was having a bad bout of homesickness and needed to see something special. I took a remote road near the back of the base. It sloped downhill and curved back and forth for nearly a mile. At some point I could see the Pacific Ocean through the trees. Amazingly, the whole world opened up before my eyes. It was a humongous white-sand beach enclosed by 500-foot cliffs. The turquoise water led directly to a crashing ocean. Surfers were everywhere.

What made this beach unique from anything I had previously seen was the surrounding cliffs and our ability to park directly next to our picnic. Car stereo systems were booming rap songs, such as "Walk This Way" by Aerosmith and Run DMC. It was completely diverse. At some point, I found myself deep in thought while listening to a George Howard's song titled "Pretty Face" on my Walkman. I literally fell in love with the song as I sat in Utopia. It was exactly what the mountain range portrayed. The cliff was known as Two Lovers Leap. Island folklore tells of two lovers from opposing villages, who were not allowed to marry, committing suicide at this location by leaping into the ocean. What a lovely story. They were nuts. If you saw this cliff you would understand. I would have died from a heart attack before I reached my first 100 feet.

Many Guam roads are only a few feet from the ocean.

Drivers can stop anywhere along the way and have a moment of solitude in a beautiful setting. Internally, the roads are winding, and I found myself at Talafofo Falls, which sits in the middle of the island. This waterfall is straight out of a Hollywood movie. There is nothing like it, at least in the U.S. The exotic tropical birds and flowers are unmatched. I saw one bird with a mixture of blues, reds and yellows. I don't know what it was called, but it was a thing of beauty. There were two other critters on the island that I could not stand, fruit bats and the infamous brown tree snake. For some locals fruit bat is a delicacy. How could they eat a huge rat with wings? It was the size of a black Timberland boot.

Brown Tree Snakes were known for blacking out power on large portions of the island at least once a week. These things came to Guam as stowaways in a cargo plane and have no natural predator there. They have multiplied out of control and to a point where most of the colorful birds are nearly extinct. They eat the eggs directly out of the nest. They have been known to completely wrap themselves around small children while they're sleeping between two parents. No birds, no flowers, no kids. Fortunately, I didn't see this with my own eyes. I never saw any children that looked like accordions, either. I did see kids who have never missed a meal. Could that be the reason the snakes came to Guam? They could eat like kings. If you don't like snakes, Guam may not be the place for you. Please don't fret; Guam isn't alone. Military cargo and household goods destined for the U.S. or other locations have been known to deliver brown tree snakes. If they come to an area without a mongoose, there will be trouble. Watch your kids!

Homeport ship life is somewhat different from underway periods. Being in port is tougher on us administrative types. We spend our entire two to three months preparing for the next cruise. We officially worked tropical hours; 0630-1300. By 1500 each day most of my shipmates were back at the barracks, wasted. Thank heavens that none of them were floating face down in the pool after work. For the guys without cars it was easy to become an alcoholic. That was the only outlet most chose to pursue. Also, many were 18 years old and straight out of high school. Can you imagine no parental supervision *and* being 10,000 away from home?

I saw one seaman who was on the anti-alcohol drug,

Antabuse, which causes people to vomit if they drink. He was so far gone that he was at the club drinking out of one glass and puking into another. The club manager spotted him and escorted him back to the ship. Peer pressure was one of the major reasons for the drinking binges we were experiencing. The younger guys were the hardest workers on the ship. Deck force, as they were known, was responsible for retrieving, painting, and replacing buoys throughout the mid-Pacific. They were as close-knit as you can get. They indoctrinated kids as soon as they arrived from the airport. Our young engineers experienced the same indoctrination. They learned how to drink before they learned how to fix buoys, lights, or engines.

Periodically, we hear stories about the most dangerous jobs in the world. Mining and crab ship operations are consistently listed near the top. There is another one that is not known to the general public. Buoy maintenance is one of the most dangerous jobs in military service. Buoy tenders were involved in the two most recent Coast Guard ship disasters.

The job seems simple: pull the ship up to the buoy, hoist the buoy out of the water, scrape it, paint it, and put in back in the water. It's really not that simple, though. First, the ship is rocking from side to side. There is a 50-foot crane overhead swinging a hook that would kill a seaman instantly if it hit him anywhere on the upper body. In addition to the crane, the buoy deck is wet and the railing system has been removed. Seamen could easily slip over the side and into the water. Buoys are also attached to 2000-pound concrete blocks called sinkers, which sit on the ocean floor. The buoys are attached to the sinkers by huge chains and bob and float on the surface.

Unfortunately, storms pull the sinkers off station. We never know what condition the chain is in or whether the buoy is in the correct position. The captain and ship's navigators determine the correct location. After the buoy is pulled on deck and repaired, the sinker is hoisted for launch just off the side of the ship. The ship is maneuvered into position. This is when the danger starts. The large chain is faked (laid) out on the deck and the bridge yells a command to let them know it's on station. Some kid with a sledgehammer hits a contraption releasing the sinker, taking the chain with it to the ocean floor. If someone is standing in the wrong location he will be yanked into the ocean, or at least his leg

143

will be torn off. Don't forget that the ship is still rocking from side to side and the crew members are standing in buoy scum and salt water.

There are so many hazards taking place at the same time that the bosses stood over everyone like hawks. This evolution has to be repeated throughout harbors under different environmental conditions. On one occasion, Seaman Cavana had to leap from a floating buoy back to the ship. He could have hung onto the buoy until the ship made another pass at it, but he jumped anyway. Actually, the captain would have preferred the latter, because Cavana slipped and was nearly crushed between the ship's hull and the buoy. He barely made it back onboard. The one thing we didn't do was work buoys at night. Stateside ships routinely operated at night, but they didn't have to contend with hammerheads and orcas. Deck force performed this operation like clockwork, and that's where their camaraderie came from.

Since there was no such thing as stress management on the ship, we got relief wherever we could. On one occasion, Lieutenant Coyle, who'd welcomed me to the ship in Japan, had the conn. He was calling out a course and it was completely opposite from where he wanted to go.

Paul Lovell, our cook, who was assigned to shoot angles, quietly said, "I wouldn't do that if I were you."

We began to chuckle on the bridge. The captain didn't hear us.

Mr. Coyle yelled out the same command and the captain yelled, "Mr. Coyle, have you ever used drugs?"

Mr. Coyle said, "Yes sir, and if this shit keeps up, I'm gonna use some more!"

That was the good thing about sailing in the 80s. Political correctness didn't exist. We also were too far away from anyone to punish the entire crew for comments. Most things were said in jest and were meant as jokes. We knew when someone was serious. We said what we felt and we either got hollered at or laughed at. It ended there and didn't turn into a federal case. In most cases, it was hilarious and great fodder for the *Bitch Log*. Life was good. PC didn't run amuck.

Eating was a bit tough. Although the base galley was located directly behind our barracks, we were not allowed to eat there. We had to catch the liberty van back to the ship if we wanted a hot meal for free. Most of us ate supper on our own – anything to avoid going back to the ship. We didn't want to eat the meals prepared by The Beast. The Beast was a guy from New England who served as one of our three subsistence specialists (cooks). The Beast would cook pork chops and ask us how we wanted them. Most of us said, "Grey, Beast, grey." If a pork chop was at least grey, it was done. He argued for hours that they were rib-eye steaks. It took the head cook to tell him that they were freaking pork chops.

One morning I had just completed the mid-watch (2345-0545), and I could smell the hot cakes and bacon aromas coming up to the quarterdeck through the pipes from the galley. I wanted to eat a big meal to help me sleep. It's tough to get to sleep at 7 a.m. while the daily operations are going on. The soothing smell of breakfast immediately turned to the infamous burnt bacon scent. Everyone on the ship could smell it – except the Beast. His Filipino chief started to yell at him, "Beast, you burnt the pucking bacon again!" I think I grabbed a plain pancake and headed to my rack. He'd just ruined my expectations.

Food was always an issue. Our ship had 53 enlisted members and seven officers. The seven officers ate in the wardroom and no one, with the exception of the mess cooks, was allowed back there. Mess cooks were usually the newest kids on the ship. They washed dishes, cut potatoes, and served the officers for 30-day stints. If no new kids arrived, they could be required to serve two tours as mess cooks.

On one sunny morning, one of the new ensigns told a mess cook, in a nasty manner, "Go butter my toast."

The kid stormed out of the wardroom and plopped down at one of the galley tables, fuming.

We said, "What's wrong with you?"

He told us and headed towards the silverware. He grabbed a butter knife and a few packs of butter. To our amazement, he began to scrape plaque off of his teeth with the knife. He smacked the plaque onto the officer's toast and covered it with real butter. I couldn't believe it. He took the toast back to the officer and returned to the galley smiling.

We lost it. I don't remember this one going in the *Bitch Log*. It stood alone. It ranked right up there with the guy on the *Planetree* who took a leak in the chief's pickle jar.

We had another Filipino cook. His name was Orlando Panjullico. We called him Orly. Orly had 20 years in the Coast Guard and 19 years sea time. He'd only made it to E5, but that wasn't a problem. E5 retirement in the Philippines is a lot better than stateside.

No one messed with Orly. He just did his job. He was the best cook on the ship. If we didn't like what we were scheduled to eat, Orly would create something different for his friends. One guy (with a hangover) asked Orly for a big omelet and received one with at least four inches of government cheese in it. He came back and asked for a little omelet; Orly gave him a perfectly prepared omelet that was one square inch in size. The guy gave up and went back to bed.

Our head engineer, CWO McDougal, hated to pay for his food. Officers didn't get to eat free. They had to deduct meals from a set amount of money given to them by the Coast Guard. He would leave the wardroom and read our bulletin board, then steal a link sausage or a burger and return to his stateroom. His meal card testified that he hadn't eaten a thing. The cooks got tired of him real quickly. They were waiting for him to do it again and he didn't let them down. He walked by to read the board, then grabbed a sausage and ate it quickly. The third cook, Paul Lovell, poked his head out of the vestibule and said, "That's $5.95 Mr. McDougal." Can anyone actually sail in the Pacific and not eat one meal? At least that's what Mr. McDougal's meal card said.

Guam presented other challenges and opportunities. Since the cable channels came from Los Angeles, the locals acted just like the S/As and low riders we saw on TV. They wore their flannel shirts buttoned all the way to the top. They bounced their cars with hydraulics or even spun the tails of pickup trucks in mid-air. A person would be an idiot to display road rage towards these guys. Most were huge. They could literally knock someone through a brick wall. For some reason, marines had to try them out frequently. It was a common sight to see a bunch of sailors and marines hanging out in town and later getting beat up by the locals. The locals let them get drunk and then beat the living crap out of them each weekend.

For some reason, they treated the brothers cool. Maybe because we could introduce them to the sisters. Whatever works. Guam was also a place where we could shop as if we were in the

States. They had everything we have here – fast food joints, car dealerships, and strip clubs. I experienced all of them, but not necessarily in that order.

I learned about lady's drinks real fast. I recall buying a lady an orange juice and the people saying, "That will be $35.00!"

I said, "I'm not trying to buy her; I was just buying her a juice."

They said, "But that's a lady's drink."

I said, "I don't give a rat's ass if it's the First Lady's drink, I ain't paying $35.00 for a damn orange juice!"

While someone distracted the big Guamanian bouncer, I crept out of this place like young Cain from Kung Fu walking on rice paper, never to return. That was close.

On Guam I learned to appreciate things that I'd had in the States, like baths. There were showers everywhere, but no bathtubs. I would spend money to stay at the Hilton just to take a hot bath. I loved the Hilton. The first time I stayed there, they forgot to calculate the items I ate and drank from the mini-bar. I thought that they came with the room, so I ate everything in it and put a major dent in the drinks as well. Nevertheless, they forgot to ring that up. Hell, I thought that was part of the deal.

While standing near a bar in the hotel, I saw and older African American guy and we began a conversation. It turned out that he was from Detroit and worked for Ford Aerospace. He asked me what part of Detroit I was from. I told him the East Side.

He said, "I'm from the East Side."

I said, "What area?"

He said, "St. Clair between Shoemaker and Warren."

I said, "I lived on Lemay between Shoemaker and Warren, but I have cousins on your street," and I began to name them, "Frank, Fella, Gwen ..."

And he finished for me, "Greg, Barbara Jean and Mane." It was amazing. There we were, 10,000 miles from home, and this gentleman knew my first cousins. He said, "They know me as Birdman, and I left home to work at Ford Aerospace. Tell them I said hello."

I could not believe what had happened. When something like that happens, I instantly feel joy because I know that the Lord did that just to let me know I'm not alone.

One of the funniest things that happened while we were in port was the initiation of the new chief petty officers. There are unofficial rituals and initiations when someone is promoted to E-7/Chief Petty Officer. Our chiefs took this to heart on the *Basswood*. I had the quarterdeck watch on one hot Friday morning and was informed by the chiefs that no women were to board the ship until further notice. This seemed unusual to me. I'd never received an order of that nature before.

Shortly after I was given this order, the two new chiefs arrived on the ship in full drag gear. The only way I recognized them was because of their mustaches and terrible legs. I thought that they were transvestites or *mahus*, as there are known in Hawaii. They were women to me that day and couldn't board the ship. They had to remain at the bottom of the gangway and say hi to everyone who boarded or departed the ship. They handled that embarrassing situation well until they were informed that they had to go to the Naval Construction Battalion (Sea Bees) and serve breakfast to the Navy chiefs. I heard that they received a ribbing that would last a lifetime. The Sea Bees are some of the toughest guys in the military. They build bridges, roads, and facilities worldwide, and in some of the most dangerous places in the world. I am surprised that they didn't come back to the ship on some guy's arm.

Chapter 21
The Angels of Pain; The ECI Excursion
------------------------☼------------------------

We finally reached the end of this home port visit and were scheduled to start our Eastern Caroline Islands (ECI) mission. I was a bit nervous because it was time to resume my sound-powered phone duties and get hollered at by the CO if I screwed up. I'd had roughly 90 days on the ship and was a bit more comfortable in my military role. I was also glad to get away from Guam and the constant office work. Our first destination was Truk, a three-day sail due east from Guam. We had to replace buoys that had been destroyed in a tropical storm and perform annual maintenance on the other aids to navigation. I began to get the hang of the terminology and I made tremendous progress in my bridge operations. My little green book continuously saved me.

The *Basswood* had its own dive team and its members couldn't wait to get to Truk to dive the Japanese fleet wreckage from WWII. I couldn't dive, but I could at least snorkel and ride my bike. The captain wanted to get started immediately, so he sent a small-boat crew ashore to set up the usual logistics prior to the ship pulling in later that evening. When the advance team arrived, they noticed a few Americans already ashore and having a ball. They were enjoying the sights, and the ladies. I guess our guys were used to having the island to themselves. What I noticed upon my arrival was a bunch of Bible-toting missionaries. I asked one of the boat-crew members if these were the same guys with the ladies, and they immediately said, "Yes." Isn't it ironic that they were being themselves when they were on the island alone, but when 60 witnesses arrived, the Bibles were brought out.

We took care of the work in Truk in a few days. The captain wanted to wrap it up fast and take four days off to allow everyone to relax and enjoy the island. The first thing we did was water-ski in Truk Lagoon. I couldn't get the hang of it – they dragged me face down until I let go, but some were worse than me. One of our shipmates bounced his butt on the water while maintaining his footing.

Our first-class boatswain's mate, Mike Lowery, said, "He better stand up or he's going to get an enema!"

We laughed because it was a good jab, but seemed far-fetched. The guy eventually fell, and when we circled around to pick him up he was floating in a sea of turds. I guess he *did* get an instant enema. He wanted us to pick him up and put him in the boat. Mike just dragged him alongside the boat all the way to the pier. It had to be extremely embarrassing because we laughed at him as he hung onto the side of the small boat. We just called him "Stinky." I vowed either to learn how to ski or not try at all. I never tried again. I didn't want to swim in Ishman's World of Shit. A man couldn't live something like that down on a ship with 60 guys in a million years.

Truk has one of the tallest cliffs in Micronesia. It was similar to the one at Tarague Beach. There was an open-air bar located on top of the cliff and we took mountain bikes up the steep road to check it out. It was one of the most amazing sights you could imagine. We could see the ship moored at the pier. It looked like a toy from that distance. The sun beamed into the cave-like place. The colorful birds landed on nearby tables, totally unaffected by humans. We shot pool and had a wonderful time mixing with the locals. We decided to return to the lowlands after dusk set in. We shouldn't have done that because more than a couple of us were toasted out of our minds. Fortunately for me, I still had most of my faculties.

Les Trailor wasn't so lucky. He breezed past us down the hill on this huge, old-fashioned three-speed bike. Unfortunately, he didn't negotiate the curve at the bottom of the hill and he and the bike went airborne into the lagoon.

We knew he had just killed himself. We sped down the hill and stopped at the water's edge, only to find Les standing in about four feet of water saying, "Ohh! Those Angels of Pain."

Can you imagine five guys falling off of their bikes in

laughter? Les was barely 100 pounds soaking wet and he looked like he was floating in the water with no legs. It was a bad situation turned extremely funny, at least until we poured him in his rack. I think he fell out of bed that night. Fortunately for him, he slept on the lower level.

Truk has a picturesque group of outer atolls circling the entire island. J. Paul was a club owner in Guam and a friend of mine. He was originally from Los Angeles and was married to a lady from a prominent Truk family. Her family ran the island's only grocery store and a few small businesses. On one Saturday morning they pulled their yacht alongside our ship and picked me up for a picnic on one of the atolls. Their yacht was nearly as big as the *Basswood*. The captain was on the bridge when they arrived and was a bit nervous as this vessel closely approached the ship. I looked up at him as I hopped from one ship to the other. He could see someone popping the top on a beer and handing it to me as I came aboard. He just shook his head and smiled. No harm, no foul.

We sailed to our own private island, where we began to picnic, roasting a huge pig underground. I took a number of pictures of this occasion, which ranked near the top of any experience I'd ever had. We couldn't dock the yacht. Everyone jumped out into four feet of crystal-clear turquoise water and waded to the beach, carrying whatever we could. There were people already on the island and they were nearly done with the pig-roast.

To my dismay, the next day I couldn't locate this roll of film. I recall putting in a new roll and didn't pay attention to what I did with the old one. I threw it away by mistake. I was floored. I pledged to make sure every photo I took from that point on would make up for the lost roll. They were good, but couldn't capture or prove what I'd seen that day.

It was time to sail to the next island, Pohnpei (Ponapé). Pohnpei looked similar to Truk; the harbor was nearly the same and it had cliffs as well. There seemed to be a trend in how Micronesian islands were formed. It was a large island with many more businesses and attractions, plus major hotels and many paved roads. The great thing about Micronesian islands was the currency. It was American, and the cost of living was the same as Guam's, which was less than Hawaii's. We spent a full two weeks working buoys and day boards. It was an extremely busy work schedule, but we wrapped up at dusk as usual. The nights were ours. Pohnpei never closed. There was something to do at all hours of the night. We could sit around the pool at the hotels and enjoy the stars. If we wanted a beer, we didn't have to go far. There was a Tiki bar adjacent to the pier and less than one minute from the *Basswood*. Whenever the ship was in port people sat on the pier and looked at it. Not only did they look at it, they poked their heads into the port holes. They even poked their heads into the bathroom and watched guys shower, at least until we closed that porthole. I can't blame them. These islands are so isolated that any activity is better than none at all. Visitors were treated like kings on Pohnpei.

I decided to rent a car on the island so that I could get around on my own without counting on the ship's vehicle. This wasn't my greatest idea. I was rear-ended and pushed to within five feet of someone's home. It was a hit and run, but I was able to get the tag number. I reported it to the police the next day and was told that it was nothing that they could do and I was responsible for paying for the rental's repairs. I thought this was crazy. They told the captain that if the ship left, I would have to stay behind to take care of my payments. I knew I didn't have $1500 to leave behind on an island after being hit in the rear. Fortunately for me, some Japanese businessmen stepped up and admitted that they'd rented the car that had hit me. It had been driven by a local girl they were, um, *dating*. They didn't want an international issue with the U.S. military. I was pleased when they paid for both repairs. There I was with whiplash and facing hardship. I'd sensed that the ship would leave without me.

At least, the captain didn't say he wouldn't. No thorough investigation? Welcome to the real world.

Pohnpei is known for two things: woodcarvings and black pepper. The men could carve any fish known to man and the ladies could weave anything they could imagine. We visited a souvenir shop and noticed a multitude of items with Coast Guard logos and designs. We were in luck. They must have known we were coming. They set it out for us. I bought a unique piece. It was a hand-woven wall mat with intertwined seashells. American eagles were woven into it, and the centerpiece was a round Coast Guard seal made out of a soft wood. I gave them $100 and they gave me the mat. We bought the entire store out of artifacts. In some cases we didn't have to buy. We could trade cartons of cigarettes, sugar, batteries, a Sony Walkman, and, yes, adult magazines for anything. If a trade is good enough, a family would move out for a couple of days so that a guy could enjoy himself, and someone else. Life was different there.

After we departed Pohnpei, we received a cable message from the cutter *Mallow* out of Honolulu, complaining that they had placed personal orders for woodcarvings from the souvenir shop and that when they'd arrived, they were all gone. Nahhhlll? We thought they were made for us, since we were the only Coast Guard ship ordered to repair their buoys. We didn't know that the *Mallow* was using Pohnpei as a vacation port. We felt that they'd invaded our Utopia and deserved what they *didn't* get. It was highly unlikely that the Fourteenth District Office in Honolulu would let them sail out of their operations area again. Needless to say, they were pissed off. Our motto was, *Better to be pissed off than pissed on.*

Our next excursion was Kosrae Island. It is amazing, with yet another cliff overlooking the harbor. It's nearly impossible to tell them apart. Kosrae was a bit primitive compared to the other Micronesian Islands. There was only one paved road that led from the airport into town. The rest of the island had dirt roads. The one thing I noticed about Kosrae was the amount of children there. They were everywhere. They literally hung off our ship. Something about a large proportion of these children caused me great concern. Many were burnt blond and possessed blue eyes. I couldn't help but think about the sailors, both merchant and military, who frequented these islands. Who were the fathers? Where were the fathers? I took more than a few pictures of this phenomenon. There were a number of children with afros as well. This was not a unique thing in this part of the world. The Australian Aborigines were of African decent. So were many Polynesians. As innocent and lovely as the women were on these islands, I could see how their bloodlines were changed forever.

Kosrae has its own unique rituals. One ritual was a bit painful. If a woman there likes a man she hits him with a rock. I got cracked in the head a couple of times. I don't know about the like thing, but I wanted to bust her in the head with a rock as well. That was a natural reaction to folks who didn't know the culture. Someone must have really loved our captain. He received a nice, big knot on the head. This was a prime example of, "If you love me, you have a funny way of showing it."

Someone must have hit one of my shipmates with a *huge* rock. I decided to take a bike ride alone and found myself lost at sunset. The bike's battery-operated light was weak and I was deep in the brush. I knew we were getting underway at 0600 and I feared missing movement. Fortunately, I found my way back onto the paved road and figured that the airport and pier were east. I made a right on the dirt road and headed back to the ship. I stopped to rest for a quick minute and heard all sorts of noises. I thought it was animals at first until I heard the words, "Ooh, Randay! Come in my wet poosey, Randay!" The only Randy that I knew was a seaman on my ship. I laughed profusely and rode my bike in complete ziz-zags all the way back to the ship. Since I couldn't draw, I wrote a nice caption in the *Bitch Log*. I let the ship's artists use their imagination and draw the cartoon.

For some reason, I had a series of midnight watches on that tour. That's just how the watch list worked. I really couldn't complain, because the mids are where I could see the drunks come back to the ship, individually and in groups. On one occasion our radioman, Woody, basically slithered up the brow (steps leading onto a deck) and onto the quarterdeck.

Woody was amazing and an avid bike rider. He was from Southern California but had lived most of his Coast Guard career on tropical islands. We could never get him excited. He spoke with this long, slow, dragged-out drawl, like, "Heeeyyy Tohnyy My Mannn," was his favorite greeting to me. He acted exactly like Tommy Chong. I suppose Woody wasn't hitting a bong here or there along the way, as he did pass all of his urinalysis tests.

This time, Woody didn't say much and was covered with scratches and blood. Since he smiled all the way up the brow, I was afraid to ask what happened. I just left it alone and watched him enter the ship for bed. Five minutes later, Sheidel, his partner in crime, came up the brow just as wasted and injured as Woody. He wasn't smiling.

He said, "Have You Seen [slight pause] Woody?"

I couldn't help but laugh. I suspected that Woody had whipped his ass, but I found out later that they'd crashed bikes while riding drunk. I didn't see Sheidel with a bike, so that's probably why he was pissed off. Every five minutes for the rest of the night someone returned to the ship. Most were drunk, officers included. They just walked really starched and stiff. They didn't know that they weren't walking in a straight line.

The work on Kosrae went extremely well and we departed early for atoll excursions. These were fun. We would pick out a small island on the map and sail towards it. We'd then anchor out and launch a small boat with the captain on board. He would ask to meet the local chief and then ask for permission to come ashore – to party! These were the most primitive islands we would ever see. They don't see many visitors. There are no landing strips and the only visitors are by sea. Most of these islands are surrounded by dangerous coral reefs, which cause most large vessels to avoid them, but not the *Wood*! We had a 13-foot draft and could basically go anywhere. We would get as close as possible and anchor. After permission was granted, the landings would commence. It was like we were invading Normandy. The only difference was the lack of weapons and the abundance of beer and barbeque. We'd bring our own grills along as well as a movie projector.

Our first atoll was Ngatik. This place was pure paradise. There was no other place in the world like it. We anchored out and waded through crystal-clear water on fist-sized stones. The white sand beach was so deep that it took a while to get our footing. The locals accepted us immediately. They began the underground pig roast and we began trading. I traded a carton of cigarettes for a thick, clear-glass ball that is used to keep fishing nets afloat. People can take these balls and place them in woven plant holders to make great ceiling ornaments. I also traded my beloved *Pictorial* adult magazine, full of lovely black women, for 10 unique sea shells and a white piece of coral that looked like an eel frozen in time. I still have these items in my aquarium. The XO made a wonderful gesture. He gave them T-Shirts. The locals just stared at him. It's 100 degrees in the shade on this island and no one wore tops, including the women. This was a true grass-skirt kind of place, and he had unknowingly insulted them. Culture dictates everything.

The best part about atoll-hopping was the evening movies. We had a large movie projector and a bunch of movies from the

Navy Motion Picture Command. We showed the movie *Excalibur*. You could hear a pin drop. I was near the projector and didn't realize the magnitude of this production. When I turned around, the island's entire population of approximately 100 people were sitting on mats and watching this classic. We sensed that *Excalibur* bored them to death. There was total silence at the end of the movie. We decided to spice it up a bit and put on *Poltergeist*. This wasn't the most politically correct thing to do to these people, but it was hilarious. They squirmed, squealed, and jumped. It was morbid. We completed the movie and enjoyed the rest of the night ashore. We later discovered that someone put the only TV on the island outside of their hut. As my shipmates would say, we were the bastards, I mean, the *ambassadors*, of goodwill.

Chapter 22
Steinbrenner, You Need to See This — The WCI
-------------------☼-------------------

We returned to Guam for another two months and prepared for our longest trip, to the Western Caroline Islands (WCI) and the Philippines. This trip would take us across the Western Pacific for nearly four months. We departed in early September, with the plan to return by Christmas. Our first stop was Yap Island. The State of Yap is part of the Federated States of Micronesia (FSM). Yap is the westernmost island in the FSM, located about midway between Guam and Palau. It is comprised of the main islands of Yap, Gagil, Tomil, and Rumung, and stretches eastward for approximately 1,200 kilometers. There are 134 low-lying atolls and outer islands surrounding Yap.

The Yapese are people of the sea who dared to travel great distances throughout the Pacific. They have been known to travel as far away as Hawaii in small canoes. More amazing than that, they took along their currency as well, their famous stone money. Yap is best known for its stone money, which is huge limestone disks with holes in the center. These stone disks come in various sizes and can be two meters in diameter. They can weigh as much as four tons, making them the world's largest currency. The holes in the center make them resemble black donuts. Those who survived this arduous journey across the sea were King wherever they landed. I would love to know the amount of people who *didn't* make it.

Another 26 coast guardsmen were assigned to the Loran Station located on Yap. Fortunately for them, the island wasn't isolated in the manner of Iwo Jima. Nearly 12,000 people make up the population of Yap. Two thousand of them live in the main town of Colonia. Our folks stationed there were in good hands. They could enjoy nightlife and a few hotels on the island. Many roads were paved, but it didn't take long to wander off of the beaten path. A mountain bike was a must.

Yap had a few interesting things about it. The local pastime was chewing betel nut. Betel nut comes from the betel palm. This palm tree can grow to 75 feet high and has leaves at least three feet long. A betel nut resembles a small green plum. They split it open, place burned limestone powder in the center, and wrap it in a leaf. They chew this stuff like tobacco and spit profusely. Unfortunately, betel nut spit is blood red. Rainstorms couldn't wash it away. In addition, their teeth turn blood red, at least at first. Years of betel nut chewing causes the mouth to turn black and the teeth to decay totally. It wasn't unusual to see a lady who looked like Jennifer Lopez, but who showed black, rotten teeth when she smiled. This is what the majority of the ladies over 20 looked like.

Another pastime was rock-throwing. The guys hated us. We were a threat to their social lives. They could hit us in the head with a rock from half the distance of a football field. They are the most accurate rock throwers in the world. If I were George Steinbrenner and the New York Yankees, I would start my recruiting efforts here. They would never throw a ball at a batter's head by mistake, only on purpose. If we stayed away from the ladies at the bar we would not be the target. If they saw one of us talking to one of their women, he would be guaranteed a pop in the head as soon as he hit the road. It wasn't a stretch to see someone in the ship's clinic getting a bump on the head checked out.

At first, Yap was a bit boring to me, and extremely hot. I spent my 24th birthday there. It actually turned out nice. My office mate, Cliff, was married to the lieutenant governor's niece. He invited us to his place for a cookout.

Shipboard tradition states that the quarterdeck watchstander must ring the ship's bell a specific number of times for distinguished visitors. Governors warranted eight dings of the bell. While passing by the quarterdeck, I noticed an overweight Yapese gentleman coming up the brow and introducing himself as the lieutenant governor. The watchstander immediately rang the bell eight times.

The entire wardroom arrived on the quarterdeck yelling, "Why did you ring the bell that amount of times?" They didn't notice the big guy with the cut-off shorts and flip-flops.

The watchstander pointed to the gentleman and said, "That's the lieutenant governor of Yap."

I could see their eyes bulge out of their heads as they regrouped to great him.

Later that evening, Cliff and I ventured out for a tour of the island and an evening with the lieutenant governor. He was extremely funny. We made a video of each person telling jokes. This was after a number of drinks, I must add. One joke he told sticks with me today. His first joke was about a trip to America, and everywhere he went he saw the sign "Hot Dogs." After seeing this over and over again, he decided to buy one. When they gave him one he shouted, "Hey, in my country, they don't give me that part of the dog!"

That was hard to top, but we all tried. I told a few decent ones, but Cliff was the champion. He said that two guys were sitting at a bar watching TV and the big guy said, "Football, that's a man's sport!"

The little guy said, "No, Fartball – now, *that's* a man's sport!"

The big guy said, "How do you play it?"

The little guy said, "You down this drink and that's six points. Pull your pants down and fart, and that's the extra point. I'll show you." He completed his seven-point play and said, "Now it's your turn."

The big guy drank the shot of liquor and yelled, "Six!"

He pulled his pants down and the little guy ran behind him and began to hump his rear and yelled, "Block that kick! Block that kick!"

I don't think we could have laughed any harder. We wrapped up that evening eating barbeque and fried fish. Unfortunately, I was informed that the barbeque we were eating was endangered sea turtle. It tasted just like Chicken. Actually, it tasted like skewed beef. It was a wonderful 24th birthday in a far-away land.

I found myself with another mid-watch during the week, but it was a bit different. One of the port managers worked the midnight oil as well. About 0300 he walked over and we chatted on the quarterdeck. His name was Dave and he was from Texas. We hit it off and he invited me to visit his oceanfront home and have a home-cooked meal with his family. I took him up on his offer and had the time of my life. His house was amazing. It was literally an open-air home. I will never forget the polished driftwood he used for stair banisters. I don't know how he did it, but the driftwood had no end to it. It traveled along the loft and down a long staircase. He had a big-screen TV enclosed in a glass closet. The one amazing thing about this home was the shower. To my amazement, there was no ceiling or roof on top of the shower. I could look up at a glistening moon. His wife was extremely kind and nicely beautiful. She found out that I had a new child on the way, and in one night she wove me a baby carrier made out of banana leaves. I still own this gift, albeit under my stairs. I will never forget this family and this occasion. I can only hope that I showed my appreciation prior to my departure from their home. Lord knows I can't locate them unless he's still there working at the port, some 20 years later.

Our next excursion took us to the Republic of Palau, the westernmost point in the Caroline Island chain. The Spanish claimed these islands in 1898, then sold them to Germany the next year. In 1946, Palau became part of the Trust Territory of the Pacific Islands under U.S. control. In 1978, Palauans elected to opt out of joining the FSM and became an independent state. Palau is a 400-mile long string of coral-reef island paradises. There is no other way to describe it. This is by far the most beautiful place I have every seen. The larger islands in the chain are Koror, Pelileu, Babelthuap, and Anguar. They contain most of the population of 19,717.

The most intriguing point of this adventure is the Rock Islands. There are over 200 small islands that rise above the waterline like mushrooms. The currents have eaten away at the limestone bases and created rock-like formations. They are everywhere. A person can literally sail to his own private island. They are all surrounded by turquoise water that is so clear that people can see the bottom of the ocean.

Working buoys on Palau was beautiful, but extremely dangerous. We expected the CO to be on edge for most of the operations. We could literally see reef as we looked over the side of the ship. It was so beautiful that we started out with a 96-hour vacation. It took two weeks to complete our work in Palau. Only the duty sections were required to work. Everyone else was free to roam the lands. I ventured out on my mountain bike. The roads were well-paved and the island was relatively commercial. It was like a mini Guam.

My ride forced me in the direction of 15 huge Palauan men and I wasn't particularly comfortable with their demeanor. They were sitting on a stoop watching a pickup full-court basketball game on a concrete slab in the center of town. As I approached the court they asked if I knew how to play basketball and if our ship wanted to play them. I immediately told them "Yes" and promised to set it up.

They told me that they liked me and I was cool with them. They told me to stop by the prison to buy some storyboards. I didn't know what they meant and I looked a bit stoic. Visit a prison? I thought that they were trying to have their way with me. Fortunately, one of the guys clued me in that the prisoners make woodcarvings and storyboards to earn money and it's normal for tourists to shop at the prison for souvenirs. I felt somewhat better after hearing this. They offered me my first cup of ice coffee and each guy gave me a nice handshake. Later in the week, our guys put on a primetime basketball show for fans. I heard it was great. I had duty. I suppose playing in front of the islanders was like being in the NBA or Olympics.

I eventually made it to the prison to look at the artwork. I was amazed at what I saw. The prison consisted of wooden gazebos with bunk beds. They could kick the fence down if they really wanted to get out. The guys shook our hands as we walked through their temporary home. There were pictures of Michael Jordan, Patrick Ewing, and Charles Barkley on every available wall space. It was completely safe. It dawned on me that they were relating to the African Americans because of basketball. Most of the prisoners were incarcerated due to alcohol incidents and minor fights. Nothing extremely violent. This was the closest I had ever been to inmates. It was nothing like an American prison. Some American would have said, in the words of the movie *Deliverance*, "You look just like a hog," while some other guy would have yelled, "You have a pretty mouth." Nevertheless, I didn't stay long and made sure that I bought something.

The captain decided that we should have an open house. We didn't want it because we had worked hard and it was a Saturday, a normal liberty day. He cancelled liberty and invited as many

ANTHONY JOHNSON

islanders as we could hold onboard the ship for a sail through the Rock Islands. We were pissed off. It was a cloudy day and wasn't the best occasion for viewing the sights. We wanted to use a sunny weekday instead. Before we knew it, here came the officers' wives. They'd flown in from Guam and wanted to see the Rock Islands. We set sail in a drizzle and pressed forward. We stayed at special sea detail for four straight hours. The CO yelled at everyone as we transited the dangerous reef. We busted our rears while the islanders and family members viewed the beautiful Rock Islands. It sucked.

When we returned, everyone not scheduled for duty departed the ship and didn't plan to return until the next morning. That's exactly what we did. A couple of us located a restaurant to grab a bite to eat. They were playing cassettes and we looked at each other and said, "Hey let's make this place our headquarters." We looked in our backpacks and pulled out every tape we could find. Before you knew it, we were playing Sade, jazz, and rap tapes on their systems. They had never heard this type of music before. They were used to "Margaritaville" and "The Wreck of the Edmond Fitzgerald", two bar-room staples. We closed the place down every night. A hotel across the street found out what was going on and offered us cheap rooms and free meals if we hung out there. We did. They kept their promise and took care of us as well, but it still couldn't top the original spot.

Palau is an experience that is indescribable. I personally challenge anyone to come up with a more beautiful island. I can recall biking over a bridge built by the Army Corps of Engineers and the Sea Bees and stopping at the apex to view the crystal-clear water below. I can clearly remember the song playing on my Walkman, Kenny G's "Songbird", not to mention the two Bartles and Jaymes wine coolers I had in my backpack.

We spend billions of dollars as American tourists in the Caribbean or Europe. These islands are unofficially the 53rd-60th states, behind Puerto Rico and Guam. They use American currency and many stateside goods and services, yet they sit idle not because of their distance, but from a lack of publicity and marketing. You can probably get to them for an additional $200 if you can make it to Hawaii. You can sleep in a hut on the beach or choose to stay at the Hilton. It seems that the rich and famous, and Japanese businessmen, want them for themselves. I'd never

162

heard of Micronesia growing up as a kid. I'd heard of Tinian and Saipan because of the Enola Gay, the deliverer of the atomic bomb to Japan. It's hard for me to spend hard-earned money in the Caribbean that will eventually go to the controlling countries of France or Britain. I would rather support the islanders in the Pacific who count on us to provide basic necessities and have shown unwavering loyalty for over 50 years.

Unfortunately, Palau has strategic importance, due to its proximity to the Philippines. The Germans and the Japanese ruled them during the previous World Wars. Palau's main source of energy is coal. How do you get coal to an island in the middle of nowhere? By ship. Who owns ships with access to large coal reserves? Us. Every port has the potential of becoming a naval base or launching point. I hope we never destroy this place by stationing a fleet in the Rock Islands!

Chapter 23
Hey Brother, Buy Something

------------------☼------------------

After a brief excursion on the historically-occupied island of Ulithi, we set sail for the big P.I. – the Philippine Islands. We could feel the excitement as we entered the San Bernardino Straits. We could see city lights on the nighttime horizon. No one slept. Everyone was topside looking at the lights until Doc, Hospital Corpsman Robert Conception, started the venereal disease movie on the fantail. A shipmate who sailed to the P.I. with the ship the previous year yelled, "Y'all don't want to go watch that!"

Unfortunately, it was mandatory. When we reached the fantail, they were watching one of those 1950 cartoon videos about V.D. I burst out laughing because the thought of my favorite Detroit Drive-In Theater commercials came to mind: "Let's go out to the snack bar." How could they show us a fifth-grade V.D. movie before we headed to the island of sin? They also warned us *not* to go to specific clubs. The most well-known place was the AC/DC Club, which was known to cause bad things to happen to private parts. I never heard of a club giving a person a disease. Maybe they should have told us to stay away from the girls at the club, because my shipmates made the AC/DC Club destination one.

We reached the coastline at dawn. The anticipation among the crew had not waned one bit. We were so hyped about arriving in the Philippines that we didn't think about the massive refresher training (REFTRA) we were about to encounter, or the two-to-three week buoy job that lay ahead. The P.I. has a way of overshadowing any negativity. No one could wait to hit the town

165

of Olongapo and the infamous Magsaysay (Masisi) Drive. This was a three-mile stretch of clubs, restaurants, and clothing stores leading directly to the front gate of the Subic Bay Naval Station. Every day is Mardi Gras in Olongapo. The captain did all he could to remind us that REFTRA would be pure hell, with 18-hour days followed by unlimited drills, some during the night. The old salts gave us the skinny. They said, "Hang out all night and you won't have to be awakened for a damn drill." Sounded like a plan to me. I have always been a night owl.

We set the special sea detail and headed in to Subic Bay. There were huge aircraft carriers, destroyers, and frigates everywhere. I thought I was in Vietnam. This would be a lifelong experience that no one in the world could take away from me. Here was this little Eastside kid rubbing elbows with military history. It was a wonderful feeling, especially since the *Basswood* was known to storm the beach, not with guns, but with a few brews and burgers. We couldn't wait for the base logistics staff to set everything up for us so that we could go on liberty. I had weathered the duty storm and was no longer the newest person in the Operations Branch. I was able to leave the base as soon as my administrative duties were done.

Subic Bay Naval Base was extremely huge. The University of Maryland had a small campus on the base. Even the library was a place to hang out and have a good time, catching up on things around the world or checking out its music section. There were unlimited bike-riding opportunities without leaving the safety of the base. I was told that they had all of the recreational facilities in order to keep teenage dependents and young adults busy. There were ball fields everywhere and I could stop and watch a full-contact football game nearly every day of the week. All of this was exciting, but I knew we didn't come this far to admire the facilities. Hell, let's cross Shit River and hit the town.

There were money exchanges at the front gate. I took out a $100 bill and exchanged it for 5000 pesos. Directly after the money exchange and the heavily armed main security gate was the infamous Shit River. The name speaks for itself. The water was completely do-do brown and there were kids riding in canoes directly under the bridge. Sailors would launch pesos over the bridge and these kids would dive in the water to find them. I had no clue as to how they located these coins. I suppose if I were starving, I would find them as well. It was sad, but funny as hell.

If the canoe scene wasn't enough, the poor kid coming up to me saying, "Buy gum" was heart wrenching. They sold individual sticks of Wrigley's gum for whatever we gave them. If they didn't like the donation, they would hit us in the back of the head with the coin. It was best to give them the biggest coin we had in our pockets. It really didn't matter, because the exchange rate was so generous to the dollar that we didn't need coins. Five thousand pesos would buy tailor-made suits, movies, restaurant meals, and tips for a taxi back to the brow of the ship. When or *if* I woke up in the morning, I'd realize that I still had money.

Everyone not on duty left the ship. The only exceptions were a few married guys who'd rather trade for a day back in Guam with their families. The hardest thing was for me to stay focused and away from the temptations. I was still a newlywed and I was thrust into the land of love and sin. I loved to laugh with people. Fortunately, in the P.I. we learned to laugh *at* them as well. I couldn't go 10 minutes on Magsaysay without laughing at someone. That's what kept me straight. To this day, I am still proud of my willpower. I had one of my old shipmates to think about. I later found out that he caught herpes from a girl at the AC/DC Club.

Speaking of the AC/DC Club, by 4 p.m. half of my ship was there. I was there, too. To be honest, it was a great club, with tall black walls with purple lighting. The clubs were the size of the largest clubs in American. The women were beautiful, but I thought about the 1950s V.D. video. I didn't stay there long. I was trying to locate the R&B/hip hop clubs. I was sure they wouldn't be too hard to find.

Can you imagine walking down a street and the first block looks like this: club, restaurant, clothing store, artifacts dealer, record store, another large club, and a strip joint – all on the same side of the street and still only about 400 feet from the main gate. There are another three to four miles to go and a person can see the same thing on the other side of the street when he returns (in the morning). Although Subic Bay was lovely on the outside, it had a dangerous vibe to it. There were so many local men hanging on the sidewalks that I literally had to walk in the street to avoid certain crowds, resuming my sidewalk stroll after passing them.

I noticed a few shipmates in an open-air pool hall. I decided to get out of the sun and the 90-degree weather to have a cold one and shoot some pool. While shooting pool, I was approached by a young adult with one leg. He hopped along on crutches, which he did with great ease. He could move better with one leg than I could with two. I thought I'd finally met the one-legged man in an ass-kicking contest. He wanted to play me for a beer. That was fine with me because I was fresh off of the Japan pool tour at Sasebo Naval Base. I was a bit cocky on the tables. He beat me.

While I was attempting to buy him a beer, he abruptly said, "I want the money."

I told him that the beer was the agreement and I wasn't giving him any money. He stormed, or should I say hopped, out of the pool hall.

He returned and began to twirl a butterfly knife while standing in the doorway, staring at me. I was a bit nervous, but I didn't show it. He was doing throat-cutting gestures towards me. I checked with my shipmates to see if they had my back – at least they said they did. He left for a minute or so and returned to the doorway, without the knife, or so I sensed. I hoped he had given it back to the person he'd borrowed it from. He gave me this puppy dog look and I returned the same. I convinced him to come back into the club for the money.

When he approached the pool area, I grabbed him by the collar and kicked away his crutches. I told him, "Don't you ever slash your throat at me! I'll kill you right here in this club." I made sure that I looked around at the other patrons so that they got a good look at me. I gave him back his crutches and bought him a cold beer. He drank the beer and left the bar. I never saw him again.

That was my first day in a great place. No matter how foolish my move might have seemed, I refused to sit on a ship for two months because that asshole wanted money instead of beer. Afterwards, whenever I walked down the street people moved out of my way like I was crazy or a king. It was like Moses parting the Red Sea. It was okay with me because the streets were like New York City and I didn't have to weave my way through the crowds any longer. Whatever works, works.

Since all of this happened before 4:30 p.m., I still had at least

12 hours to go before I returned the ship. At least that was the wise thing to do if I didn't want to be awakened by a drill. What logic! The first thing I wanted to do was get a suit and a pair of shoes tailor made.

First the shoes. I saw a nice shoe store about 25 feet from the open-air bar. I went inside and glanced through a GQ magazine until I found a pair that I liked. I quickly looked at the wall to see various animal skins hanging, all shaped like the animals they came from. I noticed a blue lizard and decided that was the one I wanted. They measured the circumference of my foot by tape. They measured the length by placing my foot on a piece of paper and sketching around it. They told me to return in four hours and it would be ready. I said, "Yeah, right," and walked out.

A clothing store was next door. I scanned through another GQ Magazine, picked out a suit, and they began to measure me. They said I could pick it up at 11 p.m. I didn't believe that, either, because it took an act of Congress to get a pair of pants hemmed in the States. I set out for a night on the town.

There were two phrases that I heard more than any others. These were, "Hey brother, buy something" and "Buy *balute.*" The first one usually came from some lady trying to get me to buy something from her booth or shop. They would say anything to get me to stop. It got on my last nerve. I think I snapped at the fifth lady who said those four words, so she changed her tactics and began to yell, "Hey, brother! Hey, dude! Hey, homeslice!" That third one got me. I stopped in my tracks and turned around. She said, "Hey, is your wife a soul sister, too?" I couldn't help but laugh at that point. Then I turned around and walked away. I felt that I was in a 1970s Pam Grier movie.

The balute thing takes a little more explaining. Balute is a half-incubated chick that is boiled and eaten right out of the shell. It stinks like hell and they are sold on every street corner. It was enough to make me puke, especially when I saw someone break off a soft wing and scarf it down. They chase it down with the juice that's inside the egg. I also noticed that there were not many dogs running around in the streets of Olongopo. I was leery of this because I'd seen dogs on other tropical islands and knew that they should have some, too. The only dog I saw was a cocker spaniel being chased by a kid.

I finally lucked up and found an R&B club. It was called the

Airport Disco. It was full of African American military members and local Filipinos. It was just like a typical American club, with rap and soul music. I was told that another club, called the Eastside Disco, was a block further up Magsaysay, with exactly the same crowd. I had a blast.

I noticed one thing about these clubs. All the Filipino women were wearing numbers. I asked someone what the numbers meant, and he replied that the women worked at the club.

I said, "They don't seem to be working very hard, sitting with the guys and dancing all night."

The person said, "That ain't the kind of work they do!"

I put two and two together and realized they were all prostitutes that were only allowed to work at that location.

It was amazing. A man simply paid the bartender pesos for the number he liked, and she was his for as long as he could afford her – which could be a long time, based on the exchange rate. I couldn't believe what I was seeing. I had a problem with the entire logic. I also felt sad for the ladies, who had to make a living off of the entire Sixth Fleet. I must say that it took all of the willpower I could muster to avoid getting caught up in that madness. Each time I felt weakened, I thought of my shipmate who was working hard trying to get herpes out of his system. The Philippines were known for the spread of herpes. AIDS wasn't really an issue at that time, as it hadn't made its way to that part of the world.

I was a bit tired and couldn't make it to 0430 to avoid the drills. I decided to take my pesos back to the ship for another day. As I walked back down the Magsaysay, I realized that I had only covered about a quarter mile from the gate. Just think, I spent at least 10 hours out on the town and only spent a portion of my 5000 pesos. I also remembered to pick up my suit and shoes, that were both finished. I couldn't believe it. I took them back to the ship that same night. I poured myself into my rack and woke up with reveille. Fortunately, they didn't have a drill during our first night. Great – maybe the CO and XO were hanging, too.

We started training bright and early. The plan was to hit us with a series of drills and to evaluate the entire crew on its success. Keep in mind the rapid turnover in personnel and the loss of expertise resulting from the 18-month tours of duty. It was a revolving door. The first drill I can recall was a mock nuclear, biological, or chemical attack. I was the bridge phone talker again.

The Navy shiprider came up to me, touched my arm, and said, "You have been hit with a nerve agent and one of the symptoms is your skin is pinker than usual."

As an African American, I assumed that I was in charge. I looked at the captain and said, "Sir, I'm in charge."

He looked at me with this gaze and said, "What's wrong with you? Get back to the drill."

I said, "Sir, if *my* skin is pinker than usual, you guys are dead!"

The entire bridge erupted into laughter – including the shiprider.

The evaluators left the bridge smiling and messed with another part of the ship; I think that was fine with the captain. There were a multitude of catastrophes they would throw at us, but there was nothing that we couldn't do. We had mastered that small, 180-foot ship. The *Basswood* had a similar reputation from previous REFTRAs. It was no secret that we knew our stuff.

We conducted nighttime drills as well. On one occasion, we were sailing in total darkness under "blackened ship." I thought I heard something on the starboard side. It sounded like a small engine. I immediately told the XO and he noticed the sound as well. He ordered our gunners and a couple of divers to take positions. The roaring sound became louder, and before we knew it a small boat opened fire on us with colored blanks. When we turned on the ship's deck and running lights, our guys were in perfect position. The shipriders concurred that we had the jump on the small boat because of the actions we'd taken before they fired on us. Another victory.

This tit for tat lasted for two weeks. We met every challenge. I was fortunate enough to be the lost person during our man-overboard drill. This was great. While I hid and rested, the officers and crew had to conduct maneuvers and rescue Oscar from the sea. Oscar was a human-sized dummy we threw overboard during the drills. Whoever had the conn was responsible for maneuvering the ship to pick up the body. This was great practice for the real thing. Unfortunately, I hid out in laundry. The heat and the vibrations from the machines put me to sleep. I didn't hear the "Stand down from drill" announcement and they really thought for a short moment that I'd fallen overboard.

We returned to port at the end of the day and the duty section had to conduct a drill to light off the P-250 submersible pump. This pump was used to fight fires and flooding onboard ship and it started like a lawnmower. A suction hose was placed in the harbor, and once started, it produced water through a fire hose. As long as the pump ran and water was in the ocean, we could successfully fight a ship's number one enemy, fire. This was a timed event and competition on base was high for it. The pier was full of Navy personnel watching the coasties work. Our first duty section broke a time of 46 seconds. We conducted this drill each evening, and before long we were breaking records and lighting off the pump in less the 25 seconds. The Navy was amazed.

Well, we couldn't hide out on the base forever. It was time to venture further down Magsaysay. This time I was determined to stay out until daybreak. A couple of us settled at an open-air restaurant and watched the sights. As soon as the food arrived, a beautiful little girl came up to our table. She couldn't have been older than six or seven years old. She was dressed in her Sunday best. She begged for pesos and we contributed. One of us noticed grownups and other children hiding around a building and calling her back to their location. As soon as she returned to them, they took the money we'd just given her. They sent her back again. Instead of giving her money, we then showered her with food, drink, and desserts. She must have sat with us for at least two hours.

Since they sold beer as well, we were able to sit there for many more hours. We watched the crew in the alley slowly dwindle down to zero, with their mouths watering at the luscious fruit and extravagant food we gave her. When she finished eating we gave her a few more pesos and had her put them in her shoe. We never saw that girl again. I did see the little boy who was chasing the cocker spaniel the previous day. He was selling barbeque chicken on a makeshift grill on a street corner. Fortunately, I didn't see any hair bumps on the chicken. I guess he caught Scruffy. I wonder how many sailors bought food off of the street.

The local guys in town could pluck our nerves as well. They

were known for placing clothing items on people and insisting that they'd bought them. I'd knock their hands off of me and the clothing items to the ground each time they did it. Unfortunately, it didn't always work.

Quartermaster Second Class Mitch England had recently reported to the ship. Mitch was extremely quiet and took a while to answer questions. If someone asked Mitch, "What is that contact ahead?" he'd put his fingers on his chin and say, "Hummm."

This drove everyone on the bridge nuts because the contact could be an aircraft carrier dead ahead, and no one had time for Mitch to figure it out. Mitch was, however, the best celestial navigator on the ship. He could plot a course by the stars in a completely darkened ocean. He was The Man on the bridge at night.

Once Mitch fell behind a bit while walking down Magsaysay Drive with a group of us. When we turned around he was wearing a large straw hat cocked sideways on his head like Huggy Bear from *Starsky and Hutch*. He had a burlap pullover shirt draped over one of his shoulders and a guy trying to put a ring on his finger. We ran back to find Mitch panicking, with his hand on his chin and saying, "Hummm, Hummm, Hummm," as he turned right and left to look at the various people around him.

We grabbed him and pulled all of that junk off of him and threatened the guys to leave him alone. We said, "Leave him alone!" and "He ain't buying none of that shit – get out of our face!"

They left us alone. As we entered a restaurant, we all began to put our hands on our chins and frantically say, "Hummm, Hummm, Hummm." I don't know if Mitch got a kick out of that, but we sure did.

We found another open-air bar on the northern part of the strip that had great food – lumpia, keliguen, and chicken adobo. Good eatin'! In the corner of my eye, I thought I saw the Easter Bunny waving at me. We couldn't let things distract us while drinking in the P.I. It wouldn't take long for a pissed-off bartender to slip something deadly in our drinks. After refocusing, I realized that it was another upper-level club sitting in an alley directly behind us. It wasn't the location that got us; it was the 15 Playboy Bunnies waving at us from the window. The discreet location of this club must have hurt their business and they used the ladies to wave folks down.

My shipmates immediately said, "Hey, there's our new headquarters," and it wasn't long before it became just that. The Navy guys on base couldn't figure out how these coasties were producing multiple photos with Bunnies, and they had no knowledge of such a location. It especially bothered them since the Fleet owned that part of the Pacific and had frequented it since the beginning of time. We were not alone though; merchant marines knew about the site, but they were older guys and let our guys take over the club. It was like a passing of the guard. That was typical *Basswood* activity: making something our own, peacefully.

We were nearly finished with REFTRA, but had one last adventure. It was called mass conflag (mass conflagration). It was also known as "The Shit Has Hit the Fan." This drill would last 30 straight hours and would happen sometime during the middle of the night. We slept fully dressed in battle gear, with pants tucked into boots and gas masks strapped to our thighs. An alarm sounded around 0230 and I can vividly recall people literally leaping out of their racks yelling, "Bring it on" or "Here we go!" The intensity level was off the scale.

We got underway and they began to hit us with every drill known to man. There were people targeted as injured who needed treatment. There were folks designated dead; they were lucky – they could sit their ass down for at least two hours. Not me. I was documenting all of these evolutions on the bridge casualty board with a grease pencil under a red flashlight. The shiprider shined another light on my board and told the CO, "Great job plotting." They left and pressed other parts of the ship. I had done my job.

When it was all said and done, we had to fake as if we were losing the ship. Technically, it was sinking and the final drill was to see how quickly we could abandon it. We broke that record as well. Thirty hours later (about 0800), we exhaustedly returned to the pier. It was over. We gathered on the buoy deck to find out our results. We had aced the entire refresher training. We had a few Subic Bay Naval Station records under our belt and the coveted Battle "E", which is a designation of excellence. It came with a ribbon for our uniforms and we got to paint a replica of the ribbon directly on our ship's side for all to see. You would think that we would be tired, but nope, as soon as liberty was granted at 0930 we went to a restaurant off base. We were too tired to think about women. We wanted to congratulate each other, grab a bite to eat, and come down off of the two-week training high.

It wasn't long before a lady offering "services" approached us in the restaurant. We were beginning to tire and felt a bit on edge. She asked if we wanted a girl. To get rid of her, one of the guys sarcastically said, "It's too damn early – is she 12?" We thought no more about it and were about to leave when, to our dismay, the lady began walking down the stairway with a young girl who couldn't have been more than 12. She was wiping sleep out of her eyes. The only words we could come up with were, "You got to be kidding!"

All she'd heard was "twelve." We quickly realized the seedy side of life in the P.I. and that we had to be careful with our words or we could flip someone else's switch. We got out of that place as fast as we could and returned to the ship to hit the rack. We would start all over again in a couple of hours.

I later returned to town alone to get a $1 haircut. This was an adventure in itself. The guy cut my hair and gave me a neck massage directly in my chair. He slipped his hand in this vibrating device and put it on the back of my neck. I thought I was going to fall asleep immediately. I was nearly asleep when I realized he was headed towards my below-decks. I woke up and smacked his hand, knocking the device to the floor. I walked out without paying. I was pissed off, but my neck felt great. No more P.I. hair cuts unless it was a woman.

I went directly to the Eastside Disco to watch the guys drink mojo. I stuck to the good old San Miguel beer. Mojo was a Kool-Aid type of drink served in large plastic pitchers. I never drank it because of its effect on the drinkers. I was told that it tasted exactly like Fruit Punch, but hit you like a sledgehammer about an hour later. They couldn't stand up. They would probably get robbed before they made it back to the base. There were so many people on the street that anything could happen. Fortunately, I never saw anything tragic.

I did hear of a case in which a sailor mouthed off to a few local club managers. Shortly thereafter, he was asleep on the bar, or at least his friends thought he was asleep. They soon discovered that he'd been poisoned and had died right there with his head on the bar. I learned that being an American in a foreign country is extremely dangerous, and everyone doesn't love us, as we tend to believe. We are instead usually despised and thought of as arrogant cowboys. It's extremely important to try to fit in and speak a couple words of the local language, in this case Tagalog. It shows that we at least recognize and respect our surroundings.

The ship voted to have a couple of parties before we departed, as if we hadn't partied enough. The first was scheduled for a place called California Jam, which was the best club on Magsaysay Drive. It was huge and had multiple levels and rooms. It had two 20-foot-by-20-foot TV screens and 30 feet of JBL speakers on each side of a large, elevated stage. Its band could imitate any American band. There were so many numbered girls in this place that the count reached at least 75. I had to take $400 dollars with me to reserve the club.

Imagine walking down a dangerous street with the equivalent of 20,000 pesos. I could rent a villa with a staff for a month with this money. I was nervous as hell walking down that street. I definitely didn't want to run into the one-legged man at this point. I arrived safely with the money in my shoe. I sat in the owner's office and he had one of the ladies bring me a drink. I felt like I was brokering a deal for Capitol Records.

The next night we had the time of our lives. The entire ship arrived, including the CO and XO. There were so many people trying to join our roped-off section that we had Security manage our crowd. Our guys were plucking numbered girls out of a line 30 feet long. I just walked around with an arm band on that said, "Coordinator." It was like we had the keys to Sin City.

Chief Gentry arranged our second party a week or so later. He was a single boatswain's mate. Chief Gentry was a joy to be around. He ran the buoy deck and took care of deck force. The youngest guys on the ship worked for him. Chief returned to the ship one day wearing a hat with one of those red slashes through it. It said, "Cherry Busters, We Ain't Afraid of No Clap!" On one small island, James and I saw him in a container crate with Lester, a John Cusack look-alike and one of two Lesters on our ship. We called one Les and the other Lester. We thought we heard two

176

women giggling. James began to throw rocks at the crate. As they pinged off of the crate, Chief Gentry peeked out and scratched his head. As he reentered the crate, James threw another rock. Chief looked out again and yelled, "Who's throwing rocks at my motel?" We ducked and ran to the mess deck like two little kids, laughing profusely. In other words, the chief was the perfect person to set up the second party.

Chief Gentry met a guy at a small bar who told him that he could invite the crew and we would receive free food and drinks. That's all anybody had to tell my shipmates. In addition, we decided to have a bachelor party for Mike Lowery and a going-away bash for Seaman Lewis. The bar was a bit wild, and we made up most of the crowd.

Our guys were on stage oil-wrestling with ladies. They were drunk as skunks, slipping in the oil and bumping the ladies heads on the wall. It was hilarious. Before long, we noticed that someone was filming us with a professional-looking camera. Moreover, there was a lovely, well-dressed couple in the middle of our crowd, and the cameras were focused on them. They eventually wandered away from the party and up a flight of stairs into a room. The cameras followed. We had been duped. The crew of the *Basswood* was the rent-a-crowd for a Filipino porno movie. We are probably celebrities over there. The chief couldn't live that one down. It goes down in the annals of WESPAC history. I once heard a Navy guy try to tell that story until I told him that I was there.

Chief was cool, and took the time to teach us no matter what we were doing or where we were. I learned a valuable lesson from Chief Gentry. On one extremely hot Friday I was caught reading a newspaper on watch. I verbally sparred with the officer who caught me. My rationale was that it was extremely hot and quiet, and I needed something to keep me awake. I was mostly pissed off because I had Friday night watch and the crew could hit the streets. When I vented to the chief, he asked one pointed question: "Were you wrong?"

I paused a little and said, "Yeah."

He said, "Well, you don't have a reason to gripe, do you?"

Since that day, I have carried that guidance with me.

We were ready to depart Subic Bay and return to Guam. We conducted dockside trials to see if everything was working properly. Many of us didn't have anything to do with this evolution; it involved only the officers, quartermasters, and engineers. A few of us were sitting on the rec deck when the lights in the room got extremely bright and the fan sped up to an unbelievable speed. We could hear the ship's power die, and then the ship went dark. We looked at each other and said in unison, "A Fire." We ran out of the rec deck and to our fire stations. I immediately grabbed my sound-powered phones, and, as suspected, we had an electrical switchboard fire in the engine room. They secured the power and put out the fire. Unfortunately, we'd burned a number of critical wires. We would not be leaving that day. Better yet, it could have happened in the middle of the Pacific, but hadn't. After making repairs, we planned to leave the following day.

Well, I had the time of my life in the P.I. Although I didn't *date* anyone, in my mind I was not a Cherry Boy anymore. I had experienced the wonders of the South Pacific in my own way. We finished our buoys, aced REFTRA, picked up a couple of cases of herpes, and headed back to Guam to make it to the Christmas party that no enlisted person wanted to attend. I think the captain at MARSEC fronted our payment and he wanted his money back. As we pulled out, we had to initiate another *Basswood* rule; we blasted Dire Straits' "Money for Nothing (and the Chicks for Free)" on the loudspeaker as we pulled away from the pier. The Navy guys shook their heads, smiled, saluted, and we were out.

Chapter 24
Happy Holidays to You, Too
--------------------:☼:------------------

We expected our sail back to Guam to be mostly uneventful, or so we hoped. The weather reports predicted a typhoon that would tail us home. There is no way in the world to outrun a typhoon with a ship that makes 13 knots at best. For the first two days we had morning muster and quarters on the fantail. I'll never forget the dark gray skies and the 15-foot seas. Imagine Michael Jackson performing one of his famous moves, leaning forward or backward with knees locked and feet firmly planted on the ground. While the ship rocked to the left, the crew leaned to the right, and vice versa. If we were on solid ground, we would have fallen on our faces. We also discovered *fantail-jumping*. When the ship pitched up and down, we could literally leapfrog forward. Instead of landing six feet ahead, it felt as if we were catapulted 15 feet, and it took even longer to hit the deck. We had to create fun and exercise underway the best way that we could.

It seemed that we never could shake that storm off our tail. We decided to head south and away from Guam, hoping that it would pass above us so we could resume our course with the heavy weather in front of us. That didn't happen. The storm changed course and followed us south. We attempted to head due east, and it seemed to follow us. We decided that we didn't have the fuel to play around in the Pacific and made a run for Guam, anyway. By the grace of God we outran the storm, as it passed just south of our location, missing Guam and Truk. We were home free, or so we thought. We received word that a Korean fishing vessel had run aground off Tinian, and there was an additional report of two women divers missing in the same

179

waters. It was 22 December and everyone was burnt out from the WCI.

Morale dropped from extreme high to an all-time low; especially for the guys with families in Guam. They hadn't seen their wives and kids since September. I know it's not like an aircraft carrier, but Coast Guard ships require a lot more care for long deployments. Milk spoiled after 8 days. The cereal eaters among us had to resort to frozen milk.

Our first endeavor was to locate the lost divers, and we'd deal with the wrecked vessel in the morning, but we'd had no need for Plan A. The authorities informed us that the ladies dove at night and had been eaten by sharks. From two people, all that remained was a half of a human lung. That was it.

Upon daybreak, we observed an amazing sight: a large, green fishing vessel beached on its side just off of one of the most beautiful white-sand beaches in the world. The ship was money-green against a white-sand background. In a morbid way it was a beautiful sight. We were informed that the Koreans were using a chart from the 1950s. I suppose they said, "That's okay, it's only 36 years old. It still works!" Well, they had tons of rotting fish onboard and additional tons of fuel. It was too big of a job for the *Basswood*, so we called in the Pacific Strike Team from Hamilton Air Force Base in Navato, California. They arrived as soon as they could and took care of the offloading of the fish and fuel. Finally, we could get back to Guam.

The captain remained in Tinian to supervise the fuel offload. The XO, Lieutenant Torasco, would have the command for the 12-hour sail back to Guam. I can vividly recall Chief Gentry asking us on the bridge if he could keep the deck lights on while they griped, or tied down, the small boat. I knew that wouldn't be possible, because this was the first time the XO had command of the ship without the CO being onboard and he would do everything by the book.

With the CO on the pier watching, the XO advised me to secure the deck lights. Lieutenant Junior Grade Coyle had the conn. As soon as I turned off the lights, I heard a loud splash and the words, "Man Overboard!" rang out from the crew members near the small boat.

Mr. Coyle froze with the throttle in his hands. He didn't say a word or order us to do anything. The XO pushed him aside and yelled, "The XO has the conn!" He immediately called out the proper commands to maneuver the ship while the entire crew conducted a head count. The person who was missing was our leading seaman, Mongo.

Mongo's real name was Kevin Young and he stood six-foot-six and at least 245 pounds. An avid motorcyclist; his arguments with Quartermaster Tim Joy over Harleys vs. Motogusies were mess deck classics. Mongo could also pull the entire iron brow from the ship to the pier whenever we got underway. Without him, it took 10 guys do the same. He was nicknamed Mongo because he reminded us of the cuddly brute in the *Blazing Saddles* movie. When the word spread that it was Mongo who was lost in the middle of a channel in shark-infested waters, our hearts dropped. The crew responded like clockwork. We had performed this drill every day underway and multiple times in REFTRA. Someone immediately threw over a life ring with a 16-inch strobe light attached to it. It was pitch black and at times we could see the strobe. The XO realized that he didn't have the maneuverability to turn the ship. Under normal circumstances, this maneuver would put the ship alongside Oscar. This was different. We had reefs on both sides of the ship.

The XO ordered the RHI boat into the water. Boatswain's Mate Third Class Hemsley was the coxswain. Hemsley traveled at maximum speed in the direction of the last sighting of the strobe. He sped in a five o'clock direction for at least 500 feet. After 12 minutes from the time of the splash, Hemsley radioed back to the ship that Mongo was on board the RHI. I can't recall the crew being as emotional and proud as it was on this evening. When Mongo got onboard I recall hugging him.

I also recall some of the younger guys bragging and laughing about how they knew they would find him. I didn't feel the same and I sort of scolded them. How soon could they forget that we found a half of a human lung in these same waters on the previous night?

We asked Mongo what was up with the strobe light. He said that he was sticking it in the water to look out for sharks. After that statement, all we could do was laugh. This scene didn't end up in the *Bitch Log*, proving that the guys were more scared for Mongo than they let on. In addition, it was two-beer and pizza night. One rocket scientist actually asked the XO if we could still have our two beers.

We pulled into Guam around 0700 to a pier full of families with signs, balloons, and flowers. It was 23 December and we were finally back home. It wasn't long before we found out that MARSEC's Christmas party would be held on 24 December and that the CO of MARSEC had spent hundreds of dollars paying for the *Basswood*'s meals. He was ticked when most of us stated that we were not going. Before long, we were *encouraged* to attend. I suppose that if he had not paid for us, we would still be underway and would have missed Christmas altogether. That was fine because we were still fresh from PI partying. We could take over this party with our eyes closed.

The party was held at the Officer's Club near the Naval Hospital. It was good seeing all, or should I say some, of the guys from MARSEC and the *Cape George*. We got along with the *George*'s crew, but we couldn't stand the shore-based MARSEC guys. They griped about being stuck in Guam and thought we had it easy because we could leave for months on end. I don't think they wanted to tell that to the married guys. We felt that free Military Airlift Command (MAC) or cheap international flights were enough to get their lazy asses off of Guam. Hell, they *could* have been stationed at Group Upper Mississippi River in Keokuk, Iowa. They continuously bitched about being in the tropics.

It wasn't long before the *Basswood* sailors took over the Christmas party. We were all dancing and clowning around.

On one occasion, a sailor approached our lovable Lester and advised him to not talk to his wife. Lester said, "Okay," and left it alone, but within five minutes we could see that Lester was fuming. He stood up and we all had that "Oh, shit!" look on our faces. He walked over to the wife and said, "I'm sorry, but I won't be able to call you. Here's your phone number back."

We laughed as the married couple left the party. We had a good time embarrassing ourselves by doing the dying cockroach dance while everyone else watched. It was usual behavior for us. This party was good, but it couldn't top starring in a Filipino porno movie.

Chapter 25
It's a Girl

-------------------☼-------------------

I entered 1987 on a roll. My wife was expecting a child back in Maryland. Something must have happened on my last night home. I guess it really does work like that. It was a tough nine months for newlyweds, with one being on worldwide assignment. We never really got to do anything that a normal couple would have done. We had to focus on it only being 18 months. I was fortunate that she had an entire family to support her back in the States. Sherri and Gregory had no intention of moving to Guam. They had never heard of it. To be honest, how could I ask them to move to a far-away island just because *I* had to go to sea? The first nine months seemed like a lifetime. The second half couldn't be as hard. We would see.

I flew back to the DC area, hoping to arrive before the birth. I planed to stay for 30 days and return to ship to wrap up my time. When I reached DC it was in the midst of an ice storm. My mother-in-law's water heater was broken and it was tough on my wife, Gregory, and the rest of the family. I think there were eight people living there during those last days of her pregnancy; it had to be hard. I assisted an uncle with repairing the water heater, only to be hampered a power outage. I had just returned from the tropics and all of my winter clothes were in storage. It was a bit rough, but it was nothing compared to what my wife would soon undergo.

I was counting down to my Coast Guard anniversary date of 9 February, when I would pass the six-year mark. On the morning of the ninth, Sherri woke me up with the famous words, "I think my water broke." I said to myself, broke what?

Most of that day was a blur. I recall her mom's friend, Mike, barreling down the Beltway to Bethesda Naval Hospital. It had to be around 9:30 a.m., because the traffic around the Mormon Temple was backed up, as usual. We did arrive at the emergency room in one piece.

I was bracing to perform whatever duties they would give me in the delivery room. I don't think we had thought of a name prior to my return. I seriously considered naming her Leilani, because that was the name I admired most in my island life. Sherri wasn't having that. During labor, I tried to recall all of that crap that was in the books I'd read. I told Sherri not to worry about the pain and to concentrate on the picture on the wall.

Her response was, "Fuck that picture on the wall!"

Well, I had to ditch the book. At 5:30 p.m., a daughter was given to us. We named her Tiffani Monique. She was tiny and exceedingly fragile. I didn't feel comfortable holding her. I could feel the bones through her skin. I recall showing her to my mother-in-law, who replied, "What an ugly baby!" I was pissed, but I didn't show it. To be honest, she was slightly wrinkled.

She had a head full of black hair. I thought to myself, "She looks like me!" She actually looked like Sherri. I was praising my own genes and forgetting that my wife had a full head of black hair as well. She didn't do it all herself. She had given Tiffani her skin and hair color. I contributed the face structure and smile. Within a couple of days Tiffani was already smiling widely. She seemed to be a happy baby. I was so proud of Sherri for sticking by me and giving me this child to go along with one of her own. I really felt like a man – more so than when I bought my first car!

I spent another 20 days home before I was scheduled to return to the ship. The hardest part of this trip home would be the departure. I knew my returning to Guam would be terrible for my new small family. The only good thing was that my tour was half done. I was literally guaranteed a position at Headquarters when I returned. I tried to convince my wife that this sacrifice would pay off for us in the long run. I would never have to go to sea again. At 24, that was a good thing. I planned to make the service my career and there would be problems if they tried to send me again. Although it was the military, we still earned rights. Completing a tour of ship duty overseas provided one of those rights.

The ride to, and departure from, Washington National Airport was one of the hardest things I've ever done in my life.

We all cried like babies. Sherri's friend Barbara was crying as well. I even saw a senior manager from HQ at the airport and he was about to cry. This truly sucked. I actually got annoyed at the Coast Guard as a way of gaining strength. I couldn't be truly angry, because our decision to live apart was our own. Who could we blame? Although we couldn't see it, I truly believed that it would enhance our lives and careers, and that something this hard should work for us in the long run. I wiped my face, looked back once, and boarded the plane.

Chapter 26
Do Prisoners Cry When Paroled?
------------------☼------------------

After a short stopoff in Honolulu to stay a night with Matt Kingsley, I returned to the grind of the ship. We didn't get to chill out in Guam as I'd anticipated. We were scheduled to remain until April. Unfortunately, winter is typhoon season and they were wreaking havoc on the buoys we'd previously set on various islands. In late February we had to return to the Northern Marianas Islands to place a few buoys back on station. In March we had to return to Truk and Pohnpei to do the same. We were scheduled to return to Japan and start our yearly ops in April. I wanted that year to fly by. I was torn between enjoying my excursions and wanting to see my family. I suppose that if I had to go to sea, this was where I wanted to do it. I would make the best out of it and try to pick up as many reminders and souvenirs as possible.

I began to snap photos continuously. I also traded more on the islands. The barracks were getting tedious. The new batch of seamen arrived with drinking problems, unlike the previous group, who became alcoholics. At the XO's direction, the master-at-arms assigned one to my room. This lasted all of one week. Traditionally, the E-5s were housed two to a room. I came back from an errand and found the door to my room wide open and my new third roommate drunk and asleep. Les Trailor and I had tons of electronics, videos, and compact discs that were ripe for the picking, not to mention the bikes and foreign artifacts.

To put it mildly, I went off on him and respectfully told the master-at-arms and the XO that it wasn't going to work and that if something was stolen from me I was going to hurt somebody.

They moved the kid, and Les and I had the place to ourselves again.

We set sail for Japan in April for yard work and firefighting and damage-control training. We would not drydock the ship, but work on it from dockside. We were also scheduled to replace the entire roach-infested berthing area. This would allow us to live in Navy barracks with maid service. As an E-5, I was slated for my own room for the next 45 days. Any privacy I could get was a blessing in that environment.

It was a year since I'd last been in Japan and I still couldn't afford anything out in town. I spent most of this tour on base experiencing things I'd missed during my first short stay. The most eventful thing was the dust and dirt the ship's renovations were causing. We couldn't cook onboard. The base delivered lunch to us on plastic prison trays. It was a mess.

Everyone had to stand quarterdeck watch, even the senior cooks, who normally went home after serving meals. I can recall one of the Filipino chiefs standing watch and announcing the arrival of the CO. At least, we thought that's what he was trying to do. When he announced over the loudspeaker, known as the 1-MC, "Now *Basswood* adriving," we lost it.

People immediately called or approached the quarterdeck to ask, "Chief, what's he driving?"

We knew he was trying to say "arriving," but it didn't matter; he'd left himself open. Once again, on a ship with 60 men, anything was worth a laugh.

I continued to whip butt on the pool table there. I don't think I've ever played as well anywhere.

Whenever I did venture out, I couldn't help but see the many "No Americans Allowed" signs on the doors of restaurants and clubs.

I can't believe that we protect this place with our sailors, soldiers, ships, planes, and missiles. You would think we were in Russia. Japan has a Defense Force. They are not offensive in their military approach. America serves that purpose. I suppose this is the agreement we signed to apologize for dropping the bomb on them and for allowing us to have all of the bases we maintain in their country. Considering that Harley Davidson motorcycles and rap music are the only things they buy from us, I think they are getting the better hand.

188

We left Sasebo and set sail for Pusan, Korea. This trip took a short 12 hours and was directly across the Korea Strait from Sasebo. Pusan is 200 miles south of Seoul and home to a large Army base. We only planned to stay for four days. I was scheduled to stand midnight quarterdeck watch on the first day. I volunteered for the first day because it was raining and I thought it was more fun to watch the guys when they returned. I could easily find out the ropes and avoid wasting time before I ventured out myself.

It was an extremely foggy night and I was supposed to log anything out of the ordinary. There was a huge empty parking lot on the pier that was surrounded by a fence. I couldn't imagine what was stored there. Around 0200 I heard the hum of a ship passing by our port side. I clicked the 1-MC for the XO. We were not allowed to use the public address system after taps. If I clicked the mike, someone on duty would come up to see if I needed coffee or assistance. When the OOD arrived I pointed out a ship that seemed larger than an aircraft carrier passing by us. Nearly 10 minutes later, it was still passing. I couldn't see it through the fog, but I observed its running lights. At dawn we noticed it moored directly in front of us.

The following morning I observed the largest peacetime tank offload in recent military history. They completely filled up the huge parking lot with hundreds of tanks. That was my first non-naval observation of American military hardware. The number of tanks in Pusan would have held off North Korea for days if necessary. I thought we were already at war. It showed the seriousness of our occupation in that part of the world.

It was coming together for me. It looked like America was deployed in every part of the world, either for the purpose of protecting people or for launching a strike from a forward position. I often wondered how long the host nations would allow us to do so. I could feel the double-edged sword. The people liked the economics of our presence, while at the same time despising our existence. This is something I could feel by looking in their eyes. It's not like looking at a person from the Far East at a store in America. There is a strange darkness in their eyes, or a phony smile while they serve us.

When I finally ventured out, I was directed to Texas Street. This was the main drag, and anything a person wanted to buy or do was on it. I went on a shopping spree that I couldn't imagine. Texas Street is known for eel-skin products, leather, tennis shoes, and bars. I didn't particularly care for the club scene there. There were no clubs that weren't centered around sex. I couldn't locate a regular disco and I couldn't go to Seoul. Students were rioting and being killed there. We were advised to avoid the drug stores because they sold medicines without prescriptions that were illegal narcotics in the States. I was told that they had opium in them.

I did find out that I had become Commander-In-Chief . This short Korean guy followed me wherever I went. If I went into a store, he waited until I came out and resumed his taunts. His only words were, "Mister DeJanitor, Mister DePresident."

My only question was, "What in the fuck was that?"

He said that over and over again until I couldn't take it anymore. I stayed in restaurants just to avoid him. I knew he would be gone after a couple of hours. Wrong! When I came out the door, he commenced with his taunt.

I got mad and told him, "I'm not your fucking janitor or your president."

I noticed that he was holding a newspaper with something inside it. He was holding it as if he was a runaway but didn't have a stick to put his ball of crap on. He gave me a two-hour reprieve and I felt relieved. It just so happened that I saw someone kneeling over in an alley off of the main drag. I stopped to see what he was doing. I saw Mr. Dejanitor puking into that newspaper he'd been holding next to my head.

I located the first taxi I could find and hauled ass back to the ship. I had completed my shopping spree, so there was no need to leave the ship again, not in Korea that is. I traded my liberty days for a later date. I assumed that if I went out he would hit me with that newspaper full of vomit and I would kill him on the streets of Pusan. I would then spend the rest of my natural life in a Korean prison, eating rice out of a little bowl with my fingers. A shipmate told me that he heard the guy eats his puke and recycles it for the next meal. It was best that I stay on the ship.

We set sail for Yokosuka again. Once again, the home on the hill played the National Anthem as we passed. I don't know how they could see that we were Americans unless they had a huge telescope. Yes, I puked again on this trip. I can roll with the best

190

of them, but I can't pitch worth a crap. This time I was on the bridge messing around. It hit me hard and quick. I tried to hide and puked over the bridge wing and onto the running lights. I also wet up the painted medals on the side of the ship. I went below and got a bucket of soapy water to toss on the running lights. I didn't take the wind into consideration and it blew the soapy water right back into my face. As I turned around to look at the bridge, everyone was standing there smiling at me. I had small white specs of liquid all over me. They thought I'd puked into the wind and it had blown back into my face. They didn't believe my story, so I just left it alone. One more for the *Bitch Log*.

As usual, we found ourselves back at the club. This time I knew a bunch of folks. I knew a lady sailor from the *Cape Cod*, which had 400 women on board. She was cute and from Chicago. A seaman named Clarence always bugged me about hooking him up with a black girl, so I thought I would introduce him to the Navy woman.

They talked for most of the night, and then she told me, "I'm going to get him to walk me back to the barracks, but I'm not giving him none."

I told her that it was up to her what they did. As they left, he looked at me and smiled as if he'd hit the jackpot.

All was quiet on the Western Front until the Shore Patrol delivered Clarence back to the ship a few hours later. They said he'd been caught peeping in the chiefs' bathroom in the barracks and they'd had him arrested. I felt as if I'd set him up. He told a few of us who were awake that the lady had told him to wait outside the barracks until she checked to see if her roommate was asleep, and she never came back. He'd started looking in windows and had peeped in the bathroom as some of the chiefs were showering.

This story was all over the ship by morning. Clarence began to approach the galley for breakfast and someone started to sing, "Do you see what I seeeee?" Someone else chimed in, "Do you see what I seeeee?" Another sang, "A man, a man, was peeping in Japan." The entire galley sang, "Do you see what I seeeee?" Another sang out, "A chief, a chief, you were looking at his beef." All together now, "Do you see what I seeeee?" I literally fell into my plate laughing. It was the funniest skit I've ever heard, and prior to 8 a.m. At this point I realized that I was living with crazy people.

We passed through Loran Station Iwo Jima again and found an entirely different crew. It was an extremely beautiful day, and the one thing I noticed was the rain squalls that circled the island. I took a photo of one of the squalls as it stood over Mount Suribachi. It was an amazing photo that I alone was able to capture. Everything I saw or did was history in the making. The crew of Loran Iwo Jima was tasked with preparing the unit for decommissioning. They would be the last Coast Guard crew to run the station. The new global positioning system was taking over many of the duties of the Loran "C" towers and they would become obsolete. Moreover, I really don't think the Coast Guard could financially handle supporting these stations in locations like Kargabarun Turkey, Lampadusa Italy, Sylt Germany, and, yes, Iwo Jima.

We returned to Guam around 15 June 1997 for another home port period. This was Captain Petworth's last sail on board the *Basswood*. I was standing by with the sound-powered phones awaiting his commands. I could recall him reaming me out in Iwo Jima when I first reported aboard. I don't know why I thought about that at the time. To my amazement, he did too.

He looked at me and said, "Johnson, pull us in!"

My eyes lit up. He wasn't giving me the conn, but gave me the right to call the commands. When a ship is within 20 feet of the pier, it's all up to the phone talker.

I responded, "Put over lines one, three, and four. Heave around easy on one. Heave around easy on four. Put over line two. Take in slack on lines two and three. Avast heaving on one and four. Secure all lines." Realizing that we were adjacent to the pier, I said, "Put rat guards and chaffing gear on all lines!" Then I looked at him and said, "Is that good enough, Sir?"

The bridge erupted in laughter and he just smiled. Mongo leaped on the pier and pulled the damn brow ashore all by himself, again.

I had the duty that evening and I was onboard when the CO went ashore. He sat on the aft winch and told me, "You have come a long way. I remember that day in Iwo."

I nearly had tears in my eyes because I'd just received confirmation that I was a real coastie. A salt. That's what I'd set out to be when I volunteered for this ship.

I was falling in love with that island paradise more and more.

We were starving for more while in Guam. We were never there. When we were home, we worked extremely hard preparing for either a district inspection or the next underway period. I was also extremely comfortable with my job in the ship's office. Work wasn't an issue any longer. I just thought about home and cherished the pictures of my family and little Tiffani wearing a navy blue baby kimono that I'd shipped home from Japan.

I knew that this would be my last Guam visit. I felt that I didn't get enough of the island. The Coast Guard's rule for ship deployments says that a cutter should not be away from its home port more than 180 days. We averaged 200 to 220 per year. I ventured out to the traditional sites during this period in hopes of getting a real feel for the place. I wanted to see the waterfalls and waterfronts. I also missed my favorite small restaurant, the Signature Lounge. It was an extremely small place with an open-air terrace out back. The food was wonderful and the hostess eagerly played my homemade jazz cassettes. The lounge was across the street from Hotel Row. We received another 96-hour liberty period and I stayed at my favorite hotel, the Guam Hilton. I continued to rent rooms to get a good bath and to get away from 60 men. The flower garden outside my room was my sanctuary.

During my remaining days, I accepted that I was going back home shortly. I had mixed feelings. I missed my family, but I felt an unexplainable loyalty to the crew as well. I couldn't wait to get back to the States, but I loved paradise. I knew that when the time came, I would break my neck to leave. I also knew that I would likely shed a tear, if not for me, then for my fellow crew members who had to remain in this hellish paradise. That's the best way I can explain living in paradise, but missing all the comforts of the U.S.A. There was no crack or an AIDS epidemic. The only drama we experienced came from *USA Today* or the *Pacific Stars and Stripes* newspapers. To be honest, the shipmates with families back home couldn't wait to return and the single guys didn't want to leave.

We departed for our ECI cruise during late July. It went smoothly and was mostly uneventful. I didn't get reamed in the rear by a reckless rental car. No Angels of Pain, either. We did well. I was extremely proud of the crew and the way I handled the sound-powered phones this time. I was cool as a fan.

We returned to Guam for a short in-port period to load up

for the WCI and the Philippines. There would be a twist. We would reverse the order and go to the Philippines first, Palau second, and Yap third. That was fine with me. I arranged to depart the ship from Palau. I didn't mind missing Yap. I didn't want to get hit with rocks by Yapese Randy Johnsons. This new twist would put the exciting part of the trip up front and the more boring part at the end.

We only spent another 45 days in Guam. The packers arrived and took an entire day to move a TV, stereo, bike, clothes, and an aquarium. They actually took a noon siesta on a cardboard box in the hallway. Now that's what you call *Hafa Adai* (haf-a-day), Guam's famous greeting. I concluded the greeting meant "Half a Day," because that's all the work anybody was going to get out of them. They shipped my car and belongings to Baltimore, and I hoped everything would be there when I arrived in late November.

WCI was a blur to me. The only thing I could think of was returning to the States. I enhanced my collection of tropical possessions and mailed everything back to Maryland. I rolled through my job assignments; I knew them like the back of my hand. I mentally rushed through that three-month period, something that I regret. I stopped and smelled the roses, but I didn't pick them. It felt as if I was being paroled and I wondered how I would survive back in the world. How ironic is that? I continue to believe that ship life mirrors prison life in many ways. Maybe I should take a cruise to break up that mind set.

We completed the buoy work in the Philippines and headed for Palau, my favorite island. My replacement was Leroy, who'd lived with Mack and Mark while we'd been at Headquarters in the early 80s, and who had provided me lodging during my stop in Honolulu.

Leroy had become a worldwide Coast Guard traveler as well. He had served in Europe, Guam, and Hawaii. Ironically, I found myself working late – keeping promises – while Leroy was undergoing the usual *Basswood* break-in – clubbing. On my last night I was in the ship's office preparing overpayment relief letters for two shipmates who owed the Coast Guard over $5,000 each due to administrative errors out of their control. I wrapped it up at 11 p.m., but was too tired to venture out on the island. The next morning it would be all over. I later found out that my letters relieved both members of their debts. I wouldn't spend that last day any differently. I was their yeoman.

I woke up bright and early and was scheduled to fly out around 9:30 a.m. It was Saturday, and many guys would be asleep when I departed, or so I thought. The van had just returned from the airport and was full of wives. I poked my head into the van, and they all began to give me hugs and say "Thank you for everything. You took care of us." It was one of the biggest compliments I could ever receive. The quarterdeck watchstander piped me ashore. To my amazement, the buoy team turned around their small boat and returned to the ship to wave goodbye. A few hung-over crew members poked their heads out of hatches and portholes to say so long. The ward room emptied and all the officers came on-deck to say goodbye. It was heart-felt. I became truly sad inside, but I didn't show it. I joked and said my goodbyes.

Leroy, Doc, James, and Les drove me to the airport. Before I knew it, the plane was flying over the ship. I looked down and began to cry. I cried so hard that I couldn't turn away from the window to respond to the flight attendant. All I could think about was leaving, and I knew they all wanted to leave as well. It was my time and not theirs. That prison-departure feeling was present. Although they were in paradise, I felt sorry for them. Everyone becomes somewhat envious when someone departs, and they want to be next. I would miss guys named Mike Lowery, Lester, Stan Hall, Les Trailor, Doc Conception, Ray C, Jeff Diamond, Eric (Boats), Tim Joy, Jim-Bob, The Thue, Skeletor, The Beast, Mongo, and many others. My *Basswood* days were over, never to be replaced. "Now, Petty Officer Johnson departing. Now, Petty Officer Johnson ashore."

Chapter 27
Objects May Seem Closer Than They Appear
-------------------☼-------------------

Washington, DC was once labeled "Chocolate City" due to its majority African American population. It had a positive spin to it because of the power that came along with the positions many of these individuals held. Seven years later, it's known as the Murder Capital of the World, a title formally held by Detroit.

I can recall asking a group of guys sitting on the stoop of a building if they knew how to get to the Carter Baron Amphitheater. I wanted to see the jazz violinist Noel Pointer.

They replied, "It's right down the street, and we're trying to get there, too."

I gave them a ride. I can't believe that I did that. I could use their help and they needed mine. I took them and they paid my way into the concert and covered all of my refreshments. Today, someone would find me in a ditch.

It's funny how things have changed. During our first month in DC in 1981, Mike and I met a lady on the National Mall and she invited us to a house party. We had a wonderful time and felt like honored guests. It was an extremely friendly town. It was rough, but a person had to mess with someone to get in trouble.

Today, no one drives under 50 mph, anywhere. Everyone has an attitude. Sixteen-year-old drivers grit on people as they cut them off. Others drive to work as if they love to work. How can they say they hate work and drive like a bat out of hell to get there? These speeders are not the cream of the crop at their various workplaces. I'll never understand. I'm not pressed to get to work. I'd rather arrive 10 minutes late to work than to the morgue on time. Nerds curse other drivers out on the highways for going too slow. I can feel the tension in the air. Most large American cities have changed, and not necessarily for the better. I sense that the pressures of successful city life have gotten to most people. Unfortunately, they don't know it yet. Maybe they will realize it when they notice themselves driving 100 mph to the 7-11 to get a Sunday paper.

I looked forward to my second tour of duty at HQ. I couldn't wait to see my family and what my daughter would look like. I'd last seen her in February '87, and I was returning in November. When I saw them my wife was as beautiful as ever. My son had grown fairly tall, and my little one looked like me. She had that thin Johnson hair and my fat face when she smiled. Sherri had purchased a nice apartment in Largo, Maryland, right around the corner from the Capital Center, where the Washington Bullets played and most concerts were held. It was a quiet neighborhood. We would get down to starting our lives, basically as newlyweds.

I had already arranged to work in the Personnel Reporting Unit at Headquarters (Persru) before I left the ship. It was responsible for all human resource transactions. The Persru was made up of a least 25 yeomen, all pros. I knew a few people in the office, mainly Petty Officer First Class Rick Larson, who led the teams. Rick was as close as a person could get to Mark Worde; he was extremely cool. We were considered the cream of the crop in HQ. Our working hours were 7:00 to 3:30. The hours were not long, but they were intense.

The office had no cubicles, just open space. We learned by listening to our peers. If the person talking was retiring a senior officer, we knew enough to keep our ears open. This is how we learned our craft. Our customers were too senior for us to learn by trial and error. Mistakes were documented for the entire service to see via national error feedback reports. Rick, Master Chief Grantham, Senior Chief Haverill, and Chief Warrant Officer Miller ran the shop. Janet and Shelly were the team leaders under Rick. I couldn't have asked for a better situation. It was continuously busy, but it was a fun assignment. This was a funny group of office workers.

The funniest guy in the office was Petty Officer Tony Williams. Tony could tell a story so well that our customers refused to leave until he finished. Tony was famous for his encounter with an admiral. The admiral had approached Tony for a new ID card. The seniority of the customer made Tony panic, and he couldn't calculate the dates properly on the application. He started mumbling numbers that didn't make sense, like "Nineteen sixty, nine forty-two." Ten minutes later he figured out the date and completed the document. The application was only a half-sheet of paper with 15 blocks of information. The admiral looked at him over the top of his glasses as if Tony were nuts. We were looking at him as well.

Tony blurted out, "Whew, all done."

We tried not to laugh. He got up to get it approved and realized there were no chiefs to sign it. He flipped and started running down the hall yelling, "Chief! Chief! No chief! No chief!"

It was funny as hell; the admiral looked at us and said, "You guys better get him some help."

Eventually one of the chiefs returned and he got the document signed. We laughed for weeks. What made it more hilarious was Tony acting out the same scene at our requests. No one can do it like the person who did it.

I received the last names covering I through L, assuming I made out because there couldn't be many bigwigs with those last names. I blew it. I wound up with at least 15 heavy hitters, including seven current and future admirals. I promised the office that I wouldn't lose it and run down the hallway looking for the chiefs, who were probably at Fort McNair's Tenth Hole having a cold one.

I wasn't the best in there and I wasn't the worst. One yeoman had a puffy desk blotter; we just thought it was warped. One day the chief was looking for something on that desk and raised the blotter. Walla! Leave papers, allotments, and other important documents that required processing. Nothing major came of it because the person was transferring soon. I felt noticeably better about myself.

We had true pros, like Yeoman Second Class Judy Dulles. She was prior Army and took a loss of stripes to join the Coast Guard. She worked her way back up to E7, and has recently retired. I did feel sorry for her once. She made first class and had to endure the *tacking on* ritual. Tacking on was a hazing practice in which a senior person hit the person being promoted in the upper arm to mimic the pinning of the stripes to her or his shoulder. Since Judy was fairly petite and a gorgeous person, I assumed she would get off easy. Not in the plans. Carlos, who was senior to us, tagged her so hard that *my* shoulder hurt. I couldn't believe it. I thought she'd stolen his lunch or something. She sucked it up and went on her merry way. Carlos made you think long and hard about getting promoted. We would be *under* the brig today if we hit one of our women, *or* men. Oh, how times have changed.

Carlos was the next funniest guy in the office. We had to be on our toes with him. He got me a couple of times. I had an allergy attack and took some Sudafed. He overheard me telling my team leader, Shelly, that I was having a hard time staying awake. He quietly stood behind me and started to yell. "Shellyyyy, I'm sleeepyyy. I took some Suuudefeddd!" He used this squeaky voice and the whole office laughed uncontrollably. I had to laugh at him, too.

I refused to let that be the last laugh for the week. I had to top it or that's the last thing anyone in the office would remember. After looking through a *Far Side* book by Gary Larson, I came up with a good one. Tony kept talking about his glasses, and we all used to tease him about how thick they were. When he complained about his glasses one more time, I yelled, "Tony, your glasses already say, "Objects may appear closer than usual."

The office erupted. I was home free for the week – or so I thought. Later that week someone came in with a fat lip. It was so swollen that Tony said, "You need an I.V. on your lip. I'll go down to medical and get you one of those I.V. bottle carts so that you can at least move around the building." He was home free for the weekend.

This was truly one for the *Bitch Log*, but we didn't have one. Headquarters can suck at times. Needless to say, it was amazing that we got anything done. It was hard to tell because our customers would never leave. Anyone watching would think that we didn't close at 3:30. We would leave at five. We told jokes from 3:30 to five. Our customers have said that the place has never been the same. The main thing that is missing is the true customer-service mentality and level of morale. We didn't depend on our bosses to provide morale. We provided our own.

Our bosses would have said, "Liberty's cancelled until morale improves," anyway.

That's the difference in today's customer-service approach. It's terrible. I believe it has led to online shopping. No one wants to deal with the employees anymore. I would rather shop online than deal with employees, especially at Walmart. I'm literally interrupting them on their cell phone or in their conversation about the club with their co-worker. If that's not enough, some poor old senior citizen, who just witnessed me purchase something, asks to see the receipt I placed in the bottom of my bag. On second thought, I may want that job one day. When Southland creates 7/11.com, we'll know that things have gone too far.

The one item that we maintained in the Persru that we couldn't disregard was confidentiality. We handled the service records and affairs for the military half of the 2000-plus employees in HQ. We did unfailingly well in maintaining the privacy of the folks who had unfortunate incidents with the law or the system. As usual, we found (or inserted) humor into most situations. The Coast Guard had the wonderful foresight to issue credit cards to junior coasties to make traveling easier. Unfortunately, the card they issued was called Diners Club. Why in the world would they give a card with that name to a bunch of brothers?

Within weeks, one guy was escorted out of the building in handcuffs. He used his to purchase bikes. My rationale was better: the card said "Diner" and "Club." I'll bet my paycheck that most culprits thought the same thing and ate out a lot. The portion of the card that says "Club" should be self-explanatory. The logic in this would have persuaded Mr. Spock to use it for that purpose. If we'd been given Visas, these guys would still be overseas. Another acquaintance of ours received prison time after she forged another *friend's* name on a Base Exchange charge account. I don't think whatever she bought was worth federal prison.

There was another confidential case in which a married officer couple was caught in a threesome with a young enlisted girl. The enlisted girl was given a negative discharge that will follow her for the rest of her days. The officer couple was allowed to resign and each received a $30,000 severance package. Who created that rule? These swingers preyed on this young blond and probably gave her money to do it.

Another guy went AWOL for a week, and when we located him he said he was on the run for snitching on some Maryland drug dealers. He was given a urinalysis which turned up positive. He may have been home free had he not told his office that he was out of town at the funeral of his sister. The office took up a collection and sent flowers to his home town. When the money was returned, the investigators were dispatched.

Some were caught in the drug-testing scam, "Give me pee and I'll pay you." It didn't work – the second party was pregnant. I thought Lemay Street had the rocket scientists.

Rick Larson transferred to Seattle and was replaced by Chief Rich Angel. I knew something was wrong when someone said, "Good morning, Chief," and he said, "What is so fucking good about it?" Rich was unique. He was both fun and mean at the same time. It wasn't personal, racial, or anything we could grasp. He just had bad days. We learned not – repeat, not – to make any mistakes on his bad day. The next day he would invite us to his house for a party or take all of us to the Tenth Hole. He didn't take any crap from customers, managers, or whoever else entered the Persru. I liked Chief Angel because he was hard but fair. I think he liked the brothers more than anyone else. For some reason, we all got along with him.

Chief Angel was married to a woman officer in the building. I do recall her walking behind him into the building on some mornings. Either that was their rule or she was just too damn slow for him. Knowing him, it was more likely the latter. Nevertheless, it was enjoyable to see an E-7 married to an O-3 lieutenant. It probably wasn't a great sight to the senior officers who witnessed this relationship. It was 1989, and things were changing. In the past she would have lost her career for dating him.

Shortly after Chief Angel's arrival, Petty Officer First Class Doris Hull approached me about a job. Doris had more years than any other African American woman in the Coast Guard. It was an honor for her to know my name. She was highly respected and was working in the Commandant of the Coast Guard's office. She approached me in the hallway to ask if I was interested in replacing her in the Commandant's Office once she made chief. I loved the Persru but it was a sweatshop.

I said, "Yes, just let me know what I need to do."

She said that someone would contact me. If this occurred it would be a tremendous thing. I would be the first African American man to work directly for the head of the entire Coast Guard. There were other guys who worked for the Master Chief of the Coast Guard or drove for the commandant, but not one to push papers for them.

Within a week someone contacted our office chief, CWO Miller, to inform him that the Commandant's Office wanted to interview me as soon as possible. He called a meeting with the Persru leadership and said, "We may be losing one of our star performers."

Chief Angel was livid. He squirmed in his chair and said "shit" about five times. He didn't want to retrain someone to handle the group of records I had accumulated. I was by that time responsible for maintaining files on nearly 150 administratively attached members. These members were assigned to overseas areas, colleges, and defense contractors around the world. I had become good at it and the job required tact that the new, more arrogant breed of yeoman didn't seem to have. CWO Miller said, "What in the hell do you want me to do about it? It's the Commandant's Office who's calling. This is a good thing. They only ask us for people."

I welcomed this change because I was starting to compile my own blotter full of leave papers. In addition, the original crew started to transfer one by one. The writing was on the wall. No more 3:30 jokefests. It had begun to get tedious and I needed another challenge. I'd recently taken the E-6 Servicewide Examination and had a possibility of making yeoman first class. A few days later I received an interview with Captain James Roy and CWO4 Richard Faults. The interview went extremely well. The Personnel Department was notified to transfer me from the Persru to the Commandant's Office. It would be a career-altering move.

Chapter 28
Work for Admiral Who?

---------------------☼-------------------

Istarted working on the Commandant's staff in April 1989. Admiral Paul Yost and Vice Admiral Clyde T. Lusk served as commandant and vice commandant, respectively. Admiral Yost was the leader who closed most of the Coast Guard clubs, including the Icebreaker Lounge. He also ordered all beards removed other than those of members who had medical reasons for keeping them. I could feel the intensity in this office. I could go for weeks without seeing him because he rarely visited the back office.

On a few occasions he would enter our area and yell out, "How's the back office doing?"

We would all rise to attention and CWO Faults would speak for us: "We're doing fine, sir!"

That was the extent of the commandant's interaction with a major portion of his staff.

There were a few other petty officers in this office and one civilian, Carolyn Lawton. I had previously worked with one of the petty officers, Dan, during my days in Enlisted Assignments. Dan was a chain smoker and lit up at his desk. No way could he do that now. He said that was okay as long as he blew the smoke into the hallway. Since he sat by the door, it wasn't a problem. Dan knew that office like the back of his hand and was the backup for Mr. Faults. Mr. Faults had first arrived in the office as a first-class yeoman in 1977. He made chief, and they changed the position to a chief's slot. He made warrant officer and they changed it to a warrant slot. He rode warrant officer from CWO1 to CWO4, and had served for 30 years. He provided continuity for the most important office in the Coast Guard. Who was going to tell the commandant that he must transfer?

April was the other petty officer and would soon depart the Coast Guard. Yeoman Second Class Jennifer Hope replaced her. We handled every single document destined for the two Coast Guard leaders. The responsibility level was tremendous. I couldn't believe that I was working for the head of the entire Coast Guard. My primary job was to manage the congressional and classified correspondence. This was probably the most critical job in the office. Admiral Yost didn't want his documents to return to the Hill late. I had to master the *Who's Who* on Capitol Hill.

On one occasion, we were asked to save the ashes of the late Admiral Benkert, who had previously served as commandant. I kept them in the safe until one of our ships arrived for an event and would take the ashes out for burial at sea. One particular afternoon Admiral Benkert came calling. We kept the safe slightly open to avoid slamming it each time it was opened or closed. On this occasion, it slowly slid completely open, squeaking along the way. We all looked at each other and said, "Admiral Benkert is ready to go." That was enough for me. I kept the damn thing closed no matter how loud it sounded when it slammed shut.

Not only did Admiral Benkert reside in the safe, it also contained the complete files from the *Blackthorn* and the *Cuyahogo* – the last two Coast Guard cutters to sink and take lives with them. I also maintained the file for Simas Kudirka, who defected by jumping off a Russian ship onto a Coast Guard cutter only to be returned back to the Russian ship. It changed international asylum law as we know it today. He was convicted of treason and sentenced to 10 years in prison. Four years after his incarceration, it was discovered that his mother was born in Brooklyn and had returned to Russia as a young child, technically making him a U.S. citizen. He eventually returned to America to reside in New England. With that batch of goodies in the safe, who cared about classified documents?

It was amazing to watch the inner workings of the Coast Guard from the top down. Captain Roy was the gatekeeper for the admirals. He was a huge guy and commanded respect. I sensed that he would soon be an admiral himself. It was strange to see other admirals practically kiss his rear in order to get their issues before the commandant. Since these officers were senior to him, I'm sure it put him in an awkward position. It didn't seem to bother him; he handled them magnificently and with great respect. I learned from that.

The next manager in our part of the office was Commander Tom Jamison, who was the commandant's speechwriter. He stood about six-foot-four and was dark-haired and chiseled. He looked like the actor Alec Baldwin. No man-crush here, but I must say he was handsome. He had tremendous class – until he whipped out the peanut butter and onion sandwich for lunch one day. I learned a lot from his style. He was the smoothest white guy in the entire building (after Rick Larson transferred). I sensed the sisters in the building had a crush on him as well. He was one of those *General Hospital* kind of guys. Whenever he sat in the outer office, I could sense an increase in female traffic. The secretaries increased their document pickup. I assumed he liked looking at them, too, since he knew every last one of their names. We could look, but touching was out of the question.

We had drivers, cooks, and security personnel – who would arrive armed – at the push of a button. Each person had an emergency button in his or her desk that would call Coast Guard Intelligence if someone posed a threat to the office. If someone came in on me, I would not use the button. I wanted to use the Curb 60 in my desk. Pepper spray can't hold a stick to the old Curb. It will literally put an attacker's eyes out. We tested it by wiping a little of it on the skin under our eyes. The skin felt horribly hot and irritated. It seemed as if someone had placed a hot blade on my skin. I couldn't wait to use it on some derelict asking to reverse a dishonorable discharge or to fix a pay problem.

The admiral's secretaries were Susan and Edna. They were extremely nice ladies and set the entire tone of professionalism in the office. The heart and soul of the office was Ms. Carolyn Lawton. She was the only civilian in our immediate area and her role was supporting the senior executive liaison from the State Department, Rick Scissors. Carolyn was tiny but feisty. She didn't take any crap from anyone and would say exactly what was on her mind. She was known for telling Mr. Faults that if she would have been my mother, she would have smothered me at birth. I don't know what I did, but that wasn't good. She was my girl and the only other African American in the office. We laughed at anything and everything. We kept each other sane. Carolyn had two kids of her own, and I can best describe her son as being like Theo Huxtable from the *Cosby Show*. The stories she told of him made all of us laugh.

Practical jokes and the myriad of visitors made our critical jobs enjoyable. On one occasion, Commander Jamison wanted his wall-size world map hung on the wall in his office. We called Chief Warrant Officer Murth, who was the facility manager for flag officers and their immediate staff. He looked at the frame and commenced to tie fishing line around some hooks that hung from atop the drywall near the ceiling. Dan and I looked at each other and quietly thought, "No Way!" How in the hell did he think this little line would hold a six-foot-by-seven-foot picture frame?

We began to say, "Sir, do you think …"

He cut us off and said in a curt voice, "This line is 500 pounds of pressure per inch."

It sounded like some physics crap that forced us to say, "Whatever," and walk out of the office. Thirty minutes after installation, CRASH, BAM, BOOM. The commander was out to lunch so we knew he was safe. We all began to laugh profusely. Someone picked up the phone and called Administrative Services and said, "Could you send Mr. Murth up to the Commandant's Office and have him bring a broom and dustpan?"

Dan was the chief of the practical jokes. On one Monday morning he completely reversed Mr. Faults's large wooden desk, but kept the desktop supplies in their original position. I couldn't tell the difference until I noticed the leg well was facing the outer office. When Mr. Faults arrived he smacked his knees as he tried to sit at his desk. He never said a word or made a peep. We nearly burst our hearts trying not to laugh. He continued to work for the rest of the morning with his legs scrunched against his desk. We went to lunch and returned to find the desk turned around correctly. The issue never came up again. It was truly amazing.

Dan had a ritual of leaving at 1530 sharp. He opened the office at 0600 and felt no need to stay late. On Friday, Mr. Faults decided to turn the clock hands up two hours and placed it at 1525. Dan never realized the change. He logged off the computer, arranged the papers on his desk, and grabbed his hat.

He said, "Have a nice weekend," and walked directly out of the office. We lost it. He returned five minutes later and continued to work without saying a word.

They were brutal practical jokers in that office. We just sucked it up and laughed on the inside when the joke was on us, too embarrassed to discuss it. The next week, Mr. Scissors fell asleep at his desk. Unfortunately for him, Dan found him. Dan pushed his clock ahead an hour. At some point in the afternoon, Mr. Scissors woke up and stormed out of the office, thinking he was late for an important meeting. He returned to the office smiling five minutes later and reentered his suite, not saying a word.

The office was pure fun. We worked together like a basketball team. Everyone had a role and played it well. It was amazing that the most critical spot in the Coast Guard was the most relaxed. The back-office tone was set by Vice Admiral Lusk. When he wasn't signing the important documents on his desk, he sat and chatted with us. It was the total opposite of Admiral Yost, although Admiral Yost's style wasn't a bad thing. It was what it was: a matter of styles.

We would soon undergo a change of command. I can vividly recall compiling recommendation packages for the next commandant. I personally handled the package for the junior-most admiral vying for the job, RADM J. W. Kime. RADM Kime was in charge of the Office of Marine Safety and Environmental Protection. He led the post-Exxon Valdez oil spill operations and had made a name for himself. In his request letter he posed the question, "Who in the Coast Guard is better qualified and has the expertise to deal with emerging environmental issues?" No one, I suppose. He was selected. I felt a sense of joy simply because I'd worked his package and noticed that statement. He was the eleventh-ranked person in the Coast Guard. Everyone above him was destined for retirement.

It was an impressive approach and highly successful, considering the impact on Prince William Sound. He skipped the rank of vice admiral completely and received his fourth star. All I cared about was whether he would continue to say, "How's the back-office doing?" Since we were the ones who put the documents on their desks, it would be great if they spent a little time checking on the crew. I was looking forward to the new team, especially Captain Roy's replacement, Captain Richard Ferr. I'd heard from one of the African American leaders in the building, Chief Eddy, that he was extremely nice. The office was running fine as it was, but the change was welcome. Captain Roy made rear admiral and was transferred to the war college next door at Fort McNair. I knew he would make it and I wouldn't be surprised if he made commandant himself one day.

The new regime reported aboard in May 1990 and we could feel the change in styles immediately. Admiral Kime frequently passed through the back office and made us feel like we were a major cog in keeping the operation running. Captain Ferr's style put everyone at ease, especially Carolyn. She was the only civilian in our portion of the office and she felt like an outsider at times; military culture has a way of unknowingly pushing civilians aside. The captain consistently joked with us, but expected nothing but professionalism.

My responsibility in handling congressional documents increased. I was allowed to determine each constituent's issue, who should sign it, and, most importantly to the admiral, how long it should take the Coast Guard to respond to it. They didn't want a drop-off in our submissions to the Hill or to the Department of Transportation. Our productivity increased due to the new relaxed environment. The Exxon-Valdez issues subsided somewhat, but we found ourselves in the middle of Desert Storm. The classified documents increased in size and scope. We never really noticed because we were working hard and playing hard at the same time.

The main reason we didn't notice the increase was because of the food. Edna kept us well-fed with such desserts as her signature dirt pudding. At one of our luncheons, she placed a flower pot on the table. It had silk flowers in it and gummy worms sprawled inside as well. As I looked at her, she took the plants out and plunged her spoon directly into the black dirt. She came up with a mixture of Oreo cookie crumbs, vanilla pudding, and Cool Whip. If you haven't had this layered delicacy, you are missing something special. Most of the others had seen it and didn't act surprised when she began to eat out of the flower pot.

Dan transferred to Portsmouth, Virginia and was replaced by Tom. He was a bright young kid who loved rap and the hip-hop culture. It was nothing to see him zooming down the streets near

HQ while kicking mad sounds out of his ride. Needless to say, Tom owned more rap music than I did. We also received a new commandant's driver, Greg Lombardi. This Italian guy came right out of the *Sopranos*, and drove like a bat out of hell. Whenever I rode with him, he would make trips through some of the roughest areas in D.C. His favorite car wash for the admiral's vehicle was on New York Avenue, Northwest. He was more comfortable going there than I was. He could put on the flashing blue light and we would be there in five minutes. Unfortunately, my stomach would be in the trunk when we arrived.

Greg was fun to be around. He was also a storekeeper by trade and he handled budget items. He was the first driver to request civilian attire to fit in with other executive drivers in the area better. It was weird. While parking in front of some of the most important buildings in D.C., the police would ask him to move along while in uniform. They would leave him alone or let him circle in civilian clothes. Go figure?

Greg wasn't the only bat-out-of-hell driver. Captain Ferr once asked me to go to Bolling Air Force Base exchange with him to pick up something. That was really cool for me. Not since Captain Phelps had a senior person treated me as a son or little brother. He also drove a candy-apple-red Nissan 280Z. I recall pulling out of the parking level and stopping at the exchange. I can't recall anything else.

We were usually treated with the utmost respect in this assignment – at least most of the time. On one occasion, I was asked to get a late congressional letter from a HQ office. I visited the office and was directed to an African American commander who was in the process of preparing it. I respectfully advised him that the admiral wanted the document to leave the building before close of business. He told me that it was 3:30 and he would miss his car pool. I told him that it was the admiral's wishes and left his office.

At 4:30 he arrived with the document. He looked around and realized that I was the only one around at the time. He said, "Is the Admiral here to sign it?"

I replied, "No, sir. He had to leave for the day."

He began to raise his voice to me and said, "You mean to tell me that I missed my ride home and no one's here to sign it?"

I told him that it wasn't really his concern, considering that I had access to an autopen with signatures for the three seniormost admirals in the building and the Secretary of Transportation. I could put the large, 2½-foot disc in the machine, the document under the pen, and hit the pedal. Done.

I didn't really care for him, anyway, because he had a reputation for not speaking to junior African American military personnel. As his decibels elevated, I became calmer. He didn't realize Vice Admiral Daniel was standing behind him. The new vice was a burly, salty kind of coastie. He was so salty that he would walk out of his office and not notice his shirttail hanging out of his pants. The vice commandant! He would also eat lunch at a small table in the middle of the cafeteria at times instead of eating in the flag mess with the other admirals and senior executives. All I can recall was the admiral giving the commander the come-here signal with his index finger. The commander followed him like a little puppy dog. I was all smiles.

That tour was so meaningful to me because it tremendously enhanced my professionalism and confidence. It also had its perks. I was able to attend the Senior Petty Officer Leadership and Management (SPOLAM) course in Petaluma. It lasted two weeks and it was a blast. I was picked up at the airport by my old *Basswood* office mate, Les Trailor. He and a bunch of friends picked me up and drove me to the base. We were supposed to hook up again, but that was the last time I saw him. He subsequently retired and I've lost touch with him. Petaluma brought back so many memories. Mike Macon was teaching Yeoman School and my buddy from my Enlisted Assignments days, Kelvin Washington, was stationed there as well. It was a mini reunion. I wasn't 18 anymore and I could really smell the roses, and the cows. I arrived in late November and was able to enjoy a few Christmas parties in sunny California.

Shortly after SPOLAM, I was able to make another short trip to Cali. This trip was as short as imaginable. I arrived in the office one morning and noticed that the admiral was scheduled to visit Pacific Area (Pacarea) and return the next day. I said, "What I wouldn't do to go on this trip."

Captain Ferr overheard me and came out to his doorway. He said, "If you can get to Air Station Washington by 1000, you can go!"

I looked at Mr. Faults and asked if I could get an overnight bag from home. He said yes and I was off. This time *I* was the speeder. I called Mike at 4 a.m. Pacific time and told him that I would be there. He told me to take a bus from the airport and his wife Cindy would pick me up from the stop in Marin County. That was perfect.

I flew on the latest commandant's plane, a Gulfstream. We were there in four hours and I was able to sit in the cockpit for the landing at San Francisco International. It was too cool. When we landed, the Pacarea admiral asked if I needed anything. I told him that I needed to get to the airport to catch a bus across the Golden Gate. He directed the duty driver to take me to the airport and pick me up in the morning – case closed. For the cost of the $10 bus ride, I was able to break bread with my best friend and his family clear across country. It doesn't get any better than that.

On the return flight, I was able to sit in the cockpit as we entered DC airspace. As the plane cruised on autopilot down the Potomac River, I got a glimpse of the Georgetown waterfront on the left and the large office buildings in Roslyn, Virginia on the right. I never realized Georgetown University had a football team until I saw their field. When I think of Georgetown, I think of Patrick Ewing, Alonzo Mourning and Allen Iverson. About 90 seconds out, the pilot resumed control of the plane and made a quick right turn past the Pentagon, and before I knew it, we were touching down. There is nothing like sitting in the cockpit of a jet while landing. Unfortunately, my stomach remained in coach.

We discovered shortly after the California trip that Captain Ferr would soon be promoted to admiral. This was amazing. He was such a firm leader and a wonderful person. He led by respect and responsibility, in reverse order, that is. He gave us the responsibility, and in turn he earned our respect. Other changes in personnel would soon take place. It was time for me to consider moving on. I wasn't given a new tour of duty when I took the job in the commandant's office. I didn't want to transfer again, as I considered Washington my home.

Chief Langdon, who had recently transferred to the recruiting office in Alexandria, Virginia, approached me about an opening is his office. He'd previously worked in the next suite for the Master Chief of the Coast Guard. It was an intriguing opportunity. I'd never thought about being a recruiter and selling the Coast Guard to young people. I mentioned it to Captain Ferr, and he said, "You'll be excellent for recruiting!" It was an option. I could maintain my household one more time. I was halfway through my career and it was time to start developing a marketable skill. Who knows, maybe I could sell cars when I'm finished.

I began to fill out my dreamsheet and put together a recruiting package. Fortunately, the lead recruiting office was two floors up. I was summoned to an interview immediately by an intimidating Master Chief, Bill Crozier. He stood about six-feet six-inches, and the only thing I can recall is that his pinky fingernail was extremely long. I couldn't for the life of me figure out why he let it grow so long. I hoped he used it to pick the wax out of his ears. Anything else would be completely unsafe – for him or her. I thought the interview went well, but I didn't think I'd blown him away.

I was wrong. He said, "Come with me." I followed him down the hall and into the assignment officer's office. He told the assignment officer, "Cut him a set of orders to Recruiting Office Alexandria immediately!"

The guy said, "Not a problem, Master Chief!"

I would soon be a recruiter. What in the hell did that really entail? I couldn't tell you then.

The recently promoted Admiral Ferr departed and I had my traditional transfer party in the back conference room – Chinese food. I would really miss that crew. They were professionals who knew how to separate work from play when it really counted.

Admiral Ferr attended my small party and he said one key thing to me: "You will make warrant officer!" Prior to that, I never thought about making such a transition. The enlisted force and senior officers revered warrant officers. Many mid-level officers thought warrants were pains because of their candor, which is granted by experience. There are times when others see things in me that I fail to see in myself. I had that feeling before, when I'd been told to get out of cars back home. It was an honor for an admiral to say that to me in a room full of people.

In September 1991, I set my sights on Old Town, Alexandria, Virginia.

Chapter 29
1-800-Get-USCG

---------------------☼---------------------

I always thought SK1 Ishman thought of me as a thug. He put me through the ringer early in my training. I suppose he was testing me to see if I could cut it, if I was a leader or a follower. I think that's why he made me right guide, where I stood out in front of the company. I place great importance on my path after boot camp, mainly because my recruiter didn't tell me about my training options. Neither did he place me in the Delayed Entry Program, which would have boosted my time and pay while I waited four months to enter the service. Ironically, he was a brother, too. Maybe he thought a little less of me than SK1 Ishman did, as Ishman didn't get to see my surroundings. I don't think the recruiter expected me to make it through the training.

I'm grateful to my former CC because he cracked the door, but allowed me to kick it in. In 1992 I saw my recruiter, SK2 Bert Stillman, at the Coast Guard's Martin Luther King Memorial Basketball Tournament when I was attending recruiter training at Reserve Training Center Yorktown, Virginia. It was standing room only, and someone yelled, "Stillman, get your ass out of the way." He was videotaping the game.

I politely stood next to him and said, "Is your name Bert?"

He slowly said yes, but began to look at me closely. I reminded him that he'd been my recruiter in 1981. He looked amazed and surprised. I reminded him of his visit to my house and about the orange van that was parked near my home that he wanted to buy. He asked me what my rate was. I replied, "YN1."

Ironically, it was one rank higher than his. After 11 years, he'd failed to put on a stripe. He could now work for me.

215

I reported for duty at Recruiting Office Alexandria, Virginia with no fanfare. There were three other recruiters assigned to the office: Chief Yeoman Chuck Langdon, Electrician's Mate Calvin Erwin, and Boatswain's Mate Vince Patterson. I knew everyone except Vince. They consistently ranked in the top three of all recruiting offices in the nation.

It wasn't long before I had my first firm discussion with the chief. I was new man on the totem pole, and I expected a certain amount of extra duties or hazing. I soon learned the ropes and began to develop my own clientele of recruits. Calvin gave me my first applicant. They didn't tell me that he had been disqualified for drug use. They told me that all I had to do was process a waiver package on him. It didn't seem difficult. As part of the waiver package, I was asked to make a home visit and assess his living situation. He lived in a sprawling suburban home, but it was crowded with many family members. They were sleeping everywhere in a darkened home at 12 noon. I processed him for service, and he was disqualified again for drugs. I felt somewhat set up, because HQ assessed each recruiter's decision-making process as well.

I decided that I would pursue my own recruits and not work with someone whom the other recruiters had once processed. The chief and Calvin began to task me with a lot of odd requests. At times I felt that Calvin was creating the taskers. I didn't mind, because it would serve me well in my learning curve. I sensed that something else was going on, but I couldn't put my finger on it. After all, it was still the Coast Guard, not the most diverse organization in the world.

On one Monday morning, I woke up at 0300 in order to drive the new applicants to the military processing station in Dorsey, Maryland. They had to catch their plane for Cape May and it was imperative that they arrived before 0530. After returning to the office, Chief Langdon asked me to solicit interviewers for our officer-recruiting drive. He said that I knew everyone at Headquarters and it would be easy. No problem for me. I got back on the road and worked the halls of Headquarters for interviewers.

The next morning he said, "Tony, could you change the message on the answering machine because you are a DJ and you have a nice voice."

Vince looked at me funny, and I returned the glare. I told the chief, "Chief, the next time you want me to do something, just ask me. You can keep the personal comments or extra details to yourself!" I was fed up with the sly remarks related to work issues.

I sensed he was ticked off, because he immediately stormed out of the office. I mentioned to him that we needed to talk. He ignored me and continued out of the office. Calvin soon followed. I sensed he thought I was submissive because of my happy-go-lucky personality in the commandant's office. It wasn't the constant requests that bothered me, but the tone in which he gave them. He never gave those orders unless Calvin was in the office.

As soon as they left the office, Vince said, "Man, you should have seen his face! I was wondering when you were going to say something!"

I told Vince that I didn't mind the orders, but I didn't like the side comments. We were all men and if they needed something, just ask. I thought that the chief never forgave me for speaking up. Our relationship was never the same from that point forward. I had four years to go. So be it. I was sent there to work, not to love someone. Vince didn't care, either; it was comic relief for him. Vince was imposing at six-three and 230. He looked like a tight end who would rip somebody's head off. In reality he was an articulate teddy bear and one of the best recruiters in the nation. They couldn't afford to mess with him. They lived by his numbers.

We finally moved into our new digs across town. Very nice. New furniture, kitchen, storage space, and shower facilities. We didn't have a say-so on the furnishings. The chief's wife picked out the furniture, color, and everything else. That was okay, because it was better than the Old Town office. The new offices were attached to expensive high-rise condos with an indoor pool and a carpeted indoor basketball court. We could use the facilities free of charge. We at last had a place to host clients properly — and a nice toilet. I sensed that this place would boost the morale of the office. We also received a new car and van. Prior to the move, I was tasked with picking up one of the government vehicles from a separate lot and bringing it to the office. The best thing was not getting out of a warm car to drive a cold one. I could walk directly into the office and start work.

The only way to learn recruiting skills was to listen to the other recruiters in action. I listened to Calvin a lot. Calvin was a fine recruiter and knowledgeable about policy. Vince's recruiting style consisted of intense energy and a since of humor. He literally laughed kids into the Coast Guard. The chief had his own office, but sat in the outer office with us at times. I still sensed a bit of tension between us.

On one occasion Calvin advised a recruit that we were not taking applicants with GEDs. He also stressed to the applicant that he would have to try again in a few months because GED applicants could only make up 1% of our annual recruiting goal, which we had already met for the year.

A few hours later, I received a call asking if we took GEDs. Chief Langdon must have been listening to my responses to calls from inside his office. I began to tell the applicant on the phone that we would not accept GEDs, and before I could finish by saying "at this time," the chief stormed out there and yelled, "Didn't we tell you that we took GEDs?"

I put the person on hold, and said, "Chief, if you allow me to finish my conversation with the applicant, I would clarify that info with him."

I finished my conversation by telling the person that we normally take GEDs, but that we were booked for the year.

I felt that he was waiting for me to slip on something and had immediately pounced on me. It was an embarrassing situation. I knew it wouldn't be long before we had another issue.

I received my evaluation in the spring of 1992 and my communication marks were notably low. I asked him how my communication marks could be so low while I was actively putting people in the service. I also asked how he could make that assessment without seeing me speak publicly or to anyone outside of the office, especially since 60% of my time was spent outside of the office. I told him that he'd only observed the side of me that has to respond to walk-in applicants.

Walk-in applicants are more likely to have issues in their background that could result in a disqualification or fraudulent enlistment. I was a bit tougher on walk-in applicants than individuals I personally recruited in the community. Case in point: I sent two applicants for a test and physical, and one of them told me that the other had mentioned that he killed someone in DC was trying to get away. Needless to say, that applicant slept with one eye open. When they returned, I was pleased to find out that the alleged killer received a score of five on the entrance test. I politely told him that he would have to study very hard and come back in a couple of months. I mentioned this to the chief and he said that I had a point. He said that we would visit the next school that called the office. Twenty minutes later, the D.C. Street Academy called and asked if we could attend their Career Day event. Vince and I looked at each other and smiled. It was on.

The chief accompanied Vince and me on our excursion through Northeast D.C. I could see the chief's nervousness as we approached the fully-barred high school that was the size of an elementary school. He said, "Is this it?"

We said, "Yeah, it is."

We entered the auditorium and took our place among many professionals. We were asked to stand up and introduce ourselves. The first guy stood up and said his name and agency.

Someone yelled out, "Who's that fag?"

The guy quickly sat down.

I said to myself, "Welcome to D.C. Public Schools." Vince stood up and introduced himself in a confident way and the crowd applauded him. The same thing happened to me. Madeline Wood, a gorgeous TV personality for Black Entertainment Television (BET), stood up in an extremely tight purple suede skirt suit and someone yelled, "GOD DAMN!" His voice sounded as deep as Shaq's.

We tried to keep a straight-face as the chief was astonished. He was next. He stood up and said, "Chief Langdon, U. S. Coast Guard" so fast that we could barely understand him. He sat down just as fast as he announced his name. I think they let him slide because he was with us and in the same uniform.

Before long, there was a small commotion in the back near the window. I heard the window slam shut and a girl say, "Ouch!"

A guy yelled, "Bitch, I'll bust your ass!"

Vince and I looked at each other and tried not to laugh. We weren't laughing at the situation, but that Chief Langdon is witnessing this stuff first hand. It seemed that they were arguing over who would close the window at the principal's request. It was a far cry from the suburban schools in Northern Virginia he was use to.

We met a bunch of kids and passed out a few goodies. We noticed that the plastic letter openers that Headquarters gave us to pass out to school children were shaped like prison shanks. I could visualize students running through the halls screaming, with objects with Coast Guard emblems on them lodged in their backs. We promptly decided not to give those out. We did give out blue-and-gold bumper stickers. We ran out of those quickly. Soon afterwards we noticed the lovely vice principal walking down the hallway. As she passed us in her nice, blue designer suit, we noticed that she had at least eight bumper stickers on her backside. We beckoned to her with the come-here gesture and slowly began to pull the stickers from her beautiful suit.

I continued to keep my eye on the chief, who by that time was speechless. You see, D.C. Street Academy was the place for students who were kicked out of every other school in the District. It was also a school for recently paroled juveniles or single parents attempting to complete their high school requirements. In short, it was kind of rough.

They had a wonderful lunchtime spread for the guests. Lunch hour was sort of uneventful. I suspected it was because there were no students in the school. They all left the school by car or on foot and returned with Chinese food, Wendy's, McDonald's, Popeye's Chicken, or some combination of these. The scene amazed me. Not only were we *not* allowed to leave the school when I was a child, we surely couldn't return with Chinese food. I looked at the chief and said, "Things have changed."

Things finally calmed down around 2 p.m. Vince and I decided to sit on the floor with some students in one of the carpeted classrooms and shoot the breeze. The chief sat on a nearby desk. Shortly thereafter, a guy and a girl had the most interesting conversation I have ever witnessed in a school.

He said, "Girl, what are you talking about? I'm the shit!"

She said, "You ain't got nothing but a two-minute egg."

The chief was looking back and forth like a tennis match.

The guy said, "I'll take you in the basement and bust you out."

She said, "With what?"

He pulled up his shirt to disclose a nappy chest and said, "With this!"

She said, "That ain't nothing."

He pulled down the front of his pants to show an even more beaded pubic area and said, "What about this?"

While Vince and I were rolling on the carpet laughing, the chief jumped up and yelled, "Now, that's enough! It's time to go." I suppose he couldn't take any more.

We politely got up and told the students goodbye. They gave us hand slaps and hugs, and we were out. I snickered all the way back to the car.

In the car, the chief said, "I had no idea what you guys go through in these schools. Are all the schools like this?"

We lied and said, "Yeah."

We returned to the office, and the next day my communication skills mark was raised to a six out of a possible seven. Vince and I understood that these visits were not about whether we could put a young person in the Coast Guard. We attended these types of schools just to show a positive presence, spark change, and generate career ideals among the students. If we were able to get around the red tape and put one of these kids in the Guard, it was icing on the cake. The Coast Guard didn't take recruits who were single parents, were attached to the criminal justice system, or had three or more moving violations. Our rules eliminated as many as eight out of 10 inner-city applicants. The qualifying score of 40 or higher on the Armed Forces Battery Test (ASVAB) didn't help, either. What a great learning experience for the chief!

After one year in recruiting, things began to change drastically. Calvin retired and Vince was accepted to Officer Candidate School. Chief Langdon applied to become Recruiter in Charge of the office in Houston, his hometown. We had some great times with the chief, but I felt an underlying uneasiness after the time I spoke up about the answering machine. I kept the faith that it wasn't a racial issue because the Coast Guard, at that time, was making progress in diversity and the acceptance of others. At least on paper.

Senior Chief Engineer Gary Neese, Health Service Technician Karla Timmons, and Aviation Machinist's Mate Willie

Robinson replaced them. We began to roll right along without missing a beat. Gary was adamant that we couldn't recruit sitting in the office. He insisted that we hit the road, and that's what we did. Willie handled all of DC. Karla took care of Northern Virginia and I oversaw Southern Maryland. We maintained our status as a top-three recruiting office.

Whenever I stayed in the office alone, something weird happened. As I began to close the office one Friday evening, two applicants entered and inquired about joining the Coast Guard. One guy remained quiet and I could barely understand the second gentleman. He talked as if his mouth was wired shut. I quickly gave him the medical pre-screening form. I wanted to weed out whatever issue he had as quickly as possible. I sensed that the second gentleman wasn't interested in military service at all. I suspect he was the transportation for the other guy. The wired-mouth guy wrote on the pre-screening form that he had "Coppersessive Rubution Cunseling."

I stared at it for a few seconds before I said, "What is this?"

He said, "That's Comprehensive Rehabilitation Counseling."

As I looked at the traffic backing up in the direction of the Woodrow Wilson Bridge, which I had to cross, I just shook my head. I said, "What is wrong with your mouth? Is your mouth wired shut?"

Speaking from a crooked mouth he said, "No, that's from the Lithium I'm on."

I was through. I said, "Well, here is the name of the book you'll need to study. Please pick up a copy of your driving record from Pikesville Maryland." I would have said anything to get him out of there. As soon as they left, our regular homeless lady entered and held up her "Hungry" sign. I gave her a buck, escorted her out, and locked the door behind us.

Senior Chief Neese was selected for chief warrant officer and was given orders to leave recruiting. I was expecting my third chief in three years. Before he was scheduled to leave, we were informed that our office had to lose one person. I suppose four people were too many to cover large portions of two states and the District of Columbia. We were furious, and worried as well. This meant that Karla, Willie, or I would have to leave when the new chief arrived. I still had about 18 months to go on that tour.

Willie had three years to go and Karla had nearly four. None of us was ready for an early transfer.

While attending the Recruiting Officers in Charge Conference at the Xerox Training Center in Leesburg, Virginia, I was surprised to find out that I would be the next recruiter in charge of Recruiting Office Alexandria, Virginia. This was as scary as it was an honor. I would be responsible for the whole shebang. My peers, Willie and Karla, would now work for me. I also had two reservists, Storekeepers First Class Beverly Barns and Antonio Sanchez. I also was responsible for two college students who were undergoing a minority scholarship program. We put minority students at historically Black or Hispanic colleges through their last two years in school in exchange for their recruiting efforts during school and three years afterwards as commissioned officers – a great deal for them, and a tremendous amount of anxiety for me. I gladly accepted the role, and to my amazement we never missed a beat. Moreover, no one had to leave early. I also found out that Senior Chief Neese had recommended this idea to the head of recruiting, who had agreed and authorized it. This move made me the only E-6 recruiter in charge in the Coast Guard.

It later dawned on me that a previous case may have stood out in the mind of the captain in charge of recruiting. I had a woman recruit who was slightly overweight when she first applied. She also had a suicide attempt in her medical file. She wanted to enter the service so badly that she not only lost the weight, she became a fitness instructor as well. In addition, the medical processing facility decided that her "suicidal gesture" had been a minor attention-getter aimed at a former boyfriend and should not keep her out of the Coast Guard.

All was well until the morning she was scheduled to fly to Cape May. It seems the Baltimore area officer in charge, who controlled our operations at the processing center, decided on his own that she wasn't a qualified candidate. This chief overruled a number of physicians, counselors, and me. She called me from the facility in tears. I immediately called the master chief in Chesapeake and he sided with the Baltimore recruiter. I couldn't believe it.

It's funny how small the world is, and even more so the Coast Guard. We received word that an irate Coast Guard captain was on his way to see the head of recruiting over an unknown issue from our office, and that we needed to go to HQ to address it immediately. Ironically, the applicant was the captain's daughter and he had monitored the entire recruiting process. When we arrived at the building, the senior chief noticed the applicant and the captain entering the building together. We were too late to head them off at the pass and prevent them from entering the Recruiting Division unannounced.

When we reached the office, the two were already discussing the issue with the captain. I tried to eavesdrop on the conversation but wasn't successful. When she came out, she smiled at me as she left the office with her father.

The recruiting captain asked for the senior chief and me to come into his office. He asked me, "Why did you go the extra mile to get that young lady in the Coast Guard?"

I replied, "Sir, I have been working with her for six months and everything I asked her to do to become eligible, she did it. I just believed in her."

The captain said, "Good call. I believe in her too." He picked up the phone and called our bosses in Chesapeake, Virginia and asked the commanding officer if there were any openings in Cape May – *Today?* From what I can tell, the person on the other end said, "Yes!" The captain hung up the phone and said, "Get her on a plane to Cape May immediately."

We said, "No problem, sir!"

I took her back up to the processing station and she departed for boot camp on the next available plane. After a few weeks, we were informed that she broke her ankle in training. I was devastated. I called up Cape May and was told not to worry. She had impressed the entire base with her enthusiasm. They decided to let her heal for eight weeks and resume her training. She graduated after four months when most recruits depart in two. Most go to ships, but she went to Coast Guard Station Miami. That's why I believed in her.

Leading an office presented other problems that I mostly kept to myself. A friend once recommended our services to a young woman who she saw working at a car wash. The lady arrived one evening prior to closing time. I was alone in the office. After realizing who she was and who sent her, I began to screen her.

When I finished the screening and informed her that she was in too much debt for us to put her in the service immediately, she began to look sad. I turned around in my chair to get a new box of Kleenex from the cabinet behind me. When I turned back around, she had pulled her skin-tight white jeans down.

I sat there with my mouth wide open, nervous as hell. I politely told her, "Miss, you don't have to do that! Would you please pull your pants up and I will do whatever I can to get you in the Coast Guard." I knew that I couldn't, but it was the fastest way to get her out of my office. Moreover, I wasn't about to lose my job over a situation like that. After she left, I put her application in the back of my applicant box and I never heard from her again.

When all was said and done, I had enlisted over 160 enlisted members in my four years. We processed so many officers for entrance that we were considered officer recruiting experts. We were so good at recruiting people with degrees that the selection boards had a problem with continuously selecting our applicants. They didn't want it to seem as if we were receiving preferential treatment since we were the closest office to Headquarters.

It had become time for me to move on from recruiting, but I had no clue where I wanted to work. I really didn't care as long as it was inside the Beltway. I decided to visit my old Enlisted Assignments Branch and see what was available first hand.

I ran into Ms. Felicia Chapperell. She had only worked for the Coast Guard for approximately 40 years. She said, "Tony, what are you up to?"

I said, "I'm recruiting but it's time to move on."

She followed me to the Detailer's Office and said, "Give him anything he wants" and walked away. She really had nothing to do with enlisted assignments, but she reigned supreme in that division.

The detailer looked at his computer screen and said, "I see you were on the *Basswood*, so sea time isn't an issue." Then, to my amazement, he said, "I have an opening at the ICC, do you want it?"

I said, "Hell, yeah!"

The ICC was the Coast Guard Intelligence Coordination Center in Suitland, Maryland, housed in a plush, top-secret Navy building ten minutes from my house. I was totally familiar with them because I'd had their service records when I was in the Persru. Intel, here I come!

Chapter 30
How Did I Get a Clearance?

------------------☼------------------

The assignment at the ICC required me to update my secret security clearance to Top Secret/Special Compartmented Information (TS/SCI). This is one of those "If I tell you, I'll have to shoot you" clearances. I was worried about my surroundings in Detroit coming back to haunt me. We never truly know how people that we may have left behind feel about us. They could tell an investigator anything. They would know it worked when they'd see me back on the block, next to them. I was confident that I didn't leave any enemies behind. I was right. The investigators visited Lemay Street, and I suspect that they said, "If he can make it out of here, he's fine with me!"

I was concerned that a separate internal investigation would take place, one in which someone in my chain of command would feel that I was living above my means or paygrade. Two Coast Guard petty officers, who happened to be friends of mine, were investigated that same year because they'd bought a house and car in the same year. The investigations were terminated when it was discovered that their wives were high-ranking government employees.

I was in the same boat. I was asked to come to the ICC for a security interview. Since it would have taken an act of Congress for me to gain entry into the National Maritime Intelligence Center (NMIC), which housed the ICC, I thought it best that they interview me at my new home. At least it wouldn't be a surprise during the investigation process. All went well and I reported aboard ICC in August 1995.

The NMIC was the most luxurious military facility I had ever seen. It was located adjacent to the Census Bureau, but had a separate security fence. Navy Federal Credit Union members were the only outsiders authorized to enter the facility. It was a beautifully constructed concrete and mirror-glass building that portrayed a futuristic image. There were three floors, or at least that's all we could see. I couldn't help but believe that there were two or three floors beneath us that we didn't know about. You know, Maxwell Smart style. I can neither confirm nor deny their presence.

I arrived at a large atrium only to be escorted to the office by Petty Officer Valerie Chaney, the yeoman I would replace. We had to swipe ID cards and enter pin numbers just to enter the elevator or pass a turnstile. I would perform yeoman duties for the staff of 30 and be the administrative assistant for the commanding officer and technical director (TD), who was basically the civilian executive officer. Right off the bat, the TD and I hit it off. His name was Jim Prondzinski. He was particularly smooth and well-dressed. The first person I thought of was Commander Jamison from the Commandant's Office. I recognized immediately that the TD was highly influential in the operation of the place. Although the captain had the position of power, the TD wielded the intelligence expertise and had developed a wealth of contacts. The captains rotated every three years and the TD provided the continuity. Moreover, everyone came to him for everything, especially advice.

The one thing I recognized about the ICC was the professionalism displayed by the staff. They did their own thing. There wasn't the usual supervisor-subordinate flavor that appears in other military office environments. Some of these individuals were War Room watchstanders. They worked seven days on and seven off, 12 hours each day. When they were off, no one – repeat – no one bugged them. There was no calling them to ask a question or the whereabouts of a project or product. The others were either intelligence or imagery analysts.

I loved all three worlds that existed in that office. I loved going to the Watch Floor. It was a typical three-story room with 20-foot TV screens and world maps. I thought I was in the movie *War Games* every time I dropped off a document or passed a message. The intelligence analysts provided assessments on negative worldwide events and trends. I learned more about the drug business than you can shake a stick at. The Cali and Medellin cartels became household names. There were pictures on the wall of captured international drug lords. I can't recall any names other than Pablo Escobar and José Gacha. They had red Xs through their faces because they were killed during capture.

I learned just as much from the imagery analysts, especially Telephone Technician Brad Nash and Aviation Technician Stan Varner. They were responsible for providing analysis of satellite images of foreign vessels and other items of interest. They taught me the intricacies of imagery. Since I was a geography buff, I became obsessed with satellite footage. I was able to locate an Internet website that sold overhead shots of any address a person entered. I saw my own home from space on a nice, clear day. I also saw the swimming pool in my father's yard. Two days later, the website was turned off. I'm glad that I wasn't the target of a hit squad. Coupled with Mapquest and Yahoo People Search, we couldn't miss a target with the information available today.

One thing that pleased me about the ICC was its diversity, with seven African Americans on a staff of 30. Those were pretty good numbers for a small Coast Guard facility, especially an Intel Unit. The TD literally hand-picked the staff or provided as much input to the process as possible. I think he liked Soul-Food Day during Black History Month; he could count on some good eatin. We celebrated every holiday that existed. I consumed more shepherd's pie, corned beef and cabbage, and green beer than you can shake a stick at. I felt like a leprechaun. During the Black History Month Soul Food Day, I noticed one officer eating a piece of pig's feet the size of my foot. I don't think he intended to get a big one out of the pot, but he didn't know how to break it off. It was hilarious when other African Americans were telling him, "You're a better man than me." I think he felt snookered a little. Nonetheless, he scarfed it down like he'd been there before.

Not only did the ICC party, the NMIC had the best office Christmas party in the Federal Government. Getting 100 people to do the electric slide in a cafeteria at 11 a.m. on a Wednesday before the holiday was something that had everyone else beat. Not only did they dance, they gave away things like $1000 gift certificates to Circuit City. Our annual holiday parties took a back seat to no one. The entire ICC Alumni Association was invited and usually showed up. I had the opportunity to DJ one we had in Annapolis, Maryland. My enjoyment came from the young white kid who asked me to play "Ain't Nothin But a 'G' Thang" by Dr. Dre and Snoop Dog. I politely whispered to him, "I don't think I can get away with that one tonight."

We worked extremely hard at the ICC, but I think we played even harder. I also found more time to give back to the community. I missed recruiting, but not feeling the pressure of quotas. I became a mentor at Suitland High School in suburban Maryland.

This came in handy after a young lady from the school disappeared. They located her dead body a week later behind a local grocery store. She had been stabbed repeatedly and bashed in the head with a broken bathroom sink. When the details were sorted out, she had been killed by a group of youngsters, led by a wannabe Blood. This young adult wanted to start a Bloods chapter in the DC area. They thought she snitched on them in relation to a crime the group committed earlier.

I couldn't sit still. I gave a series of anti-gang speeches to groups of students over a two-week period. It was the least that I could do with what I had experienced in Detroit. My main message was that they don't know how disruptive gang life can be to a neighborhood, school, or environment. To date, there are no large-scale gangs in the African American community in Southern Maryland. They mostly operate in crews of seven to 15. I can't speak for the Hispanic and Asian gangs that are cropping up all over the country, though.

Two tragic events occurred during my tenure at the ICC: the death of Secretary of Commerce Ron Brown, and, you guessed it, The OJ Trial. God bless Ron Brown, but has there been better television than the OJ Trial? No. It had everything. There was the chase, bloody footprints, and things that went bump in the night. Unfortunately, they went bump behind the room of that burnout, Kato Kaelin. Everyone can recall where they were when the police were following the white Bronco down the highway at 20 mph. I was watching the New York Knicks play the Houston Rockets in the NBA Playoffs.

I normally left work at 1630, but never before 5:30 while the OJ trial aired. We turned it on each night and discussed it in great detail. I was one good tie away from being Johnny Cochran.

Fortunately, we didn't have any Mark Furmans in the office to discuss the trial with us. We were very civil. We left no stone unturned. To date, I know more about the details of the OJ trial than the names of my neighbors. I know people perished, but it was good TV.

Unfortunately, I realized something negative after the verdict. I realized that many of my new NMIC friends failed to speak to me immediately after it. This was ironic, because I am a gregariously friendly person, especially in a new building upon arrival. I spoke to everyone during those first two months. I knew exactly who returned the greetings and who didn't. It was obvious that the results of the OJ trial have affected many in this country. I think the results have driven a wedge between the races that will take at least 30 years to overcome, if at all. Some of the same people who spoke to me the morning before the verdict did not speak to me for the remainder of my four years at the NMIC. I never stopped speaking to them. I refused to lower myself to their level even if they continued to diss my greetings.

I never displayed where I stood on the trial because I sensed that it was bigger than the actual murder of two innocent individuals. I didn't want any racial repercussions stemming from my reactions.

That didn't stop Carolyn and Lisa. They were clapping like the mother in Eddie Murphy's *Nutty Professor*, "Hercules, Hercules."

I said, "Well, that's it!" I picked up the rest of my lunch and went to my desk. Everyone else was in total disbelief and silence. I suppose that blacks were too happy and whites were too mad – no in-between.

Things really started to click for me in the intelligence field. I could quickly make a name for myself. Most of it had to do with Mr. Prondzinski hyping the achievements of his folks, which any good boss should do. It wasn't long before I was selected the ICC's Enlisted Person of the Year. This award allowed my photo, which was produced in the building's multi-million dollar photography studio, to be posted in the corridor near the employee's entrance. I'm not a shy guy, but I have many shy moments. Walking by my picture several times a day could get to me, and the words, "Hey that's you" didn't help the situation at all. It did help in convincing my new colleagues that I was a squared-away sailor. I felt the respect that was given to me within this mostly Navy building. It couldn't be a bad thing. In addition, I was allowed to park directly in front of the door for one year. That was worth the price of gold on a cold winter day in metro Washington.

A couple of months after the student's murder and my speeches, I received word that I was the recipient of the National Association for the Advancement of Colored People (NAACP) Roy Williams Meritorious Service Award. Who, me? The ceremony would be held at the annual NAACP Conference in Pittsburgh, Pennsylvania. I was informed that my recruiting efforts, coupled with my anti-gang seminars, were recognized as the best Coast Guardsman effort in the nation in support of community service in minority areas.

I couldn't believe this was happening to me. An ex-BK sitting on stage with Kweisi Mfume, Merly Evers, and C. Delores Tucker! The importance was underscored by the arrival of Secretary of Transportation, Rodney Slater and Admiral Robert Kramek, the Commandant of the Coast Guard. They filled up the commandant's jet with every senior Coast Guard African American and Hispanic officer in Washington, two of whom were my mentors. These were Commander Larry Barrow, who coached our basketball teams as a junior officer from 1982-84, and Commander Steven Rochon, who as a lieutenant junior grade sat with the young enlisted guys each morning to eat breakfast. Commander Rochon would later be selected for admiral, only the second African American admiral in Coast Guard history. He constantly encouraged us by saying that we could excel in the service and make it as far as we wanted to go. The sight of these guys touched me dearly, and I'll be forever grateful for their knowledge and support. My wife was flown up to Pittsburgh to experience the event with me. She'll take a free trip anywhere.

Pittsburgh is one of the most underrated cities in America. I thought I would see old smokestacks from condemned factories. I was surprised to see some of the loveliest high-rises in the country. The Pittsburgh Plate Glass (PPG) Building looks like an 80-story glass castle. The downtown area was completely clean, and the subway system was free, unless one crossed the river. We didn't have to walk anywhere. The NAACP chartered buses to take us from event to event. I recommend Pittsburgh to anyone.

Especially downtown. I can't vouch for the hood. The hood is the same everywhere.

The most enjoyable part of this whole trip wasn't the awards presentation; it wasn't meeting the historic civil-rights activists either. It was shooting the breeze with the Ojays as they were checking into the same hotel to perform the next day. They were so down-to-earth that a casual observer would not have known that they were international superstars. I marveled at how young they looked in person. Money can't buy you love, but it can sure put off Father Time.

After all of the festivities, I returned to the ICC and resumed my pursuit of becoming a chief petty officer and warrant officer. The rules had recently changed to allow first class petty officers who placed in the top 50% on the Servicewide Exam. Fortunately, I placed 53 out 300. That placement allowed me to compete for warrant officer ranking. Who knew what could happen?

I also learned a lot about imagery from Brad and Stan. On one occasion, they were feverishly trying to locate the debarkation point of a Chinese alien-smuggling vessel. We were looking at sites in Baja California, Mexico. With little intel related experience, I noticed a place called Pt. China (pronounced Point Cheena). While Brad discussed other ports and facilities, I couldn't help but think, "Hell, if I was coming from China and saw a place that said Pt. China, that's where I would go." I brought that to Brad's attention and he focused on it as well. I though of intel as common sense coupled with technology. Over the next couple of weeks, I heard the name Pt. China mentioned throughout the shop. I never asked if my guess proved fruitful, but I assumed it did. Within weeks, Brad was the recipient of the Billiard Award for the best intelligence analyst in the Coast Guard, beating out a host of senior intelligence analysts.

We conducted another urgent national security operation in response to the shooting down of two commercial planes, resulting in the deaths of four pilots flown by the Cuban exile rescue group, Brothers to the Rescue (BTR). BTR successfully rescues exiles from Cuba to Miami. Castro threatened to intercept, shoot down any additional flights, or to sink boats entering Cuba's territorial waters. The Coast Guard and Navy became deeply involved in the cat-and-mouse game that developed. I was asked to stand a couple of 12-hour shifts on the Watch Floor. It was fun. This was my first long-term stint in the War Room. BTR conducted a memorial and wreath-laying service just outside of Cuban waters. The Coast Guard was tasked with monitoring this event. Navy and Air Force resources were mobilized as well. I didn't have much to do, so I stood behind Commander Gill Davis, who was one of the hard-nosed senior officers at the ICC. He was the consummate professional sailor and intelligence analyst. He ran the Operations Section and the Coast Guard Watchstanders. He was no-nonsense, but had a great sense of humor, when we could get him to laugh. I was used to guys like that because they remind me of Captain Petworth.

Commander Davis supervised the Coast Guard portion of the BTR ops. I stood behind him and his deputy, Lieutenant Scott. They were mentioning something that sounded like Zukes. I had no idea what they talking about. Someone mentioned, "It may be in *Jane's*." I quickly slipped out of the Watch Floor and went to the main office to get the *Jane's Fighting Ships* guide that was on the coffee table near my desk. I looked in the index and located the Cuban Border Guard, and one class of patrol boats was called *Zhuks*, which are 40-ton Russian-made patrol boats. The next time someone mentioned it, I gave the *Jane's* book to the commander. *Jane's* described the dimensions and capabilities of the patrol boats.

He said, "Thanks. How did you know we needed that?"

I just said that I was listening in the background and I needed to do something to stay busy. He was impressed at that small item and we seemed to have a wonderful relationship from that point forward.

At one point, he plopped down on the chair next to my desk and said, "These kids!"

I said, "Your son?"

He said, "Yeah."

I sensed he was having some issues around the house. I said, "Is he wearing his hat to the back and his pants too big?"

He said, "Yes."

We agreed that he basically had a little *brother* living in the house. I mentioned to him that times had changed and these kids love the hip-hop culture whether they are black or white. We laughed and went back to work.

ICC was proving to be a major stepping-stone in my professional career. I gave the Servicewide Exam and the Warrant Officer Selection Board one more try and had to wait for the results. Needless to say, I was a bit nervous about them. I was becoming somewhat more militant and politically astute as well. I guess the deaths of Ron Brown and the whole OJ saga impacted my defense mechanisms. Nevertheless, I had honed my administrative skills. I flipped the switch. I could easily make OJ jokes around the shop or walk onto the Watch Floor with the flair of an intelligence analyst. I could talk to a group of kids at a local school, or brief the commanding officer of the NMIC on Coast Guard administrative processes.

The ICC was the perfect switching facility. Morale events were commonplace, but a crisis was always around the corner. The constant keypad entries and the swiping of access cards have a way of letting me know the seriousness of the place in which I was employed. Minus the few folks who avoided anyone of color after the OJ Trial, the NMIC was an excellent place to work. As long as I had my switch nearby, I was fine.

There were no single gut-busting humor moments at the ICC, but we found ways to keep laughing. There was always Larry, the collections boss, who asked, "Did we have any mail?" at least three times a day. He was a retired chief radarman and he never stopped moving. When I saw how hyper he was, I wanted to put some bottles and cans around the office so that he could "collect" them. Larry could bug anyone to death, but he had a heart of gold. If he liked a person, chances are that everyone in the ICC would do so as well. I just kept his mail flowing and he treated me fine.

My niece Charmaine visited me for Spring Break. On a sunny Friday morning during her stay, I received a call at 10 a.m. sharp. It was supposedly someone from Headquarters who asked if I was interested in working at the White House. Thinking it was a joke from someone at work, I said, "Sure," and hung up the phone. I told Charmaine what happened and we both looked at each other.

Five minutes later, my friend Vince called and said, "Tony, we're serious!" Vince was by that time the supervisor for Coast

Guard enlisted assignment officers, the detailers in my old office. He told me to talk to Chief Warrant Officer Kasparez, who would give me the details. She said that the Commandant of the Coast Guard had just returned from a meeting at the White House and they'd asked him if he was interested in assigning a yeoman to the National Security Council to replace a Navy chief.

She mentioned that I could stay in the job for four years, which would take me to 20 years service. This would secure my retirement in the DC area. Only at that point was I taking this seriously. I told her that I was interested and to let me know the details on Monday. I hung up the phone and the feeling of elation was overwhelming. Charmaine and I laughed for the rest of the morning. She was so proud of me. Vince called back and said that he was asked if they had anyone who was capable of filling a yeoman position in the White House, and he'd said, "Tony Johnson!" He mentioned that they were sending a Coast Guard captain, who was detailed to the White House, over to review the records of potential applicants. I was on top of the list.

No one would have ever believed that I imagined that I could end up at the White House when I tried to get administrative jobs after high school. I'd also felt that way when I tried to get a summer job photocopying at the community center at the age of 14. I didn't get that job because my parents made too much money. How ironic. We didn't have enough money to live in one of those houses further up East Warren, but too much to get a summer job with the rest of my neighbors.

I often daydreamed about making it to the White House and contacting Ms. Pierce, who had been my business teacher at Finney High, to inform her. She was the one who believed in my administrative abilities and made me feel that I wasn't a punk because I wanted to work in an office instead of a factory. That mindset was prevalent in a city with an auto mechanics class in every school. I doubt that anyone would believe that I always thought I would make it to the highest levels of government, albeit as an over-hyped secretary, but nevertheless "In the House!" I suppose it's the same mindset that persuaded people to ask me whether I'd seen the President just because I lived in Washington. We perceive access is automatic. The time had come to break the news to the TD.

I felt slightly guilty about telling the ICC I was leaving two years early. That job had boosted my confidence level and given me the administrative notoriety that eluded other coasties in the DC area. No matter what happens to me in my future endeavors, I will be able to trace my success to my tour at the ICC. Prior to departing, I called at least five top-notch petty officers to give them a personal shot at replacing me in that assignment. Each of them told me that, "I heard you work too hard over there," and "No, thanks; I don't want a clearance." I thought long and hard about never soliciting people for opportunities again. I'm glad I didn't adopt that mentality.

I thought of a young yeoman I knew from Station Alexandria, Virginia. Her name was Crystal Sparks. I knew if I offered the job to Crystal that she would take it. She always told me that she wanted to follow in my footsteps. Crystal took the job and I felt comfortable that I wasn't leaving the ICC high and dry. It was time to move on to my new challenge at 1600 Pennsylvania Avenue. Ms. Pierce, thanks for everything!

Chapter 31
The House

-------------------☼------------------

What should I wear? Should I report in a suit or wear my uniform? That was the only question I had. I didn't know if I would get the job, but the honor was in the opportunity to compete. I called Vince's captain to ask if I should wear my uniform or civilian attire. He advised that I should wear civilian clothes since that's what the job required. The Coast Guard motto of Semper Paratus (Always Ready) played a role in my adult dressing habits. It didn't hurt that I use to sneak into clubs in Detroit as a 14-year-old by wearing suits. I accumulated a few suits over the years, mainly to wear while working part-time security gigs for the World Bank and International Monetary Fund (IMF). I wouldn't have to start from scratch. The captain also told me that I would receive at least $1300 towards purchasing clothes for the assignment. Sounded good to me, although most suits in DC cost at least $250 to $500 each. Off to Value City I would go. I had to report to the Southwest Gate in time to make a 10 a.m. meeting in the Old Executive Office Building (OEOB).

I arrived at 9 a.m. and approached the uniformed Secret Service agents at the guard shack. They looked imposing but I felt at ease because they were all brothers. I thought, "Clinton, brothers," makes sense to me, and I may like it here if I get hired. The OEOB stood about 40 feet from the West Wing door. There were cars of all types parked diagonally on the tiny street between the White House and the OEOB. The entire compound was enclosed by the same security perimeter. I assumed that none of the parking spaces would be mine, and there must be underground parking for the minions, probably right under that tiny street. After giving them my name, they gave me a red badge with a huge white letter A on it. I asked if that was it. They asked if I had the room number. I did. I was sent on my merry way.

As I walked towards the side entrance of the OEOB, I noticed at least 20 jet-black Chrysler Conquest cars parked in an interior lot. They all had tinted windows and antennas all over them. They were sleek and imposing. I assumed that I would be driving one of those if I had to take one of the directors to a meeting. As I entered the OEOB, the first thing I thought was, "This building is old as Hell!" The tiles were black-and-white 12-inch diagonal chessboard squares. They were so old that I could see pits and cracks that had to be hundreds of years old. Ironically, the floor was glistening. The ceiling seemed 50 feet tall. There was a series of spiral staircases that were at least 15 feet wide. I noticed that light illuminated the staircase, but I couldn't locate the fixture. I looked straight up to the ceiling and saw the loveliest stained glass. The sun beamed down on my forehead. It was truly amazing. I decided not to take the nearby elevator and continued up to the third floor, the location of the National Security Council (NSC).

I couldn't help but notice most of the NSC doors were closed. The titles on door amazed me as well: Office of Legislation, Office of Intelligence, Office of Near Eastern Affairs, and, at last, the Office of Global and Multilateral Affairs. I rang the doorbell. The doorbell? I heard a click and the heavy, three-inch-thick wooden door popped open. I walked into a deep-blue carpeted room with a metal spiral staircase to the left and a coffee table with every major newspaper on the right.

At the desk directly in front of the door stood a gentleman who said, "Hi, I'm KB." He was the Navy chief yeoman I would replace if hired. Ken was an extremely confident African American sailor.

I looked to his immediate right and saw an African American lady. I introduced myself and she said, "Hi, I'm Beverly."

They seemed extremely pleasant, but I could feel the intensity of this environment. I sensed a high-morale looseness about the office, but I also felt the *don't-fuck-up* aspect of it as well. Beverly said that Dick was in a meeting, and asked Ken to take me to meet Captain Fred Rosa, the Coast Guard officer who served as the Director for International Crime and Narcotics. He was on Dick's staff and was the person who reviewed my record. Captain Rosa was a scholarly looking person with tons of work and files all over his office. He was extremely nice and he mentioned that there were four other applicants that they were going to fly in for interviews. He told me to call him Fred. That would be hard to do, knowing that he was a Coast Guard captain. He told me that I had to call him Fred because Mr. Berger wants to be called Sandy. The last time I'd called a senior military member by his first name I was chewed out. He seemed busy and we didn't bother him long.

The first thing Ken said after we left Captain Rosa's office was, "Man, you got the job!"

I said, "How do you know?"

He said, "When Dick sees you, don't worry, you got the job." He told me that since I was hired, he needed to give me the royal tour. We crossed the driveway between the OEOB and the White House and entered the famous West Wing. I couldn't help but notice the cars again and wonder, "Where would I park?"

A long, white awning covered the entrance. In the vestibule sat a large wooden mailbox with a polished brash drop hole. KB said, "If you want to mail something to someone at home and you want it stamped, White House, put it in here."

We continued on towards a set of French doors and another Secret Service desk. KB flashed a badge and I showed my A badge. We walked right in and began the grand tour. He took me up a set of stairs. He said, "This is Sandy's Office." Sandy was short for Samuel Berger, the National Security Advisor to President Clinton. His assistant was an extremely nice lady named Dora. KB seemed to introduce me to everyone while saying, "This is Tony, my replacement." I felt uncomfortable because I hadn't had one interview. Dora asked me if I wanted to see Sandy's office. It was a huge office with expensive furnishings.

We continued on with the tour. We were winding through so many corridors that I couldn't have retraced my steps if I tried. Before I knew it, we were in a circular vestibule containing a roped-off office. KB told the Secret Service agent standing nearby that we were going to look in. I stepped up to the rope and poked my head into the room and quickly noticed it was the Oval Office. I couldn't help but notice the artifacts on the desk and the intricate carvings on the bottom facade on the tan wooden desk. I couldn't believe where I was standing, especially since I was a guest and not a White House staffer.

We departed the Oval Office and we took a turn down a set of staircases and before I knew it we were standing outside a large steel door. It almost looked like the door to a gas chamber. As soon as we approached the door an imposing figure in a perfectly cut suit came out. He and KB hugged and KB introduced him as Calvin, a Navy senior chief. They led me into an area known as the PEOC, the President's Emergency Operations Center – the infamous White House bomb shelter. We passed a series of small rooms with tiny cots and the guys said, "That's the President's room. ... That's the Vice's," and so on.

I said, "Where in the Hell is mine?"

They looked at each other and laughed. I quickly assumed that if President Clinton was to sleep in a six-by-six-foot room, I should KIMBAG, or kiss my black ass goodbye. We continued on to a large conference table with many video monitors encased in a large wooden and glass case. I couldn't wait to get out of this place. I couldn't help but think about the situations that would make that room an option. Nevertheless, it was a true honor to see it on my first day. We headed back to the office for my interview.

When we returned, Dick still had not arrived from his meeting. I was sent in to meet Mr. Len Crowley. He was a Senior Executive Service member and a retired Army colonel. He was the director in charge of United Nations Peacekeeping Missions and operations in Bosnia and Kosovo. He used the nearest empty office to conduct the interview. It contained a large fireplace, which seemed commonplace throughout the compound. He hailed from Detroit as well. We spent the first 20 minutes taking about Detroit and the Coast Guard. I can't recall discussing the job at all. He was nice and placed me at ease. It was a great icebreaker for my interview with Dick.

Dick returned during my interview with Len. Beverly led me into a colossal office that was two stories tall, with another large fireplace. There he was, standing there with a cordless keyboard, facing a cabinet containing a large TV monitor, surfing the Net on AOL. It was intimidating but I tried not to show it. He was Richard A. Clarke, the nation's foremost terrorism expert. I had read Dick's bio on the Internet before the meeting. Any man who puts his high school, the Boston Latin School, on his bio has to be a work of art. He was a Penn and M.I.T. graduate and had served every president since Nixon in some major capacity.

We met halfway and shook hands. He said, "I'm Dick Clarke, nice to meet you!" I introduced myself and noticed Captain Rosa sitting in one of the chairs. Dick had a large sofa in his office and I could smell the strong aroma of coffee coming out of a cabinet. He had a large electronic whiteboard in his office with so much stuff scribbled on it that I couldn't read it. I was afraid to read it, anyway. We began the interview and I flipped my switch. I sat up straight in my single-breasted grey suit with a shiny black-and-grey tie. I started telling him how interested I was in imagery and explained its relationship to how we caught drug boats and illegal migrants in the Coast Guard. This was stuff that I stole from Brad and Stan, but used it to enhance my interview.

I never thought I would use any of the back room stuff from the ICC. I also talked about working on the staff for the Commandant of the Coast Guard and that I processed Admiral Roy's son into the Coast Guard's Officer Candidate School. Dick didn't say much. I don't think he wanted to. I think he wanted to hear me talk. Whenever I paused, he remained quiet. So I kept talking. I was concerned that I was talking too much.

When I finally stopped yapping, Dick looked at Fred and said, "Fred, we have our guy! Make him an offer and tell the others thanks!" I'm sure they'd never seen a black man blush before, but there's a first time for everything. We all stood up and shook hands, and I departed Dick's office on top of the administrative world. I flipped my switch back and shot the breeze with Beverly and KB. They were grinning at me and telling me congratulations.

KB only had one week to break me in, and Beverly, patiently, would do the rest. There was another lady named Carolyn, who worked across the hall in Fred's suite of offices. Fred told me to report to work the Monday after next and I would meet Carolyn and the other directors.

I finally asked them, "Where will I park my car?"

They laughed at me and KB said, "On the Ellipse after I transfer."

I didn't tell them that I thought I would park with the cars just outside the Southwest Gate. I just couldn't foresee any of them parking outside. I literally thought there was a large underground parking facility below the White House. I realized quickly that I was at the bottom of the food chain. They told me to take the subway until KB departed and then I would get his parking pass for the Ellipse. Fred told me that my working hours would be from 8:00 a.m. to 7:00 p.m., minimum, five days a week. I expected this because everyone said they worked long hours at the White House. I *floated* out of the OEOB and onto the subway. I had accomplished something that no one in my neighborhood could have imagined: a job in the White House!

Monday morning came in a blink of an eye. I entered the compound via the 17th and G Street entrance. Wouldn't you know it, *all* of the Secret Service security members on this gate were African Americans as well. I was starting to see a pattern. The first thing I noticed when I entered the compound was the diversity among the electricians, the maintenance crew, and especially the support staff at the NSC. There were a number of well dressed African Americans carrying briefcases.

I thought to myself, "Damn, this is Chocolate City!" I definitely saw a pattern there. I always suspected that these high-level places were run by people who just plain get it done. I was honored to be a part of this team. I learned early in my career that the same people you see on the way up, you will see on your journey down. I never dissed the mail-delivery person or the individual who dumps my trash. I learned from the *Basswood* not to mess with the people who prepare my food. I *was* the guy people didn't want to piss off because I handled their paychecks. I was extremely pleased to see the makeup of the general staff. I planned to get to know as many of them as I could. I could never tell when I may have needed a light bulb replaced or an extra chair before a major meeting.

I was nervous on my first day, but tried not to show it. It was going to be a challenge. I didn't know how I would function in that environment. I couldn't bring any of my previous Coast Guard work rules with me. Everything was different. Intangibles were the only items I could bring to the table. I had to muster up everything I'd learned in previous assignments and in life. My role was to pick up the daily intelligence briefs, get the newspapers, and start the coffee in the morning. I would also gather up the trash for the cleaning crew in the evening. Whatever happened in between was anyone's guess.

KB took me around to meet all of my directors. I was told that I would work directly for Len Crowley, William Wechsler, and Lisa Gordon-Hagerty. William looked so young. I was amazed that he had such a powerful position. He was around 27 and seemed to be Dick's right-hand man. He was in charge of financial and international crimes, and counterterrorism. He was a Cornell Graduate and had arrived from high-level jobs in the Pentagon.

Lisa Gordon-Hagerty graduated from the University of Michigan and was the splitting image of Princess Diana. She was tall, classy, and brilliant. You see, Lisa dismantled nuclear bombs for a living at the Department of Energy prior to her arrival at the White House. She was also from the Detroit area. We were batting three for three with Detroiters. The lead actress in the George Clooney movie *The Peacemaker* portrayed Lisa's role with the government. Fred had not arrived for work. Beverly said that he showed up late and worked to at least 11 p.m.

I met two other directors, Steve Simon and Daniel Tangeman, after they returned from getting coffee. Steve was Dick's major backup on terrorism issues and Dan backed up Steve and handled nuclear, biological and chemical warfare issues. Steve was Princeton and Oxford trained. Dan has degrees from Harvard and Oxford.

Another director, Phillip Bobbitt, worked periodically. I sensed right off the bat that Beverly wasn't too impressed with Phil. He was the nephew of Lady Bird Johnson and hailed from Texas. Beverly would say, "He don't work!" I supposed he liked to hold and attend meetings, but didn't produce a lot of substance afterwards. His area of expertise was critical infrastructure protection, with an emphasis on Y2K.

There was another youthful gentleman running around who Beverly called Dr Metzl. Jaime Metzl hailed from Kansas City, Missouri. He had just completed his doctoral degree and was up and coming. There were two interns, Brian Klein and Mark Fung, assigned to the office as well. These were two up-and-coming guys. They worked as unpaid volunteers, but I think they produced more work than Phil. Dick could give them a task and it was returned completed in a couple of days.

The third administrative assistant was Carolyn. She was a career Foreign Service assistant. She had served many years at various embassies around the world. The last piece of the puzzle was the special projects and security staffer, Chuck Green. Chuck was a career Secret Service agent. His role was to take care of Dick. He ensured that Dick didn't run into any issues at any time. Chuck turned out to be one of my best friends. He had a tremendous sense of humor, as did most Secret Service agents.

We were reorganized within days of my arrival, becoming known as TNT, or Transnational Threats. Dick received a new title as well, becoming the National Coordinator for Security, Infrastructure Protection and Counterterrorism. Internally we were known to a chosen few as those who dealt with drugs and thugs. We were also in charge of the national security aspects of Y2K. I couldn't believe the staff Dick had assembled and I was a part of it.

It wasn't long before I was thrown into the fire. KB had departed and Carolyn was continuously out sick, and also nursing an ailing husband. The admin assistants at the NSC had to stand a weekend beeper watch at least once every four to six months. Beverly's watch came up one Friday while she was on leave. The NSC Admin Office said that I had to take it in her absence because it wasn't fair to give it to another office. That was fine with me, except I had no clue what to do in an emergency. I was told that if I didn't receive a call by 3 p.m. on Saturday, I was home free.

Three p.m. Saturday came, and no calls. I was elated. Around 8 a.m. Sunday morning, the damn thing vibrated across my headboard shelf so hard that I banged my head jumping up. I called the Situation Room and someone said, "Tony, this is Ericka from the Africa Directorate. We need you to come in as soon as possible!"

I said, "No problem, I live in Clinton, Maryland and will be in within the hour!"

I hung up, got dressed, and hit the road. I got a close parking space this time. I entered the West Wing and reported to the Situation Room (Sit Room), where Ericka met me. She worked for Gail, the Senior Director for African Affairs. Gail was the spitting image of a young, non-alcoholic Bridgett Neilsen, with a short-white crewcut. She was at least 6-foot-3 and fly. I saw a major reporter from ABC News trying to hit on her one day as she walked to her car. She blew him off. You are likely to see anything on the corner of Pennsylvania Avenue and 17th Street.

Ericka informed me that we had to set up an emergency conference call for President Clinton to talk to two African presidents who were threatening each other with war. This was right up my alley, except for the part that I didn't have a rat's-ass clue what I was supposed to do. They sent me to the West Wing desk, where Sandy's deputies, Jim Steinberg and General Donald Kerrick, worked, to pick up a correspondence manual. I quickly recalled how Beverly would put the packages together for Dick and the other directors. I knew that I needed tabs and certain types of letterhead. I knew I needed the light-green paper for the President to sign and the regular bond for the cover letters. I really didn't understand how they put them together because they would use Tab A to introduce Tab B, which introduced Tab C. I knew that Tab C had to say that we recommend the President sign one of those damn tabs. That was enough for me.

I returned to the Sit Room with book and letterhead in hand. Before I knew it, I had typed the documents and Ericka had made some minor corrections and given them back to me to print in final. The President signed one of those damn tabs and the calls were made. Ericka shook my hand and said, "Go home." I was home by 2:30 and enjoyed the rest of my Sunday.

The next morning, I received a copy of an email from Gail and Ericka to Dick. It said, "Dick, I don't know where you got him from but you better keep an eye on him! Someone's going to steal him!"

Dick had replied, "Not a chance, he's not going anywhere!" After two weeks on the job, I couldn't ask for a bigger compliment, not only from my staff, but from other serious players in the White House. I had made a small name for myself. Not a bad start.

I was fortunate to be befriended by the gentleman from the records room, where I picked up my newspapers and daily briefs. Continuing the tradition of the Clinton White House, the three main players in this office were African American as well. I spent many mornings shooting the breeze with Chris, Ralph, and John.

All were long-time NSC staffers. Chris was extremely funny and down-to-earth. Ralph had nearly 30 years working for the White House, and no one bothered him. He did his job and went home. John ran the office and was a major jazz fan; he was especially partial to Cassandra Wilson. After getting my papers, I meticulously organized them on the table near the door.

Each morning Dick held informal current-events chats over coffee with a few staffers. They read the *Washington Post, New York Times, USA Today,* the *Washington Times,* and the *Wall Street Journal* from front to back every single day. If those papers didn't arrive for some reason, I would steal one from another directorate's box. I wasn't about to enter that office without any one of the five papers. They never knew why we never missed a paper. If ours showed up during the course of the day I returned it to the office box I initially took it from. No harm, no foul. They just blamed the paper boy. I filed the classified daily briefings in a binder in Steve's office. I don't recall anyone ever reading them. There were so many other mechanisms for our directors to get important information. By the time something made the brief, they already knew about it.

My main task at the NSC was maintaining the schedule of the directors and coordinating their many meetings and documents. I had to enter the attendee's name into a system called WAVES. We didn't want to invite some distant relative to the White House without first finding out if they were a felon. WAVES would embarrass them, and us. It was critical to get to know the WAVES staff. They could make or break my time in the White House. I could view the Southwest Gate from the window behind my desk. I could literally see if all of my folks were entering the compound properly. If I noticed someone outside the gate for more than five minutes, it was a problem.

The most important group was the CSG: the Counterterrorism Security Group. The CSG was comprised of senior government officials involved in anti-terrorism operations. I faxed the classified meeting notifications to the Justice Department, FBI, Secret Service, CIA, Pentagon, and other key agencies. I was told never to use my military rank during my follow-up phone calls. If I told them I was Petty Officer Johnson, no one would have shown up. I was known as "Tony from Dick's Office." Whenever they heard from one of us, they were directed to a meeting either at the White House or via secure video teleconference (SVTC, pronounced *sivits*). I kept a plastic card with the names and numbers of the key antiterrorism players in my wallet. This allowed me to set up meetings from home, if I had to.

I couldn't believe how people jumped when we called. Dick had a motto: delegate up. That motto was for the Washington bureaucrats who delegated their meeting attendance to subordinates. Our method stated that if the principals couldn't show up, their boss had to replace them. That kept the BS to a minimum. We couldn't afford to have someone at a meeting who couldn't make a decision. Our decisions could mean life or death.

Unfortunately, there were a limited number of classified conference rooms in the entire White House. We utilized two others, with the help of our good friends in the PEOC and the Secret Service. There was one cavernous room in the OEOB, the infamous Cordell Hull. Dick hated this room with a passion. I didn't book that room for him, no matter what. We could bump anyone from any conference room in the compound unless someone senior to Dick held the meeting. The Secret Service Conference Room was our best-kept secret. It was high-tech and it seated 24. We were allowed to place chairs around the walls, and this raised the capacity to 40. Dick liked this room, but he loved the PEOC. I guess it had a serious intelligence vibe to it. It fit, since 9 times out of 10 we were discussing something devious.

The most unnecessarily bureaucratic department in the government, at least from where I sat, was the Treasury Department. Most of our meetings consisted of the principal member plus one. Treasury had to bring no less than five for every meeting. I don't think they were authorized to answer a question without a huddle. We conducted one meeting in the Secret Service Conference Room that required a principal plus one. To my dismay, 20 Treasury officials arrived and demanded attendance. Since the Secret Service worked for Treasury, they assumed we should let in as many attendees as they desired. Not in Dick's meetings. Dick was a beast in meetings. He was the most powerful non-cabinet member in the federal government, period.

I never saw him raise his voice, but it didn't take much to make him red as fire. Dummies made him see red. If someone didn't bring it mentally, they were toast. I politely entered the meeting room and whispered the Treasury Department's desires to him. He just turned his head and looked at me like I was nuts. He thought for a while, and then said, "Let 'em in!"

I looked at him like *he* was nuts. I left the room and escorted the 20 officials into the room. As they filled in space around the walls, Dick stood up and announced that the meeting was over. The agent in charge of the conference room smiled at me and made me laugh. Dick walked by me and smiled as well. The 20 officials looked dumbfounded. They were the only ones left in the room and whispered together feverishly, trying to figure out what they missed. Moreover, how would they explain it to their boss at headquarters? Maybe he or she shouldn't have sent all of them over to the meeting in the first place.

I woke up bright and early with a lot of energy on August 7, 1998. I went through my usual morning drill of touching up my starched white shirt with an iron. Tiffani was also up early, getting ready for school. I decided to turn on the TV to check out weather and traffic. To my dismay, the news didn't display weather and traffic, but buildings in rubble, instead. It looked as if an earthquake had hit them. I could see lifeless African bodies being pulled out of the carnage, while the bloodied survivors walked around bewildered and looking like zombies. I turned up the volume and discovered that two American embassies had been bombed simultaneously.

The American Embassy in Nairobi, Kenya was destroyed, the bomb killing 213 people. The American Embassy in Dar es Salaam, Tanzania was also destroyed, 11 people losing their lives there. I let out a loud "Damn." At her tender middle-school age, Tiffani came into my bedroom, looked at me, looked at the television, and said, "You want me to tell Mommy you will be late?"

I said, "Yeah," and headed out to work while she went to school.

When I arrived at work, the first thing I saw was Lisa running up and down the spiral staircase. Beverly was feverishly working her phones. Dick's door was closed, which meant that someone was going to get his ass kicked. Dan, Will, and Steve were running in and out of Dick's office. It was a madhouse. The one consistent detail about this event was that it was Friday.

Something crazy happened every Friday in our office. I don't know what it was about Friday, but the entire staff dreaded them. Something would always blow up or the country would receive a major terror threat. I could never leave work before 9 p.m. on Fridays.

As the day went on, I discovered more details about the bombings. Did UBL do this? UBL was the classified nickname for the guy we were not allowed to mention. I think he was the same guy I saw on a picture on Dick's desk. He had one of those red circles and a slash through his face. I didn't know much about this person initially. I do know that every time he was mentioned, things got extremely tense. It wasn't long before I discovered he was Usama Bin Ladin. He was a wealthy Saudi Arabian and an alleged financier for international terrorism. He had established an organization called al-Qaeda, aka The Islamic Army.

Along with one of the suspects who allegedly killed Egyptian President Anwar Sadat, Ayman al-Zawahiri, he established this organization with the goal of toppling moderate Muslim governments and waging Jihad (Holy War) on American or other Western nations. Ayman al-Zawahiri was the leader of the Egyptian Islamic Jihad organization. He could be seen in old footage yelling at courtroom members from a crowded cage during the Sadat murder trial. I think he received three years in prison for his part in the plot. That's it. They were America's number one enemy, and priority 1 in our office.

Bin Laden was pissed at us for putting American military bases in Saudi Arabia during the Gulf War. I'm sure he was pissed at other stuff as well, but having these bases near the holy cities of Mecca and Medina was a bit more than he could take. It was a convenient excuse for his terror war. The puzzle was finally coming together for me. I had set up UBL Financing meetings for Will for weeks. I thought it meant United Blood Lords or something similar. I had no clue it meant this guy. I discovered that most of my meetings had something to do with UBL in one way or another.

In the days following the bombings things were gradually heating up. My street sense was saying that we were taking too long to hit their ass back. Since this wasn't the streets and I had no say, I kept those thoughts to myself. I was starting to think that we were worried about the Monica Lewinski sex scandal. I sensed that the whole Monica thing was strapping us down.

Speaking of Monica, I never met the girl. Nevertheless, there were no shortage of "Monicas" in the compound. I could spot them a mile away. I actually think most interns thought of her as a success. They began to style their hair or buy wigs like hers. They also wore the same cheap summer suits. You know the kind, those light-grey, no-shape skirts with the matching zip-up jacket. Don't forget the black *Love Me* pumps with the fat heels. I suppose they felt that she'd latched onto the Man and they could do the same.

I was most pleased that the sisters didn't get caught up in any scandals. They kept it strictly professional. Moreover, I was somewhat disappointed in him myself. There were African American women at the White House who were extraordinarily beautiful. I'm not talking Halle Berry beautiful, but at the supermodel Beverly Johnson level. I said to myself, "Monica? Come on, Commander-in-Chief, that can't be this hard!"

Although many sisters wouldn't have sacrificed their careers for a presidential quickie, a small percentage would. That group wouldn't have said a thing. They would have kept that skeleton bone right in the closet. The dress would have been burned in the White House furnace and then taken out and shot. With our newfound forensics experience (Thanks OJ), there would have been no DNA or soiled dress to match. He would have been home free. Technically, he was already home, so to speak. The sisters may have mentioned to a friend or two, but it would have been on the DL (the Down Low). Since most of their friends would have said, "Sure, you dated the President," the case would have died right there.

Before I was so rudely interrupted by the tangent called Monica, I was discussing our response to the African embassy bombings. We discovered some of the details of the bombings. They seemed to be the work of UBL's, al-Qaeda. They liked to do their dirt on a grand scale, or conduct simultaneous attacks on targets. The scariest part of this whole mentality for me was that Bin Laden was exiled from his home nation, Saudi Arabia, but still had at least $300 million dollars worth of inheritance to work with. A man hating us with that much money and no official ties to a particular country is extremely dangerous. He can bomb things and move from country to country from now to eternity, especially since America has so many covert enemies. How could a guy like that come out of nowhere?

I thought the CIA and other worldwide intelligence organizations knew everyone and everything. The CIA scares the hell out of Americans. Couldn't they take him out individually? When UBL's ties to Afghanistan and the newly formed Taliban government came to my attention, I recalled the two guys who opened a video store next door to my recruiting office. They were from Afghanistan, and talked about how proud they were of the Mujahidin fighters who defeated the Soviet Union in the 80s. I didn't know what the hell they were talking about most of the time, but I knew they had to be on the good side, since we hated the Soviet Union. Plus, they had good smut in their video store.

I started researching the Internet to get additional facts on UBL. I found out that he helped finance and train the Mujahidin fighters, with America's blessings, in their war against the Russians. He had also lived in Sudan as a guest of the government. Sudan seemed to have two countries in one. One Muslim elitist, who ran the government, and the other African peasants trying to survive and not starve to death. Was this another case of someone who worked with America becoming an enemy? It wouldn't be the first time.

I couldn't help but think of Noriega and Saddam Hussein. They were both buds of ours who we eventually fought. What I couldn't understand was why would they blow up Africans to kill a couple of Americans? I looked at Muslims as more African than anything else. I didn't see any Americans being pulled from the rubble. Everyone I saw was a person of color. I just couldn't understand the rationale. I now know that radical Muslims practice historical teachings that go back centuries, some of which preach that a suicide bomber will become a martyr and receive 72 virgins in heaven. Hell, there weren't 72 virgins on the East Side of Detroit. Moreover, collateral damage or casualties of war aren't an issue, because they believe that good people will go to heaven, anyway. Some were just in the wrong place at the wrong time. I finally had my answers on why they blew up those Africans in their attempt to kill a few Americans. How sick!

A couple of weeks passed and things started to heat up again. Lisa began running up and down the stairs again. Beverly worked the phones and visitors came in and out, some of whom I didn't recognize. Visitors were commonplace. I returned from lunch one day and saw a guy with an earpiece standing in front of our door. I put my code in and he moved a few feet to allow me entrance. As soon as I entered I saw the Director of the Central Intelligence Agency, George Tenet, sitting in my chair with a cigar lit and his feet propped up on my desk.

I quickly looked at him, turned to Beverly, and said, "I'm going back to lunch."

She looked at me and said, "Good!" I knew that was short for "Good Move."

I went back to Swings Coffee Shop across the street and had another one. I sat there and recalled one day when I'd been in the office alone. The doorbell rang and this distinguished older gentleman walked in. He had on slacks and a short-sleeve, opened-collar shirt. He didn't look like the normal Joe, as his clothes implied.

My military training kicked in and I stood up to greet him. I said, "Good morning, sir. Mr. Clarke is out of the office."

He said, "Hi, I'm Tony Lake – and you are?"

I said, "Tony Johnson, sir. I'm KB's replacement from the Coast Guard."

He shook my hand and said, "I didn't come to see Dick. I came to steal your *USA Today* sports section."

I said, "No problem, sir. It's right there on the table."

He took the paper, said, "Bye," and left.

Anthony Lake was President Clinton's first National Security Advisor, Sandy Berger's predecessor. Military customs and courtesies served me well in this case. My switch flipped itself and I addressed one of the most powerful men in America and the world intelligence community with the respect he deserved. Two weeks later I saw him on the Metroliner to New York City. We were getting coffee and sandwiches in the food car and we looked at each other.

I said, "Hi Mr. Lake."

He said, "How are you? You get around, don't you?" He asked about Dick and we went back to our seats. You never know, first impressions mean a lot.

Mr. Lake was nominated to take over the CIA but declined it. I'll bet dollars to donuts that he didn't want people digging up his rear end during the confirmation process. He returned to teach at Georgetown instead, but maintained close ties to the President, White House Staff, and Dick. Beverly later told me that Mr. Lake would use our office as refuge when he'd been in charge of the NSC.

It was no telling who would enter our office at any time. I sat there one day and Steve Kerr walked in. At least I thought it was the Kerr from the Chicago Bulls. It wasn't. It was his brother. I tried to figure out how he would know Dick. I later found out that Malcolm Kerr, Steve's father, was a career educator and an expert on the Middle East. I'm sure he frequented diplomatic circles. Mr. Kerr was assassinated while heading the American University of Beirut, Lebanon in 1984. I assumed Dick probably mentored at least one of the Kerr boys after that incident. I kept my switch next to the switch on my desk that automatically opened the door. I may have needed both at any time.

I entered the office the following morning and Lisa was a train wreck. Steve was busy as hell. Will continued to run in and out of Dick's door, which was mostly closed. A group led by Sandy came in and went into Dick's office. They didn't stay long, and Sandy looked intense when he left.

About 5 p.m. Dick said, "Tony, I'm going to need you tonight."

I said, "Not a problem!"

He gave me about $70 and said, "Get all of the pizzas you can." I ordered about nine pizzas and picked them up from the 17th and G Street door. The Secret Service guard said, "What's going on? Whenever I see this many pizzas, something is going on. Plus, I know where you work."

I kept that "What are you talking about?" smirk on my face.

We began to wave in the entire world. I'm talking about 20 people, mostly one or two at a time. These guys and ladies looked so seedy that I was getting nervous. The last person I escorted into the office was Assistant Secretary of State Thomas Pickering. He was second in command to Madeline Albright. He stood about 6'-5"; the guard looked at me with his head slanted to the left. I smiled and took Mr. Pickering up to our suite.

Shit began to hit the fan. Beverly and I were faxing stuff everywhere and running back and forth to the Sit Room. We were grabbing supplies from the Admin Office left and right.

Around midnight, she and I began putting a stack of white binders together, with tabs from A-Z. Tab A was something akin to, "We warned you!" Tab J was "We have this evidence." Tab Z was "We're coming to kick your ass!"

We were working in what we called Ollie's Loft while the visitors worked at our desks and took over Steve's office. It was crazy. I never saw this many people running around our suite without a party going on. Beverly and I were struggling trying to put all the documents together. Around 1a.m., a bunch of people came up the spiral staircase, led by Mary. She was in charge of the NSC Intelligence Office next door, but hailed from the CIA. Following her were generals, Navy captains, and a few of the visitors. They rolled up their sleeves and assisted us in putting the binders together. I can recall one Navy admiral licking his fingers trying to unstick a page and said, "Any more Tabs Gs?" They were helping us. I never experienced senior personnel helping junior folks like this in my entire Coast Guard career. Coast Guard officers would have *supervised* us.

This would be a lifelong management experience for me. I will never think that I am too big to help my staff out when it's crunch time. In addition, I will not hesitate to advise my managers when I think an issue has become an all-hands evolution. Whether they help or not isn't the issue. I can always remind them of my NSC late-night experience. Some of the binders were later driven to the embassies involved. I hope they didn't think the packages were from FTD.

I made it home around 3 a.m. and returned to the office at 8 a.m. Lisa was literally flying through the office with her arms extended like a kid acting like an airplane. It's amazing that we could work in a place like this and not know what the hell we were working on until it was nearly completed. We worked on bits and pieces from every director but compiled it later for the big picture. Lisa was flying around because we'd launched over 100 cruise missiles at Sudan and Afghanistan. We were literally looking at CNN and counting down to 10 a.m., expecting them to say, "We interrupt our telecast to inform you ..." At 10:05 a.m. CNN did just that.

I think we eventually made it up to the loft to pop a cork or two. We had struck back at Taliban-run al-Qaeda training camps in Afghanistan and a pharmaceutical plant in Sudan which was allegedly producing VX nerve gas. A high level al-Qaeda meeting was allegedly planned at the camps in Afghanistan and we hoped that Bin Laden would be there. The best way to describe this entire smooth-as-silk operation is to compare it to the movie *Patriot Games* with Harrison Ford. He advised the character played by James Earl Jones that he thought the targeted terrorists were at a desert location. James Earl Jones later invited him to a conference room where they observed an entire covert operation via satellite. In this movie, you could see the operatives moving in on the tents through night-vision satellite technology, and, after striking, quickly backing out prior to blasts of lights caused by helicopter-launched rockets. It may not have been a movie, but it was just as dramatic as anything I have ever been a part of. The BKs couldn't touch this crew. I wouldn't want to be on the receiving end of a barrage of missiles in the middle of the night.

After the operation, we continued on with the rest of our agenda, which consisted of Y2K conversion issues. Dick asked me to call a Navy vessel that was underway in the Persian Gulf. I was told to get the XO on the line. I can recall the kid who answered the phone yell, "It's the White House, go get the XO!"

Moments later, I was advising Lieutenant Commander Monty that he had been selected as a White House Fellow and was to report to our office as soon as he could. I later learned that Commander Monty's ship launched a number of the missiles for us. He arrived the next week and took over where Phil Bobbitt left off. He was a fireball of energy. I never saw anyone acclimate themselves to a position so quickly after arrival. Monty was so good at winning people over that within a week he was carpooling with Dick. Go figure.

We never stopped looking for Bin Laden or quelling possible attacks. After receiving threats, we also recommended the temporary closing of numerous embassies worldwide. The critical infrastructure protection operation rose to the forefront. We didn't want a nuclear power plant or some bomb to blow up at midnight of New Year's Eve 2000. This topic took up a major portion of our meetings and required me to learn an entire new group of attendees. I spent most of my time in the loft processing WAVE requests and getting to know people throughout the compound.

There would be occasional visits from Coast Guard leaders on a variety of issues. On one embarrassing occasion, our law enforcement admiral gave Dick a presentation on the use of force for Coast Guard personnel. Since it was Coast Guard issue, Dick asked me to work the VCR for the group. It wasn't long before they showed Dick clips of non-lethal methods of stopping drug boats. One of the methods was the shooting of stink bombs into a small boat operated by a drug smuggler. I could sense the laughter in Dick's gut. He was too professional to laugh outright. I put on my OJ verdict face so that they couldn't see how embarrassed I was or how non-serious their idea was. I'm sure Dick was thinking, "Why don't they drive with one hand and hold their nose with the other?" Here we were in a room with a man who could order an air strike on a nation and my service was presenting him Nickelodeon law-enforcement methods. I was so glad Steve wasn't in the office that day. I would have never lived that one down.

Our office reminded me of the ICC. We worked hard, but played harder. It didn't take much for us to celebrate something. We kept a few bottles of the bubbly on ice. On occasions, Dick would turn his office into a buffet line with gourmet dishes from the White House mess. The mess was run by Navy cooks, who were available to tend bar as well. We were known for setting up a bar in the hallway directly outside our office. Dick invited a number of Coast Guard admirals to one event and all but one was afraid to drink a glass of wine. The old Icebreaker Lounge mentality had departed forever. It didn't stop Vince and me. It didn't stop a few of my guests as well. Carolyn from the ICC was at that time working at the federal building directly in front of the OEOB. It was nice having a dear friend that close to me, especially on rough days. It was also an honor to have invited one of the Fairview Five members, who was a senior FBI official, to one of our parties. Can you imagine having two guys from Shoemaker in the White House at the same time? You can't beat that with a stick.

The toughest thing about a party in a White House terrorism office was answering the phones during the festivities. It's impossible to entertain and not miss a call at the same time. Nevertheless, Beverly and I did it. We managed to mingle and keep an eye on the phone as well. We couldn't miss any calls from Sandy's office or miss anything that involved the CSG. Terrorists never stop and neither did we.

My last major endeavor at the White House was Y2K Night. I had the mid-watch and looked forward to being in the eye of the beast if something happened that night. Dick was in charge of the negative aspects of Y2K, and John Koskinen, who later served as deputy mayor of Washington, DC, was responsible for the industry side of the event. We took over an entire building and ran the operation from there.

There were computer screens and plasma televisions everywhere. The managers wore white cardigans and the worker bees wore blue. I could see the entire operation underway because there were glass walls. No view on my floor was obstructed.

I was responsible for monitoring worldwide websites and keeping an eye on a data link that monitors power plants and other critical infrastructure items. Y2K Night had finally arrived. Dick wanted to celebrate apprehending some terrorists trying to enter the country through Seattle with explosives and maps to LAX Airport in Los Angeles in their car. It seemed that we were winning on that night. As each nation celebrated the clock striking midnight, no explosions or major malfunctions occurred.

As midnight approached on the East Coast, we decided to go on the roof and look at the fireworks with champagne in hand. Our group passed Mr. Koskinen in the hallway. Dick and John congratulated each other and we took the elevator to the top floor. Unfortunately, we didn't have a key to open the door to the roof. Someone yelled, "Use a credit card," and the group laughed aloud. Chuck pulled out a credit card and swiped it through the lock mechanism and the door popped open to a star-lit night. We all burst into laughter, with Dick's being the loudest. The oldest trick in the book allowed us to experience that wonderful night.

We commenced popping corks, some of which flew over the side of the building. I hope some poor soul wasn't standing below. Within minutes we noticed a police car and ambulance speeding down Constitution Avenue and the rooftop went silent. Chuck called one of his Secret Service contacts to see what was going on. He found out that a DC police officer had just suffered a heart attack. We were relieved. Poor guy, but at least the world wasn't blowing up. Back to the bubbly.

We polished the bottles off and returned to the command center. At 3 a.m. Dick and nearly everyone else in my shop departed to nearby hotels for the rest of the night. I stayed in front of my monitors and near the food for the next five hours. I departed the Y2K Command Center at 8 a.m. and caught the subway home. Mission accomplished!

My time at the White House was the highlight of my administrative career. It was an experience that can't be matched by a similar position, should I earn another. I made an unlimited amount of high-level life-long friends, with Mr. Clarke at the top of the list. I feel a tremendous sense of accomplishment for completing that assignment. The pressure that the Coast Guard unofficially placed on me was excruciating. I was truly the first. Each time Admiral Roy or one of the admirals would see me, they would say, "Make the Coast Guard proud," or "Hang in there."

The pressure not to mess this up was the most I have ever felt in my life. It was tougher than going to sea or adjusting to military life. I felt like I had to succeed in order for the Coast Guard to continue to have administrative representation in the White House. I wanted them to say, "Those coasties are good!" That was my goal and I did my best to accomplish it. I can honestly acknowledge that reality. Two Coast Guard yeomen have followed me into that same position at the National Security Council. Now, that's success.

During my high-paced excursion at the White House, I received great news on two Coast Guard endeavors. An old Persru friend called me to advise me that I was number 11 out of 300 on the Chiefs Examination. The cut-off would be 20, so therefore my promotion to E-7 was guaranteed.

Two weeks after receiving that call, a friend named Phyllis called me and said, "I have some news for you."

I asked, "What is it?"

She said, it's the warrant's list."

I said, "Did I make it?"

She said, "Yes. You are number three."

I couldn't believe it. It is nearly impossible for an E-6 to come out that high on the list.

There were 26 people on the list, and the first 15 were guaranteed. I successfully achieved the one rank that always intrigued me. I always wanted to be like the old detailers in Enlisted Assignments. They were the ones who raised my work level, and along with the guys like Alex and Matt from Enlisted Assignments, made me a real yeoman. I would be forever grateful to those guys, as well as to my joint-service mentors from the Navy Yard, Fort McNair, and Bolling Air Force Base.

On May 31, 1999 I went to bed as a first class petty officer. On June 1, 1999 I awoke as a chief warrant officer two, five paygrades higher. That evening in the White House's Indian Treaty Room, Coast Guard Lieutenants Mike Macon and Vince Patterson took off my collar devices and placed warrant officer shoulder boards on me. My wife, many friends, and co-workers were present, but not my mom, she was in Detroit dying from cancer. I had reserved hotel rooms for her and two aunts so that they could see the White House from the inside. She apologized so forcefully that it made me cry. She was more concerned about not making my ceremony than she was about her own health.

That would always be a bittersweet day, because I put on my game face and dealt with the knowledge that all the accomplishments in the world could not replace my mother or her love. I sucked it up and enjoyed a wonderful going-away shinding. Dick, Beverly, Fred, and Lisa pulled out all of the stops. All I really wanted was some champagne and chocolate-covered strawberries from the White House Mess. They got me. The White House Mess catered the event, but I think they made the strawberries themselves. I could tell, but I didn't let them know that I knew it. Their strawberries were better than the Navy's.

Lisa and Beverly were my sweethearts. We had our administrative ups and downs, but we were family, and families spat at times. I knew I would miss them and the entire crew. I didn't worry about not seeing them again because they are the nation's foremost terrorism experts, and if I didn't see them in person, I would see them on CNN, World News Tonight, 60 Minutes, and even Oprah. All of which are true. They were the best and brightest and I am proud to have served on the same team.

Chapter 32
Epilogue

-------------------- ☼ --------------------

Many say that we are all products of our environments. That is a true statement, but it doesn't capture all of the elements that determine the outcome of an individual. I've been called a jack of all trades. The negative aspect of that is the second part of the phrase: a master of none. In my opinion, that's an incorrect statement and assumption. Who says that a person can't master the trades they have been a jack of? What if a person has five trades and has mastered all of them? Is that a bad thing?

One of the problems with America is the perception that a person must fit a mode that will place him or her in hot pursuit of the so-called American Dream. I can't forget the old coastie in Petaluma who was too old for his peers until they found out that he hit the cycle on military services while they were the jack of one. There is only one way to reach a dream, and that's to sleep. I chose not to sleep through life, but pursue every opportunity or endeavor I've damn well pleased while I'm awake. I am so tired of hearing the "I have a dream" speech, not because I'm tired of hearing the Great Martin Luther King. I'm tired of the folks in the same room who are listening as well, and yet saying, "Keep Dreaming! As long as you are asleep, we will continue to move around you!"

At some point, Americans will have to work together to facilitate the survival of this great nation. Everyone. We can no longer afford to practice divide-and-conquer, superiority, or just flat-out racism. We have common enemies who want nothing less than our total destruction. It's not that they want our land or resources; they just want us gone. Every time I hear of a bombing

263

or some other world-wide catastrophe, I can't help but think about our children. Are they prepared? They can't be. As long as they have video games in their hands, and thousands of kids in the same age group are carrying AK-47s to go along with learned hatred of America, our kids are not ready. There has to be a way to dissolve this hatred for our nation by citizens of the world. Have the powerful in this country committed so many worldwide atrocities, which are mostly unknown to the American public, that the rest of the world despises us? I truly hope not.

There is one item at our disposal that is under-utilized in our pursuit of peace. That one item is the positive aspects of hip-hop culture. From where I sit, hip-hop is a force to be reckoned with. It is the only thing in the world that can cause the youth of this nation to pause, listen, laugh, and acknowledge the struggle of others across the globe. It is a culture that wasn't supposed to last but here it is, 30 years later. From DJ Kool Herc, DJ Hollywood, and the Sugar Hill Gang, to Eminem and Nas. From Run DMC, Eric B. & Rakim, to Public Enemy - it still stands. No matter how many parents, administrators, or president's wives protest, they can't even keep this culture out of their own homes.

Every time I visit a mall and I see a young white kid with pants so wide that people can live in them, it's hip-hop culture whether the parents like it or not. I don't endorse music or the part of the culture that relegates women to bitches and whores, but I do endorse their right to produce their product. No one stops a pharmaceutical company from producing a product to control menstrual cycles, while the side effects for the drug are strokes and fainting spells. Hell, I will take the bad menstrual cycles for $100 Alex! As in any job environment or market, if you don't produce a great product, you will not last. That's true for the music business as well. One-hit-wonders are a dime a dozen. Focusing on negative music ignores LL Cool J and NAS's sustained success. Moreover, they aged with their music. Now they are turning playground merry-go-rounds into water pumping stations in impoverished countries. The kids can play and pump water at the same time. If it wasn't for hip-hop, some poor kids would have died from thirst.

Not only is hip-hop a force, but so is Marilyn Manson. If you can get past the Goth look, he is a brilliant American. If you can get past the look of death and listen to him speak, you can see that he is one of the brightest individuals in American culture today. I never agree with everything anyone says, but I do listen to see if what they say is on point more times than not. In his case, he is usually on point. He speaks to the youth who feel alienated in their own homes. He was the kid who could never get the girl or friends. Now he can't keep them off of him or control the throngs of admirers.

The youth in these subcultures are not being addressed by the American political establishment, which just wishes that they'd go away. Fortunately, they are not going anywhere; we are. We are only 20 years away from them changing our diapers and running the nation. They are trying to communicate globally through positive aspects of their culture and music while we are causing global destruction through violence against mankind and the environment. What happens if they choose not to change our diapers? In the words of SK1 Ishman, we will be in a world of shit.

Let this group speak non-violently through their cultures and bridge the gap with the children from the Far and Middle East. Nas's "One Mic" song and video can do more for world peace than a 5000-pound daisy cutter any day. The world is longing for something fresh to latch onto. This culture is right at our fingertips, but we refuse to respect it, recognize it, cultivate it, and release the positive aspects of it onto the world. Anytime rappers have more visas stamped on their passports than State Department employees, or the President, for that matter, there is a problem.

Maybe that should tell us something. If we don't make these changes rapidly and pay the public school teachers of this nation on par with doctors and lawyers, we are going to wake up one day and *we* will be the Third World. Unfortunately, we will be too arrogant to know it. We'll know it when the Soylent Green rolls down the conveyer belt and first-come, first-served really reigns true. There will be no racial, social, or economical barriers to distinguish between the groups. We will be eating green crackers together forever.

Please don't misunderstand me. Hip-hop and goth are not the answer for total world peace, but they are truly a start when it comes to communicating with youth around the world. If I could solve world peace, I would not have spent twenty five years in the

Coast Guard. When it is all said and done, it is their world anyway. We have had our chance and we truly screwed it up!

Struggle is a universal problem, and whether you are pissed at losing a girl friend or you need a peso to buy a meal, it's all a matter of perspective and environment. If people across the globe can relate to an issue that's mentioned in a CD, who are we to deprive them of that message when it may be one of the only things left to prevent them from strapping body-bombs on themselves and setting them off at the Kennedy Center.

Until these issues touch the home of the elite, these out-of-the-box solutions will not be considered. Fortunately, the youth and hip-hop communities are not waiting for us. They are bringing the gap themselves through programs like the infamous Napster. These songs are not just downloaded in the States, they are worldwide. But no, the music industry's legal machine shut it down. I can understand intellectual property rights. I just think it is the performers' call, not Sony Records'. We should sue *them* for the horrible $17.99 CDs that contain only one hit.

I have a lot of hope in the youth. I also have a lot of fear in their ability to live successful lives. They expend too much energy in their attempt to be seen and or heard. I continue to be amazed by the so-called nerds who now lead the world. They have worked harder than anyone in the world at becoming a success. In our youth's attempt to be heard, they turn off a number of individuals who would normally help them succeed. My elders have told me that, "If you are talking, you are not listening". If our children take a step back, listen, look, and learn, they will devise ways to succeed without the ruckus.

My success is not based on my annual salary or a rack of credentials. Lord knows the military pays us more near the end of our careers, and I can pack my credentials in a decent-sized envelope. My success is based on the eclectic lifestyles, environments, and happiness I've chosen to pursue. My success can be attributed to one common denominator: the Lord's decision to bless me with a decent set of switches!

AJ

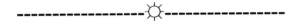

This book is dedicated to my mom,
Elaine Johnson.
Thank you for the drive to succeed.
Although you never finished formal education,
you were well-read and determined.
You demanded that we excel in whatever we endeavored to do.
Lord knows we could not bring a bad report card home!
Now I know why you are one of the only
Ladies that I know who can read a roadmap –
You charted our lives!
Luv Ya and Miss You Much!
Your Baby Boy!
Tony